D0203358

Framer Framed

Framer Framed

Trinh T. Minh-Ha

Routledge
New York and London

Published in 1992 by

Routledge
An imprint of Routledge, Chapman and Hall, Inc.
29 West 35 Street
New York, NY 10001

Published in Great Britain by

Routledge
11 New Fetter Lane
London EC4P 4EE

WIDENER UNIVERSITY
WOLFGRAM
LIBRARY
CHESTER, PA

DISCARDED
WIDENER UNIVERSITY

Copyright © 1992 by Trinh T. Minh-ha

Artwork and Jacket Design by: Jean-Paul Bourdier (detail from *The Third Eye*)

Interior text design by: Karen Sullivan
All photo designs by: Jean-Paul Bourdier

Printed in the United States of America on acid free paper

All rights reserved. No part of this book may be reprinted or reproduced or utilized in any form or by any electronic, mechanical or other means, now known or hereafter invented, including photocopying and recording, or in any information storage or retrieval system, without permission in writing from the publishers.

Library of Congress Cataloging-in-Publication Data

Trinh, T. Minh-Ha (Thi Minh-Ha), 1952-
Framer framed / by Trinh T. Minh-Ha.
p. cm.
Includes bibliographical references.
ISBN 0–415–90561–3 (HB) 0–415–90562–1 (PB)
1. Trinh, T. Minh-Ha (Thi Minh-Ha), 1952-—Interviews. 2. Motion picture plays. I. Title.
PN1998.3.T76A3 1992
791.43'0233'092—dc20 91–42876
CIP

British Library Cataloguing in publication data also available

Contents

List of Illustrations, Filmography and Distribution

List of Illustrations and Filmography

Photo design, layout and story boards: Jean-Paul Bourdier
All photos of the filmmaker are also by Jean-Paul Bourdier

R - *Reassemblage,* 1982. 40 mins. Color
Distributed by: Women Make Movies; Third World Newsreel; MOMA; Idera; Cinenova; Lightcone; Image Forum.

NS - *Naked Spaces—Living is Round,* 1985. 135 mins. Color.
Distributed by: WMM, MOMA, Cinenova, Idera, National Library of Australia

SV - *Surname Viet Given Name Nam,* 1989. 108 mins. Color and B & W.
Distributed by: WMM, MOMA, Cinenova, Idera, Image Forum, National Library of Australia

- *Shoot for the Contents.* 1991. 102 mins. Color. Distributed by: WMM. Idera. Image Forum. Cinenova

Distribution

Cinenova	113 Roman Road London, E2 OHU, United Kingdom tel: (081) 981–6828
Idera Films	2524 Cypress Street Vancouver, BC V6J 3N2, Canada tel: (604) 732–1496
Image Forum	Fudousan Kaikan Bldg. 6F 3–5 Yotsuya Shijuku-ku, Tokyo, 160 Japan tel: (03) 357–8023/358–1983
Lightcone	27 Rue Louis Braille 75012 Paris, France tel: (1) 4628–1121
Museum of Modern Art	Circulating Film Library 11 W. 53rd Street New York, NY 10019 tel: (212) 708–9530
National Library of Australia Film & Video Lending Collection	Parkes Place Canberra 2600, Australia tel: (06) 262–1358
Third World Newsreel	335 West 38th St., 5th floor New York, NY 10018 tel: (212) 947–9277
Women Make Movies	225 Lafayette St., Suite 211 New York, NY 10012 tel: (212) 925–0606

Film Scripts

NS

1

Naked Spaces—Living is Round

West Africa, 1985. 135 minute color film.

Produced by: Jean-Paul Bourdier
Directed, photographed, written, and edited by: Trinh T. Minh-Ha
Narrators: Barbara Christian, Linda Peckham, and Trinh T. Minh-ha
Distributed by: Women Make Movies (New York); The Museum of Modern Art (New York); Idera (Vancouver); Cinenova (London); The National Library of Australia (Canberra).
First published in *Cinematograph*, Vol. 3, October 1988.

(Text written for three women's voices, represented here by three types of printed letters. The low voice [bold], the only one that can sound assertive, quotes the villagers' sayings and statements, as well as African writers' works. The high-range voice [plain] informs according to Western logic and mainly cites Western thinkers. The medium-range voice [italics] speaks in the first person and relates personal feelings and observations. Words in parentheses are not heard on film; the names of nations and of peoples appear as burnt-in subtitles on the lower corner of the film frames.)

(Senegal)

(Joola)

People of the earth

Not descriptive, not informative, not interesting
Sounds are bubbles on the surface of silence

Untrue, superstitious, supernatural. The civilized mind qualifies many of the realities it does not understand untrue, superstitious, supernatural

Truth and fact
Naked and plain
A wise Dogon man used to say

"to be naked is to be speechless" (Ogotemmeli)

Truth or *fact*

The correct vibration. A body resonates to music as does a string.
A music that elicits physical response and calls for mediated involvement.
It does not simply "play"
In such a way as *not* to impinge on the viewing

An African man wrote:
Contrary to what some Westerners think, religion in Africa is not a cause for man's stagnation, nor a source of interterritorial conflicts. The more profound a believer the black man is, the more tolerant he proves to be. Wherever intolerance occurs in black territories, they are due to a cause introduced from the exterior

(A. Hampate Ba)

The circumcised young men beat time with a walking stick while chanting
They are holding in their hands feminity, water, and light

Building as dwelling
On earth, under the sky, before the divinities, among mortals, with things.
They dwell in that

They neither master the earth nor subjugate it
They leave to the sun and the moon their journey
And do not turn night into day
They do not make their gods for themselves
And do not worship idols
They initiate mortals into the nature of death

(Sereer)

The circle is a form that characterizes the general plan of the house, the granaries, the court, the shrines, sometimes the rooms, the village, the tomb, the cemetery.

(Mandingo)

life is round
This is not a fact. Not a data gathering.

air, earth, water, light.
The four elements that explain the creation of men and women in African mythologies.

earth-born and earth-bound
dusty grey-white bodies made out of clay
stark naked children.
"she made a hole and breathed air into it: a child is born"

(Jaxanke)

The sun, the calabash, the court, the arching sky
Everything round invites touch and caress
The circle is the perfect form

you'll never spread doubt in their mind by convincing them of seeing 'yes'

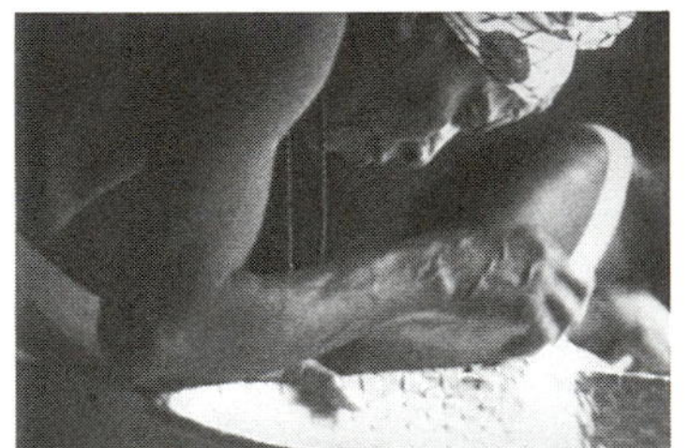

NS

when they already saw 'no.'
when all that they perceived was a hut or a mud shelter
They went away the way they came

For many of us, the hut is the tap root of the function of inhabiting. A universe (inside and) outside the universe, it possesses the felicity of intense poverty (Bachelard).

she said: man, woman and child
line / sun / star / calabash cover
turtle / big snake / fox
calabash

they help the plants to grow.
you ask me: "what is the use of these paintings?"
they help the plants to grow
they promote germination

(Bassari)

Every illness is a musical problem
"Music has a magical, energizing and creative power. The mere shaking of a cow bell is enough to make people drift into a state of excitement. It is then said that 'strength has entered them.' Elders who can hardly move in daily situation without a cane would emit war cries and dance frantically to the sound of music. Farmers who feel tired and lack enthusiasm will be fired with desire to work in the fields upon hearing the drum beats or the chants of the masks." "Even if you have eaten and are full," a man said, "you have no sustaining strength to plough the land vigorously and endure the hard work if no music flows in you."

(Soninke)

Space: even when close I feel distance

"Whether a house is lively or not depends on the way it breathes

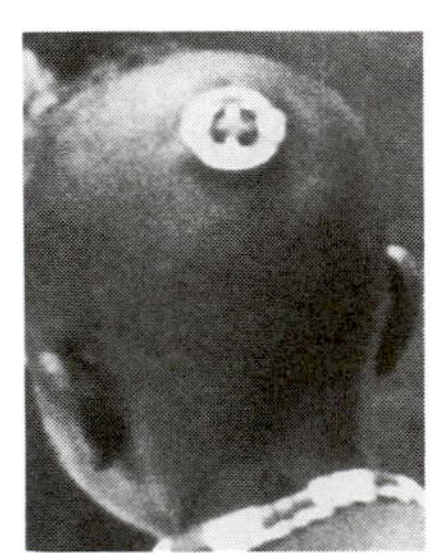

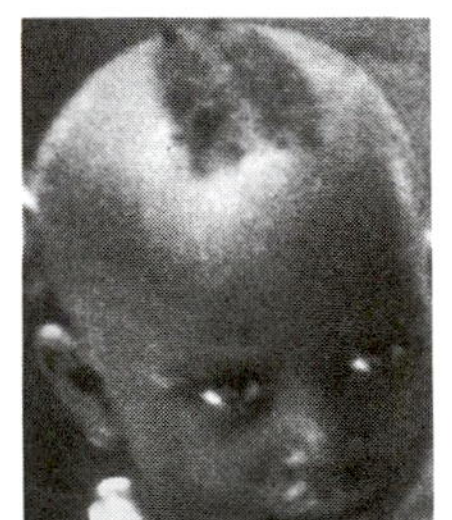

NS

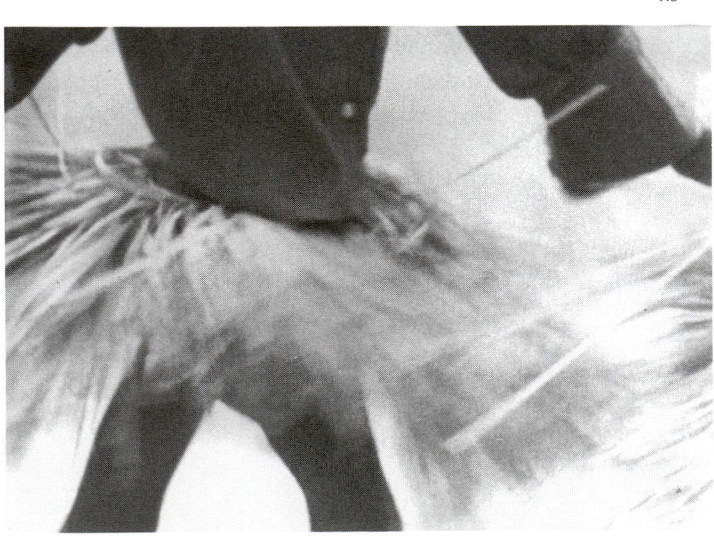

"Houses and humans are both made out of small balls of earth"

Music rests on accord between darkness and light

(Mauritania)

(Soninke)

Listen in the wind to the bush sobbing: it is our
beloved dead's breathing.
The dead are not dead (Birago Diop)

People of the earth

The reason two deers walk together is that one has to take the mote from the other's eye (proverb)

A sense of time, not only of hours and days,
but also of decades and centuries
A sense of space as light and void

Space has always reduced me to silence

A space that speaks the mellowness of inner life

Scantily furnished, devoid of concealment or disguise
"The truth appears so naked on my side,
That any purblind eye may find it out" (Shakespeare)

A house that breathes
That encloses as well as opens wide onto the world

We often took our own limits for those of the culture we looked at

All definitions are devices

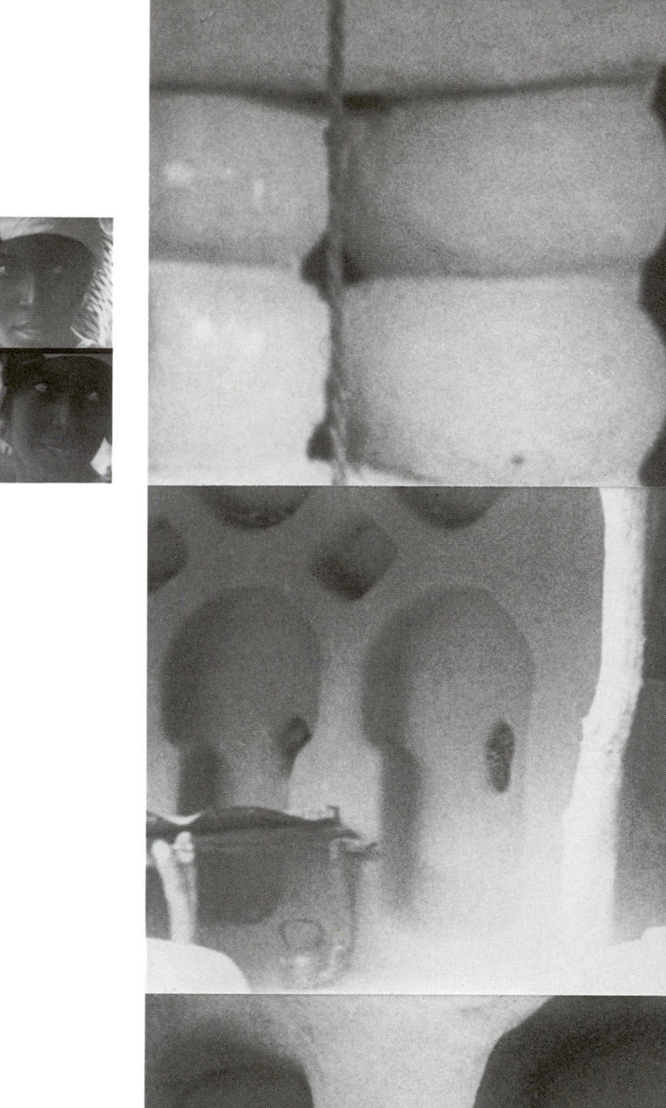

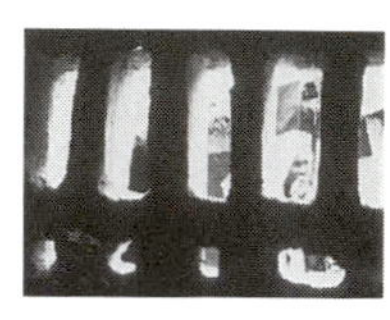

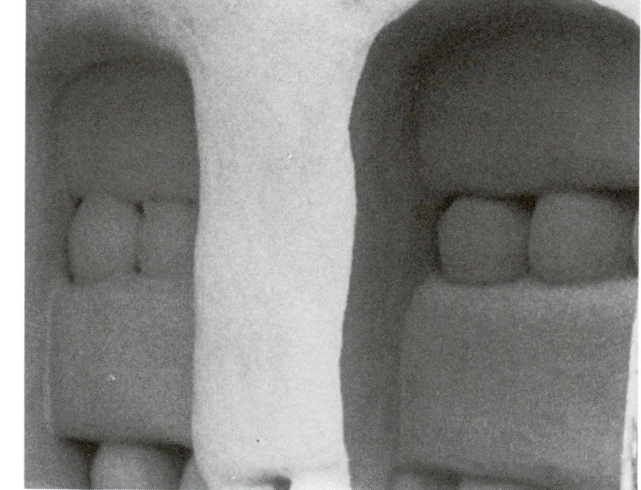

NS

Color does not exist, being first and foremost a sensation

She would often sing while she worked
The air filled with her voice
The song scanned by her regular snifflings

First and foremost a sensation

Do you see the same color when the light is red?
Color blinds. Some greyness has to remain for clarity to be

Nice colors are called 'shades'
Red attracts and irritates, while bright yellow is bound to hurt. In places where the sun dazzles and where sandscapes prevail, people dress in blue, deep blue. Shades are soothing to the eye.

Color is life

Light becoming music

She would often sing while she worked
The air filled with her voice

Songs cure bodily pains, soothe the pangs of bereavement, calm anger and cleanse the mind

To explain the scornful lower lip of the camel, Moore men have this to say: "The prophet has a hundred names. Men know 99 of them, only the camel knows the hundredth one; hence its superior 'marabout'-like expression"

(According to J. Gabus).

(Peoples of Oualata)

They help the plants grow
They promote germination

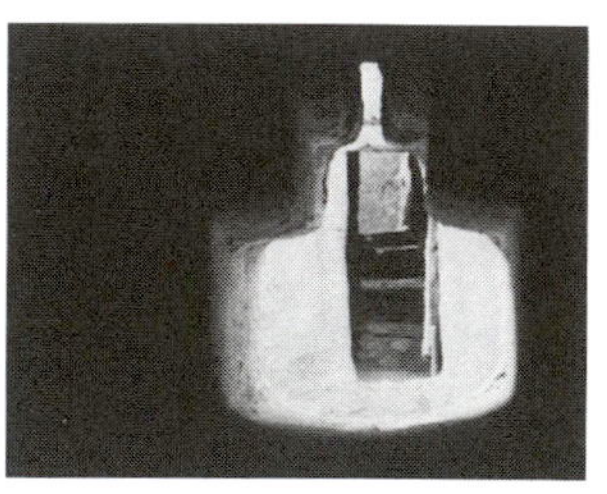

NS

A long wail tore through the air
Blue veiled figures
She sailed down the alley
Her indigo-blue garment
Flowing behind her

As if for centuries
She sat there
Instinctively veiling her face as the men came in
Unveiling it as soon as they left

Being truthful: being in the in-between of all definitions of truth

There was much covert peeping through the veils as we walked around looking carefully at the rooms and their details.

Caught each other looking. She laughed and I laughed. Soon all the women in the court were laughing together

The earth is blue like an orange

"La terre est bleue comme une orange
Jamais une erreur les mots ne mentent pas" (Paul Eluard)

Sky, earth, sea, sun
Air, earth, water, light

Outside is as bare as inside is ornate

For fifteen minutes we stood in the street, slightly off the house door, waiting until we were allowed in. Time for the men to inform the women to go back to their rooms and stay in there all the time while the visitors were present

How can you explain this excitement to live in an old house? One that ages with the imprints of previous lives?

The severe aspect of the exterior often stands in contrast with the exuberant decorations of the interior

NS

She stepped into my room abruptly and stood there staring at me intently. I stared back at her questioningly, but she remained silent. For a long time we stared at each other without a word; there was more fear in her eyes than curiosity. She turned away a few seconds, then looked back straight into my eyes and said: "Oil, I want some oil for cooking."

Walked down the empty narrow streets and thought for a while I was truly alone. I was soon to discover blinded walls had eyes. Gigglings and laughters spurted out around me as I stopped and looked carefully at the faces that swiftly appear and disappear from the discreet openings on the walls. Or above me, from the terrace-roofs of the houses. Women, unveiled, mostly young, all share the look of intense curiosity.

(Togo)

(Moba)

The world is round around the round being (Bachelard).

Religion is living without conflict

"The ground level of the house interior is the underworld, the terrace level is the earth and the granaries upper level is the sky"
"Granaries elevated on the front facade 'make the house look well'"

The cosmic house is both cell and world (Bachelard). Each dweller inhabits the universe while the universe inhabits her space.

"dark and cool, red like the sun"
. . . untrue, superstitious, supernatural
"as the sun descends, the rays enter the cattle room and touch the ancestors, speaking to them while they ask for health and protection of the family."

The Tamberma house is a sanctuary

"these mounds are the sun; for the reproduction of human beings and the expansion of the family."
The horns of the entrance and the mounds are the focus for sun ceremonies

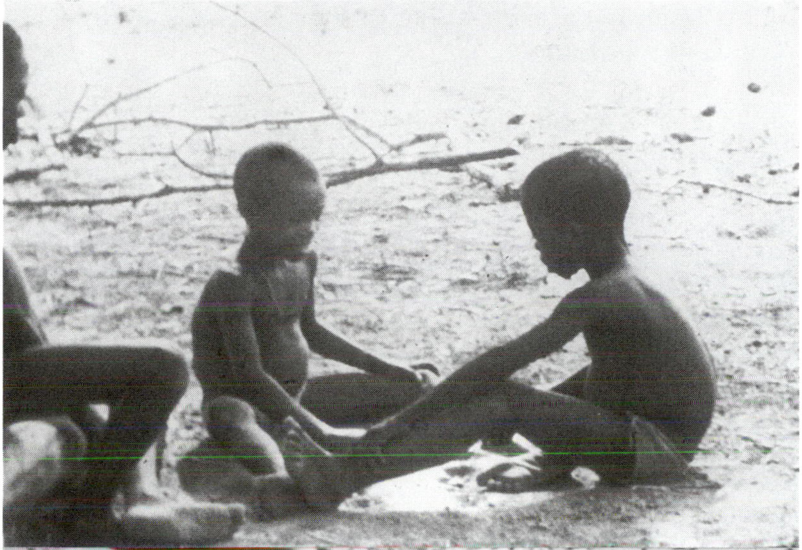

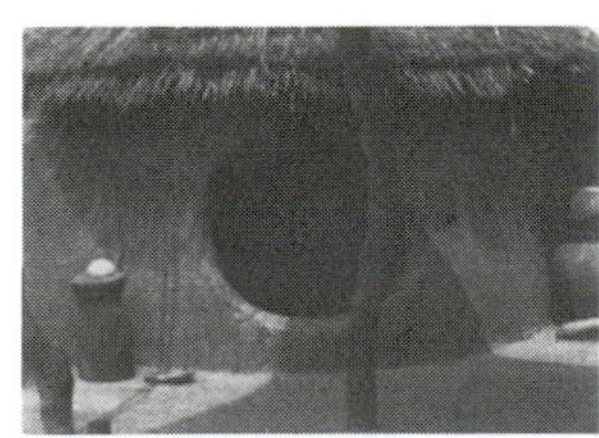

NS

Upon entering, we stepped into a somber central room where I could smell and hear a cow munching on my left; we then climbed up to the tiny oval kitchen lit by the soft morning light that came in from the upper portal leading to the terrace roof of the house.

Entering the womb of the earth, sheltered from heat and sun, from rain and wind, from all other living creatures

"The earth is round. We all know that. No part is longer than the other." When we enter, we enter the mouth—*the door***—When we exit, we step out onto the large calabash—***the court***—we call it the Vault of Heaven."**
The house opens onto the sky in a perfect circle

Rhythms are built into the way people relate to each other

(Tamberma)

"We call ourselves Batammariba, 'the people who create well with earth, the people who are builders'"
the designers, the architects

Tribute to the dead

"We say the placement of the house is that which is important"
"A house is beautiful when its back is not coming out"
"Not too high, not too low, not too far outside nor too far inside. His house is really smooth. He knows how to build, he does not leave his finger marks"
(A Tamberma architect, according to S. P. Blier)

She who wears an antelope headdress is said to portray the deceased's daughter

Third act for a funeral drama. Funeral performances are referred to as plays; the house of the deceased being the stage, a group of skillful performers, the actors, and the villagers in attendance, the critical audience. Drums, flutes and horns are the voices of the ancestors.

"sun's house is a circle. This is what we have been told"
"sun protects us all. Like mother it brings out children.
Like father it has wives, the earth and the moon"

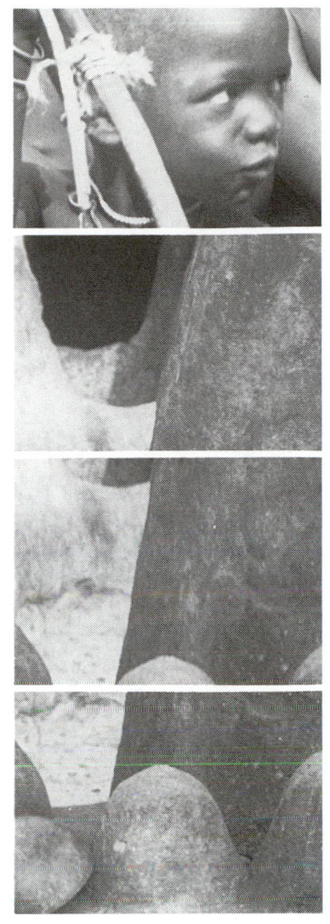

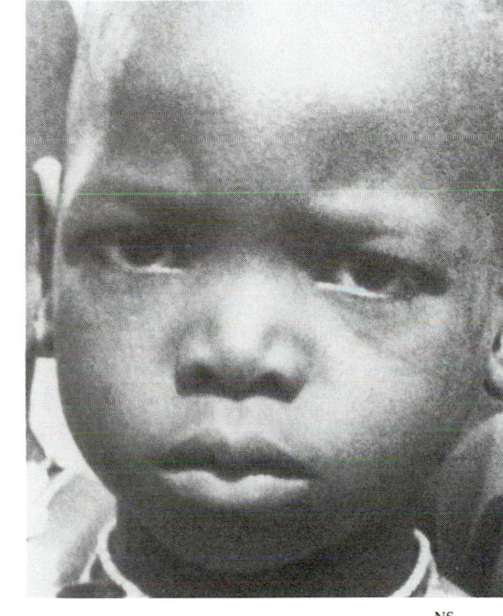

NS

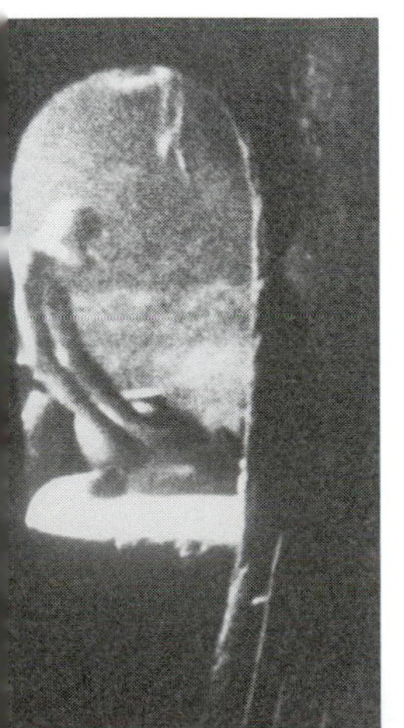

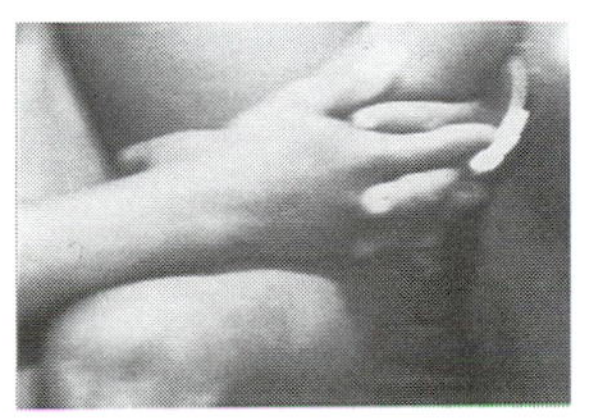

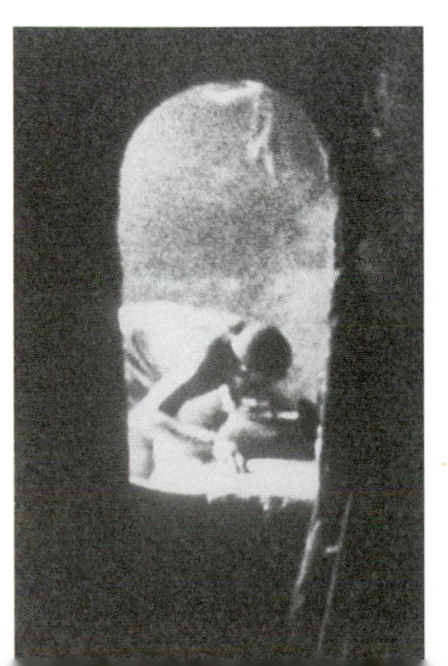

NS

"it is beautiful because his fingers leave lines and his lines are visible"

"if the woman plasters the walls such that from far away you don't see the different levels, we say the house is beautiful"

The egg-shaped granaries are raised above the terrace at the houses' front corners, closest to the sky, their opening facing the sky god who provides rain for the grain (according to S. P. Blier).

"When you climb it, it leads you to the sky." The sky is like a tree; it is formed from the branches of a huge tree

(Kabye)

People of the earth

"The more profound a believer the black man is, the more tolerant he proves to be"

In one of the rites in initiation during which a man is born again in his community, the initiate has to go naked, his body painted with red earth, color of the newly born.

(Konkomba)

"A village that neglects music and dancing is a dead village"

Red: a warm limitless color that often acts as a sign of life
Black: an absence of light, of sun, therefore of life, color

In many parts of the world, white is the color of mourning

Truth or fact?

Poetry becomes only *poetry when I become adept at consuming truth as fact*

"The house like a woman must have secret parts to inspire desire"
(according to Ogotemmeli)

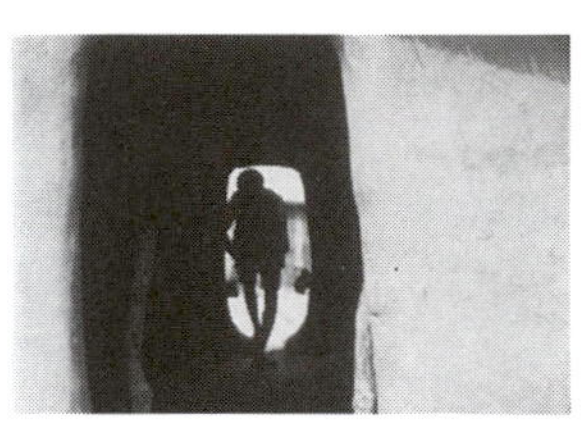

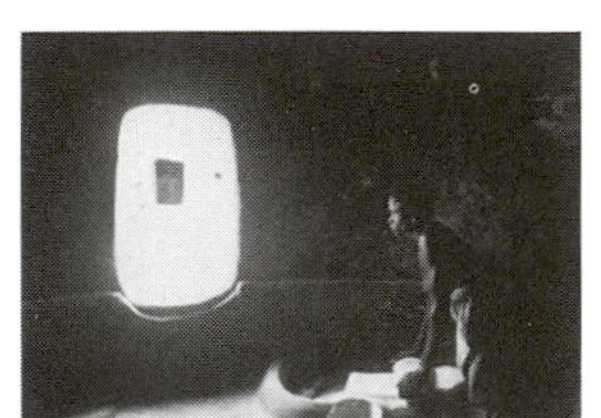

NS

Unadorned she is not desirable. Adornment excites love. If there is a connection between ornaments and love, that is because the first ornaments of all were in the centre-jar of the celestial granary; and that jar is the symbol of the world's womb
(according to Ogotemmeli)

In certain societies where sounds have become letters with sharps and flats, those unfortunate enough not to fit into these letters are tossed out of the system and qualified unmusical. They are called noises. *It is known that one of the primary tasks of ethnomusicologists is to study what traditional societies consider music and what they reject as non-music.* A music bound up with movement, dance and speech, one in which the listener becomes a co-performer, one that has no overall form except one of continually recurring sequences of notes and rhythms, one that plays endlessly—*for nobody has enough of life*—has been repeatedly called elemental or rudimentary. Is irritable to most Westerners' ears.

The sound of a swelling cry of ululation
That high wail that speaks her joy, excitement or grief

I am inhabited by a cry
Joy sorrow anger it curls out
Sharp and vivid in the night
Inhumanly human
The cry I hear, she said, is from the other side of life

Deeper insight always entails moments of blindness

(Mali)

(Dogon)

"Step into the footmarks of your ancestors. Tradition may weaken but cannot disappear." *A Dogon prayer*

Scale as an element to impress, to dominate or to speak up a mutual vulnerability?

A journey in these villages may have a cathartic effect, for a man seeing a hundred-storey building often gets conceited

NS

There is also a way of viewing nature as a challenge to man's conquest; therefore, of seeing in the smallness of man and woman a need for im-prove-ment

Ogo, the first who stood against God Amma, and introduced psychological diversification in the universe, was transformed into a Fox and thus reduced to speaking only with its paws on the divination tables

The figures are drawn on the smoothed sand by the diviners before sunset. The Fox, which comes out at night, is lured onto the tables by means of peanuts which the diviners have carefully scattered over them. The next day, the diviners will come back to the site after sunrise to read the traces left by the Fox. Their interpretations vary according to the latter's itinerary whose imprints may join, border, or avoid the figures. The divination table is the Earth turning under the action of the Fox's legs.

The divination table is the Earth turning under the action of the Fox's legs.

How "very much content am I to lie low, to cling to the soil, to be of kin to the sod. My soul squirms comfortably in the soil and sand and is happy. Sometimes when one is drunk with this earth one's spirit seems so light that one is in heaven. But actually one seldom rises six feet above the ground" (L. Yutang).

"When you climb it, it leads you to the sky. The sky is like a tree; it is formed by the branches of a huge tree"

Togu na: "the mother's shelter," "the house of words," or "the men's house" is the reference point for every Dogon village

The life-force of the earth is water

The remaining facade of the large house with its eighty niches, homes of the ancestors.

Reality and truth: neither relative nor absolute

I can't take hold of it nor lose it
When I am silent, it projects
When I project, it is silent

NS

"The calabash is a symbol of woman and the sun, who is female"
Signs are things that move about in the world
Signs are the things of all men and women

11616 signs express and indicate all things and beings of the universe as well as all possible situations seen by the Dogon men

Each sign opens onto other signs
Each sign contains in itself a summary of the whole
And the drop is the very ocean

The Dogon house is said to be a model of the universe at a smaller scale and to symbolize man, woman and their union. The central room, the store rooms on each side and the back room with the hearth represent the woman lying on her back with outstretched arms, ready for intercourse as the communicating door stays open. The ceiling of the central room is the man and its beams, his skeleton. The woman and the man's breath finds its outlet through the opening on the roof

(according to Ogotemmeli)

(Burkina Faso)

(Birifor)

Spider web and dust have aged with them

"Bathed in the sunlight, one after the other they took turns to speak to the sun, keeping in touch with it from dawn to dusk"

The sun touches them as they ask for health and protection of the family

"It is beautiful because when you enter you see there where the sun penetrates, where there is light, and the rest is dark"

Houses with a sculptured head on the roof are said to belong to hunters

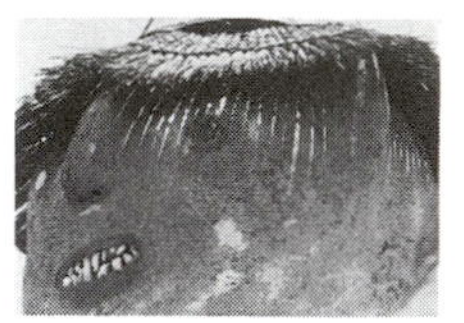

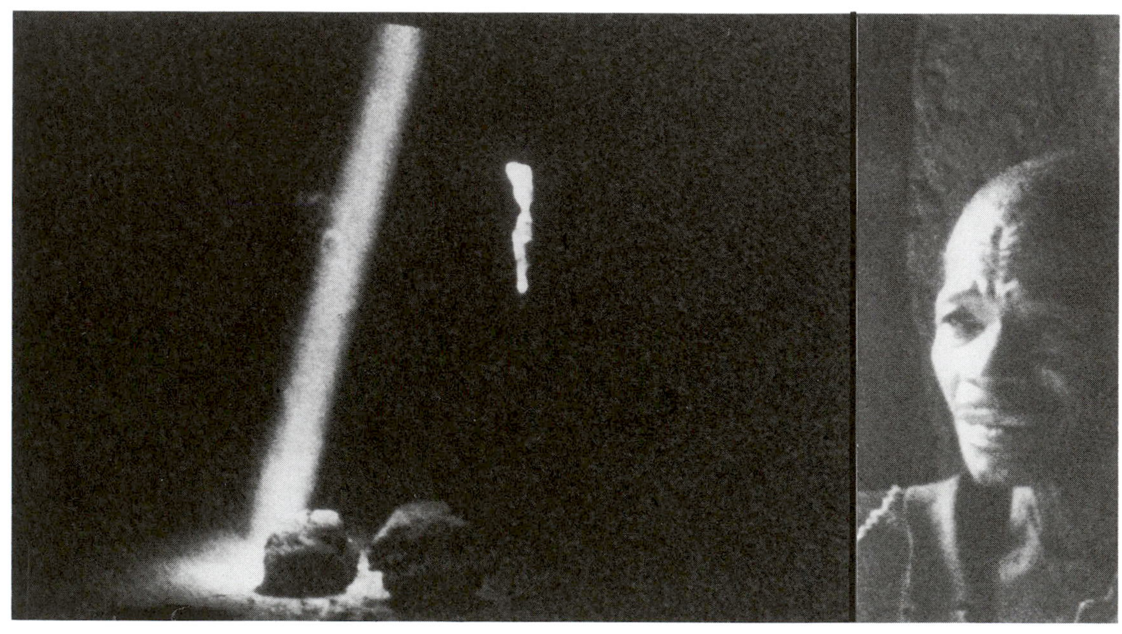

NS

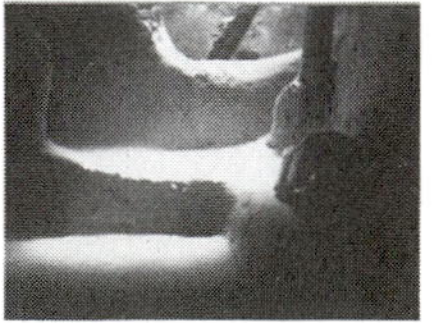

The supernatural, *term widely used in pro-scientific milieu,* **is an anti-scientific invention of the West,** *a wise African man observed* (Boubou Hama).

The diagnostic power of a fact-oriented language

The sky is
A calabash
The water jar is
A woman's womb

Blindness occurs precisely during the short moment of adjustment; when, from full sun we step into the dim inside. Abrupt transition from bright to dark for a change. To advance, we must go sightless, time to cross an immaterial threshold that links the social to the personal

The dead are not dead
When night constantly floats in certain parts of the house

It never appears to me in its totality. Here, a small round hole; there, a carved ladder leading up to the source of light; a wall; another wall; a bench; a straw mat; her water jar; a long dark room ending in several nest-like spaces. The whole thing is scattered about inside me. I can only see it in fragmentary form.

An act of light lets day in night
Makes far nearer and near farther
Why is it so dark?

Everything is at the same time transparent and opaque
Irreducibly complex in its simplicity

Not really a dwelling or a living space as an observer said, because of the overall absence of windows

When men go hunting in parties they know the rules of precedence; they know him who is higher than another; they understand when one says "I speak, you remain silent." . . . There are dangerous things in the bush and a small quarrel may bring many arrows (V. Aboya, according to Rattray).

Before the hunters set forth, they were told this by the man in charge of the hunting parties:

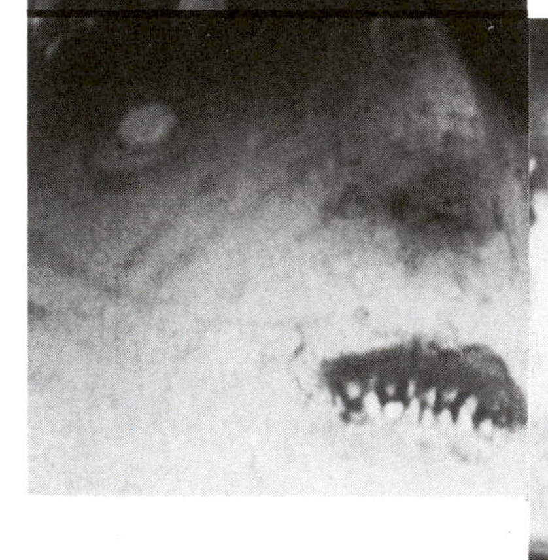
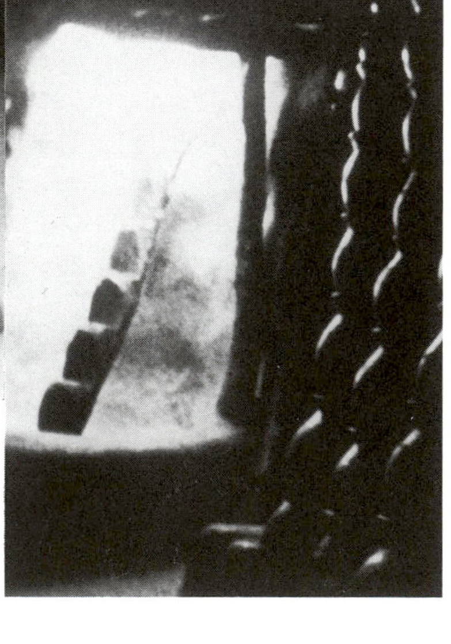

NS

"If we meet a lion, let it be like cold water
if we meet a leopard, let it be like cold water
if we meet a snake, let it be like cold water
but if a man wishes to quarrel while out hunting,
let him get headache and belly-ache,
so that he may have to return home" (according to Rattray)

(Voice stammers on 'anthropological') *An anthropo . . . an anthropo . . . an anthropological shot: one that turns people into human species*

Both ancestors and children are 'builders up of a compound' When a man dies, his son, upon sacrificing a sheep, will ask this man to join his father and grandfather in guarding the house properly. When a man has no children, he is sometimes laughed at, and told "what are you, if you were to die, they would break down your house and plant tobacco in it." (V. Aboya according to Rattray).

A light without shadow generates an emotion without reserve (R. Barthes)

Entering and exiting as love-making.
The door remains open, for a house with a door closed is an infertile house.

It is by way of the 'house hole' that the rays of the noon Sun enter into the house to look at the family and speak with them. Family eats around it. The food cooked and spilled while eating are so much offered to the Sun. Women give birth under it to secure the Sun's blessings.

The house like a woman must have secret parts to inspire desire

The womb image of the house
The nest-like power of curves

Floating around in these dark spaces is the subtle smell of clay, earth and straw

There is a saying that "a man should not see all the dark corners of another's house."
"If light be called the life-blood of a space, darkness could be called its soul"

Color is first and foremost a sensation

"The house's eyes. It looks out and sees like a woman."

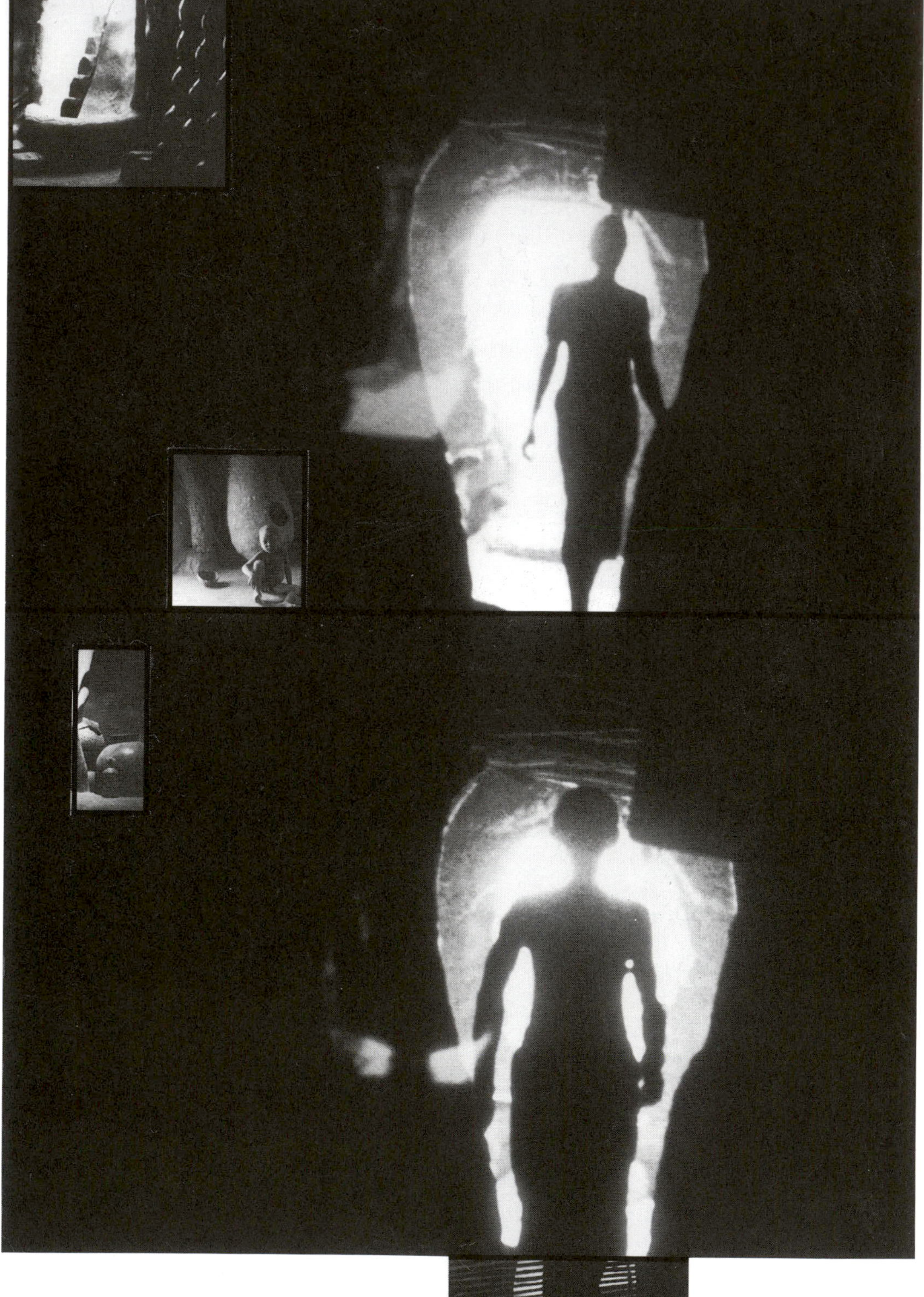

NS

A male is buried facing east, a female facing west.

"A man faces eastward, that he may know when to rise and hunt. A woman looks to the west, that she may know when to prepare her husband's food"

(V. Aboya, according to Rattray)

(Bisa)

The world is round

Are you seeing it? Hearing it? or projecting it?

Unadorned, she is not desirable. Adornment excites love. If there is a connection between ornaments and love, that is because the first ornaments of all were in the centre-jar of the celestial granary; and that jar is the symbol of the world's womb

(according to Ogotemmeli)

The earth is an overturned calabash. For the death of a man or a woman, the priest sprinkles in the air earth taken from the center of the circle formed by the calabash while making a circle around the house.

here, patience is one of the first rules of education

Orange and blue; warmer or colder; more luminosity, more presence.
Timing acts as a link between natural and artificial light.

The earth is blue like an orange

You can't take hold of it, but you can't lose it

So please let the smoke go and let the seed die to its outer shell

Be a stranger to myself

No matter what we call it, we will miss it
Relieved of so many words, we went naked

Objects in her surrounding. . . . The naming of spaces rarely refers to their function. It refers instead, to the various parts of the human body.

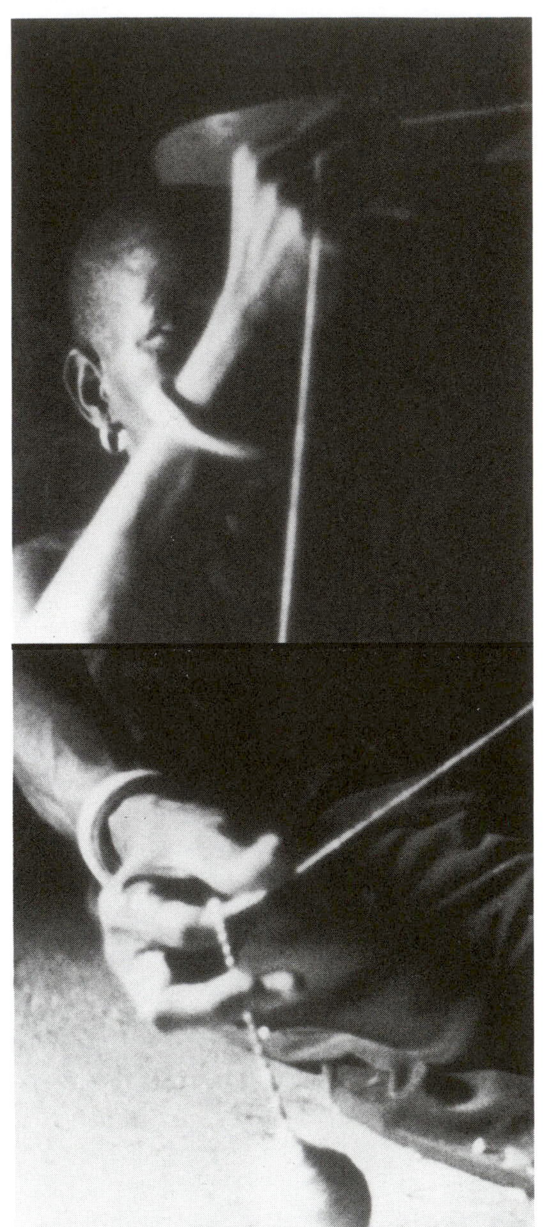

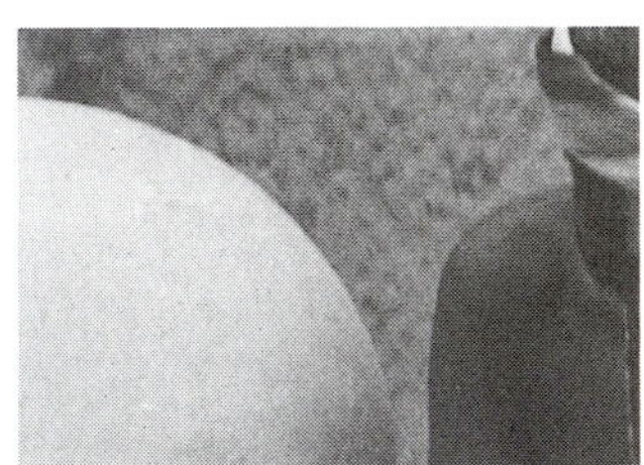

NS

The house is composed like the human body: the earth or clay is the flesh; the water, the blood; the stones, the bones; and the plastered surface of the walls, the skin

Sun rolling in space
"The bobbin, which is wound off in spinning is the sun rolling in space"
(according to S. P. Blier).

(Benin)

(Fon)

They call it giving. *We call it self-gratification.* **We call it self-gratification.**
They call it give-and-take. *We call it take-and-take.* **We call it take-and-take.**
They call it generosity. *We call it conditioning / The beggar's mind.*
We call it conditioning the beggar's mind
Today, to survive the poor can hardly refuse to accept
They say they don't give anymore
Because we are ungrateful
The ungrateful acceptor / *The expecting donor*
They say they don't give anymore because we are ungrateful.
We ponder: will the donor species survive?

We substitute expectation for hope and easily speak about "falling short of" or "failing to come up to" our expectations
Strategies of rupture and incorrectness need some airing

A cloud of oratorical precaution / Fear
Fear of making / out of a crystallized I

Any expectation, even that of peace, brings restlessness

Questions and answers: a mutual deception

Life on the water
Never can one walk home and feel the contact of solid, secure ground

NS

Floating, flowing constantly
The house suspended between water and sky

What they name generosity / *arrogance*
A mutual deception

You should be able to accept with simplicity / *simply accept*
From we, us, who are neither a source of authority nor a seal of authenticity

They see no life / When they look
They see only objects

The dead are not dead

Humble enough to accept without trying to return

Be a stranger to myself
And the drop is the ocean

The earth is blue like an orange

An instant's freezing
To be lived directly
Silence: people having faith in each other

Void is always capable of being filled by solid
And I look at the myriad of reflections
the entire lake within me
Unable to quench it
Quench an endless thirst

The charm of its nudity lights up our desire for both retreat and expansion
The more naked the space, the more it fires my imagination

Blue like an orange
And orange becomes blue
Earth becomes Sun
Sun becomes Water
Water becomes Sky
And blue becomes orange, like the Earth

(Senegal)

(Peul)

The circle is the spirit in eternal motion

While giving there is no thought of giving
While accepting there is no thought of accepting
"Who could ever think of the gift as a gift that takes?" (H. Cixous)

Going beyond logic to experience what is large in what is small
Clear, simple, irreducibly complex in its simplicity

To build out of dwelling
A philosopher observed that "man's homelessness consists in this, that man still does not even think of the *real* plight of dwelling as *the* plight (M. Heidegger)

We dwell altogether unpoetically
But dwelling can be unpoetic only because it is in essence poetic (Heidegger)

Have you seen such a look in a child's face? Such a look?
A sunlit smile that sticks in your eyes

Spirit in eternal motion

For many foreign observers, these people have no notion whatsoever of the private garden. This is hardly surprising: there is no point in fencing off a piece of land as one's own; their houses are situated such that wherever they wander they own the entire landscape.

The earth is an overturned calabash

(Joola)

they are holding in their hands
femininity, water and light

people of the earth

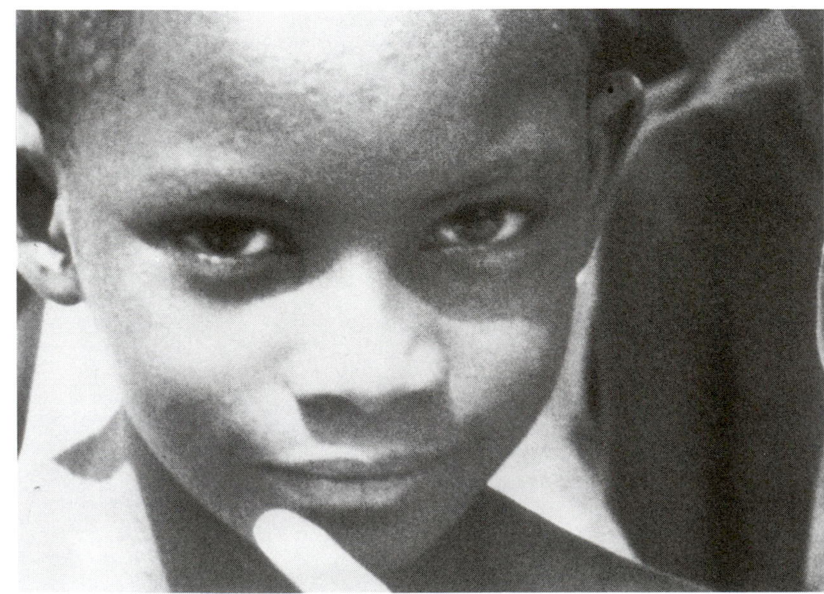

NS

Those whose serenity of understanding and simplicity of spirit is the despair of bigger men

The reason two deers walk together is that one has to take the mote from the other's eye (Proverb)

"Life with its rhythms and cycles is dance and dance is live"
(Opoka, according to J. M. Chernoff)

The Joola people: renowned for having raised a fierce armed resistance to the French colonial administration at the start of the century.

For the one who travels in this restfully green part of Senegal today, the Casamance, the dreamland of research workers and tourists alike, it is quite difficult to imagine no foreigner had dared to venture here without an armed escort a few decades ago.

Light, air, earth, woman, palm leaf, dust, children

Space has always reduced me to silence

They can't really afford this, they said
But bought it anyway
Flew to Africa
And waited with an anguished excitement
For the paid shock of exoticism

A Joola proverb says: "those who are proud of their nudity will be insolent once clothed"
This is not a fact

Light, air, people, sound

The impluvium: a house built around an inner court with an inwardly inclined roof and as some said, "a tank to catch rainwater"

Some call it the "Senegalese Florida," ideal for the visitor who hungers for tropical adventures made to measure

A life-generating power

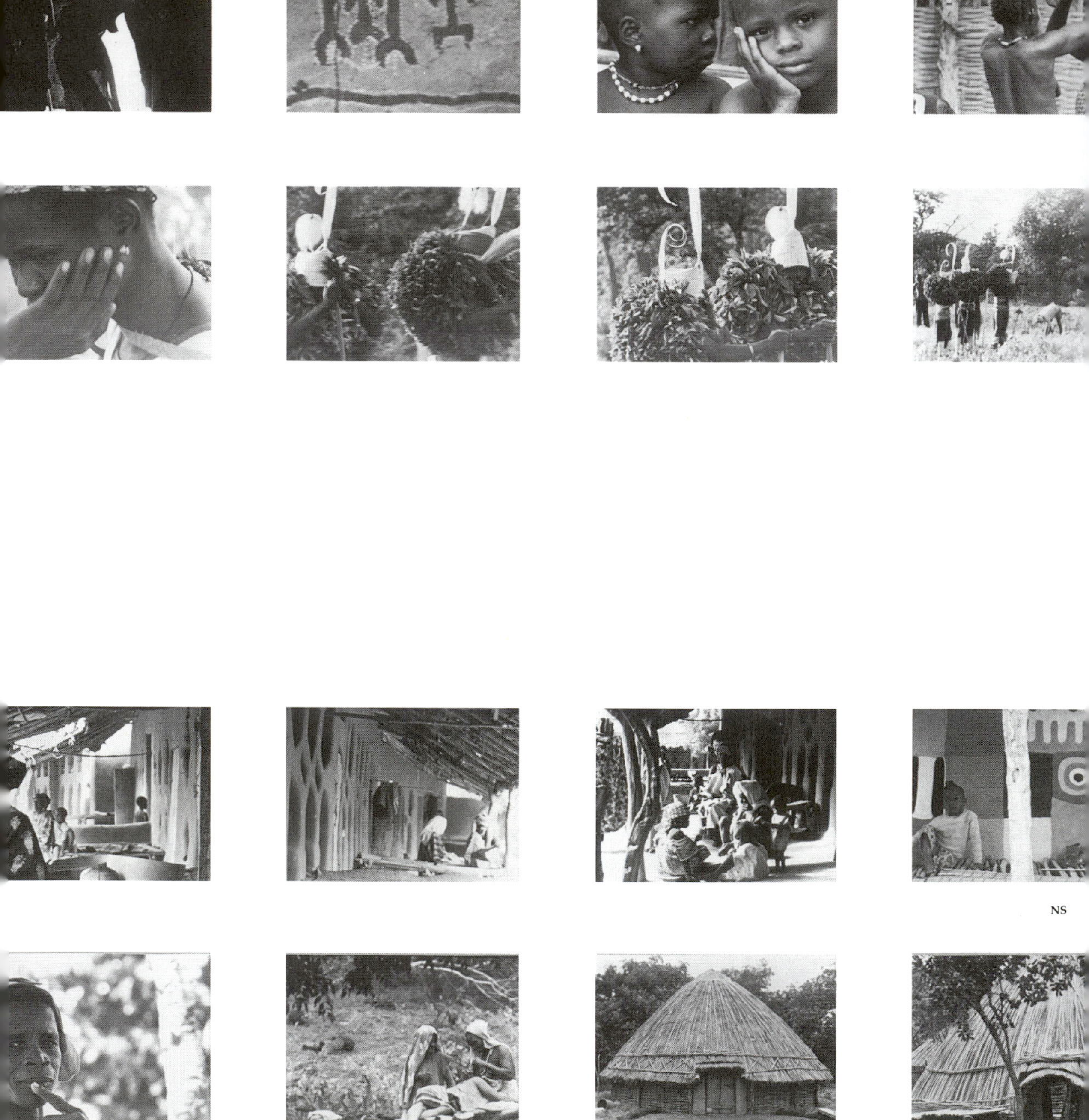

NS

"A house without a fence is not a house," the old man says

An earthen castle, according to a tourist guide book

A place for communion / Sharing
A sun chapel

They took turns to speak to the sun, keeping in touch with it from dawn to dusk
"The dead are often buried in their own rooms which will remain locked forever. The room will crumble with time on the grave"

Infinitely secure in its nudity / *Insecure in its infiniteness*

A damaged house is a damaged family. Very often, family and house bear the same name.

Femininity, water, and light
An interior court
A time clock / A sun chapel
A reserve of air, light, water

Each woman prepares her own meal. Each household has its own hearth located all around the court under a circular covered gallery.

A pit
A tank for catching rainwater
A place for reunion
A place for rest and conversation

Music rests on accord between darkness and light

Every religion is based on a lie device
All methods may be viewed as lies
At best, they create a situation

Rhythm creates a storage of energy

Eager for an indigenous answer, someone walked around asking: "What is music?" People would look at him as if he had said something funny or strange. They would laugh and say: "Don't you know?"

NS

"A dance that does not attract many villagers and foreigners from afar is said to turn out badly, for the spirits have not come to attend it."
The animation of a dance is a sign of the spirits' presence. Dance and music form a dialogue between movement and sound. One who hears the music understands it with a dance. The dancers do not imitate or express the music heard; they converse with it and dance to the gaps in it. Both marked and unmarked beats. A different beat, one that is not there, one that you add because you feel it and fit it in. Your own beat. Your own move. Your own reading.

It usually signals arrest and has long been forgotten as a wind instrument.
The whistle here is a musical cue for change

Dramatic action is stimulated by the flute-, horn-, whistle- and bell-players who do not form part of the drum ensemble. They wander round the circle of dancers, blowing, striking a few notes on their instruments to urge them on

A drummer explains that one should not breathe too strongly while performing if one does not want to miss the rhythmic formulas and to get tired too quickly. One should take in reserves of air during the pauses, between each dance

Every illness is a musical problem

"My wrist is fast": that is not drumming. As you are beating, it is your heart that is talking, and what your heart is going to say, your hand will collect and play. And unless you cool your heart, your drumming will not stand. When you heart cools, your arm will cool too, and as you are bringing your strength, you will also be leaving it. At that time, the drum will cry well. . . . The one who has learned to play well can beat a drum and the sound will spread out and you will hear it vibrating inside the ground. But the one whose heart gets up and he is beating hard, his drum will not sound.

"Drumming has no end," the drummer said. "No one can know everything about drumming; everyone knows only to his extent. If you know everything, what are you going to do and know it?" . . . In our drumming way, no one blames another. If someone doesn't know, you don't say "this man does not know." If you say that, you have demeaned yourself. Maybe as you say you know, someone too knows better than you, and as you are bending down looking at someone's anus, someone is also bending down and looking at yours." (I Abdulai, according to Chernoff)

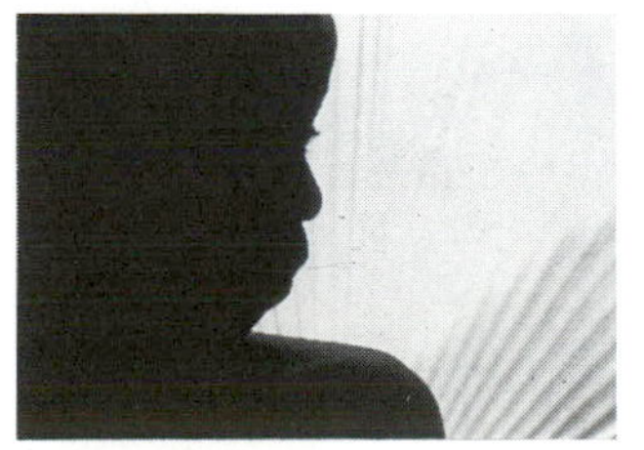

NS

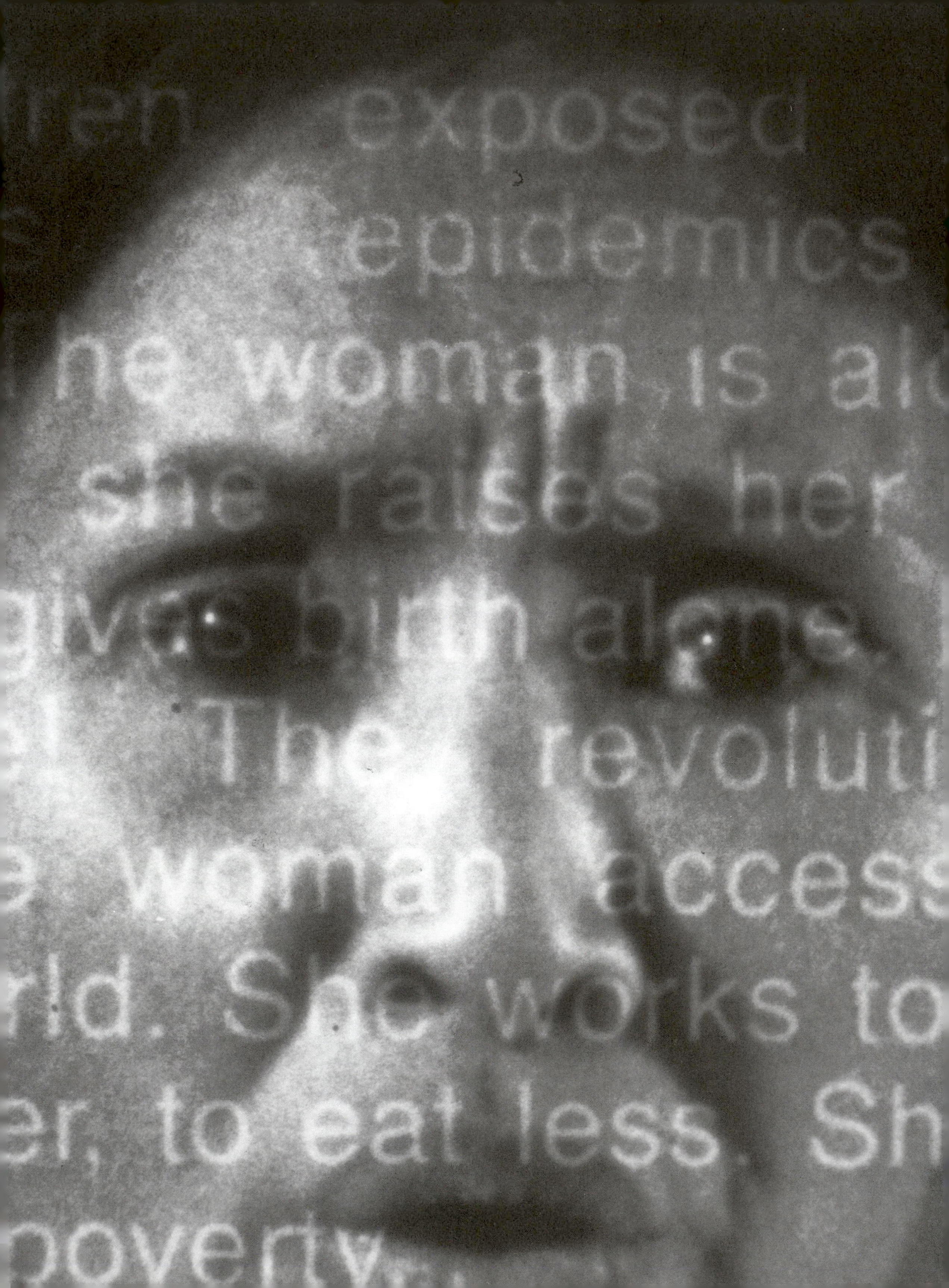

ren exposed
epidemics
he woman is al
she raises her
gives birth alone
The revoluti
e woman access
rld. She works to
er, to eat less. Sh
poverty

2

Surname Viet Given Name Nam

1989. 108 minute color and B & W film.

Directed, written and edited by: Trinh T. Minh-ha
Mise-en-scene, lighting design, and associate producer: Jean-Paul Bourdier
Cinematography: Kathleen Beeler
Narrators: Lan Trinh and Trinh T. Minh-ha
With: Khien Lai, Ngo Kim Nhuy, Tran Thi Bich Yen, Tran Thi Hien, Lan Trinh, and Sue Whitfield
Distributed by: Women Make Movies (New York); The Museum of Modern Art (New York); Cinenova (London); Idera (Vancouver); Image Forum (Tokyo); The National Library of Australia (Canberra)

In this film, women speak from five places; these are represented here by different typestyles. There are two voices-over reading in English (italic & plain); a third voice singing sayings, proverbs and poetry in Vietnamese (bold), with translations in a smaller typeface; interviews in Vietnamese subtitled in English; and interviews in English synchronized with the image (indented plain and italic texts).

Than em nhu tam lua dao
Phat pho giua cho biet vao tay ai?
(I am like a piece of silk
Floating in the midst of the market,
knowing not into whose hands it will fall.)

Dat nuoc nam trong con bao to
Con toi nam trong con bao to
Toi muon lam sao dem than yeu nho
tre tro con toi
Nhung trai dat truyen rung, truyen rung
va chiec noi con toi truyen rung, truyen rung
(The country lies under a heavy storm
my child lies under a heavy storm
I wish to use my fragile body
to protect my child
But the earth is shaking, shaking
and my baby's cradle is shaking, shaking) (Sister Phuong, "A Lullaby")

(Quoted on screen:)
In principle, a foreigner is already a spy . . . Even a socialist . . . Or even you. We live in constant suspicion. There is no mutual trust.

Ly, 37 years old, employee, Vietnam 1982

***(Voice off:)** "Our two salaries are no longer enough. I do some sewing in the evening, for the cooperatives.
(Sync:) "We receive, from time to time, a package from my brother who lives abroad. He sends us 2 kilos of MSG, 3 kilos of wool. We sell them back in the free market and buy whatever we need [with the money]. It's a satisfying exchange! This is the same situation for almost all families. . . . How can we do otherwise? My mother lives with us. My father is departed. Six of us live in two tiny rooms. My mother is 60 years old, she is still strong and in good health to take care of the housework and to cook our meals. This leaves me some free time to do my sewing.

**Note:* All interviews conducted in Vietnam (here with Ly, Thu Van, Cat Tien and Anh) are excerpted and translated from the book *Vietnam, un peuple, des voix,* by Mai Thu Van (Paris: Pierre Horay, 1983). These interviews are reenacted in the film, with: Tran Thi Hien, both as Ly (her role) and as Hien (her real voice); Khien Lai as Thu Van and as Khien; Ngo Kim Nhuy as Cat Tien and as Kim; Tran Thi Bich Yen as Anh and as Yen.

"Let's say that my job is better [than others]: I belong to the restaurant service. Sometimes I go to the embassies when there is a reception or a dinner. I feel less isolated. . . . I do see the foreigners coming and going. . . . [But] we can't develop any relationship with them.

"In principle, a foreigner is already a spy. . . . Even a socialist. . . . Or even you (*Ly smiles*). We live in constant suspicion: between husband and wife, between parents and children. . . . Suspicion is everywhere. There is no mutual trust.

"When a foreigner gives us something, it may be because of pure sympathy for us; but it is often thought that they want to obtain something more from us. . . . You have to know how to compose yourself to be admitted in the heart of the system.

"Sometimes I revolt against the fact that our children can't have a bit of meat or fish, whereas the foreigners can sneeze at them. But Vietnam offers whatever it has best to the international diplomats and governmental staff. They should come and see, at least once, what a meal in a Vietnamese family is composed of!" (Interview with Ly)

Trong dam gi dep bang sen
La xanh, bong trang lai chen nhi vang
Nhi vang, bong trang, la xanh,
Gan bun ma chang hoi tanh mui bun.
What is more beautiful than a lotus in a pond?. . . .
Yellow stamens, white petals, green leaves:
Always near mud, it never smells of mud. (Trans. Nguyen Ngoc Bich)

He kept hold of her: "You try to run but I won't let you. Young woman, are you married yet?"
And she replied: "Easy, young man, you're spilling my rice! Yes, I am with husband, his surname is Viet and his given name is Nam"

(Voice off:) "[When I first met the women of the South,] we looked at each other with distrust, if not with hostility. Slowly we started talking to each other. From distrust, we have come to dialogue. And this was a radical turn that changed my political understanding. Before, I learnt in the political courses that capitalism was the exploitation of man by man. Period." (Thu Van)

(Quoted on screen:)
A society that imposes on its people a single way of thinking, a single way of perceiving life, cannot be a human society.
Thu Van, 35 years old, health technical cadre, Vietnam 1982

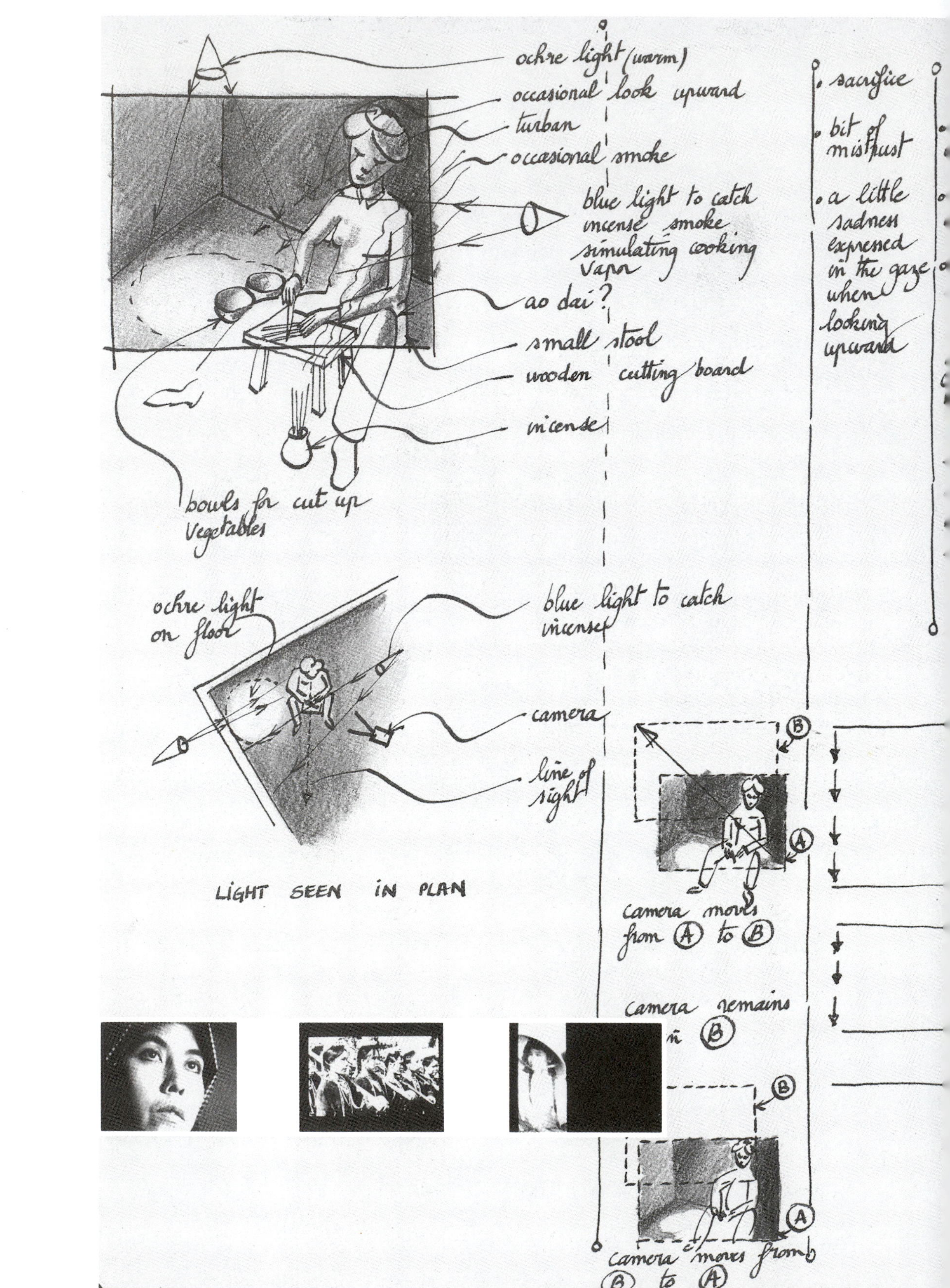
ochre light (warm)
occasional look upward
turban
occasional smoke
blue light to catch incense smoke simulating cooking vapor
ao dai?
small stool
wooden cutting board
incense
bowls for cut up vegetables
sacrifice
bit of mistrust
a little sadness expressed in the gaze when looking upward
ochre light on floor
blue light to catch incense
camera
line of sight
LIGHT SEEN IN PLAN
camera moves from A to B
camera remains on B
camera moves from B to A

Ly, 37 years old, employee, Viet

cutting green onions liseron carotts etc...

I have 3 children, that's quite e
~~years~~... Our two salaries are no
end of the day ~~to meet~~ [for] our mont
I do some sewing in the evenin
in the evening. [~~With much wil~~
We receive, from time to time, a
us 2 kilos of MSG, 3 kilos of woo
whatever we need [~~with the mo~~
~~situation for almost all families~~

stops cutting to arrange pant on right leg.

My father is departed. ~~Six of us~~ [We are]
is still strong and in good healt
This leaves me some free time to

Ly takes a vegetable from an adjacent place on her left

Let's say that my job is ~~less repe~~ [bette]
Sometimes I go to the embassies
isolated. We do see the foreigne
relationship with them.

Ly looks upward toward the left of the camera and below it level. Her gaze is very lively and becomes a bit dead afterwards while she looks slightly to the right as if talking to herself.

In principle, a foreigner is alre
We live in constant suspicion; b
children... Suspicion is everyw
~~work.~~ There is no mutual trust.
~~so as not to betray our intimate~~

When a foreigner gives us some
it is often thought that they wa
~~emphasis is laid on mutual suve~~
to be admitted in the heart of th

Ly finishes cutting and places some of the cut-up vegetables in 2-3 bowls (toward the end of the paragraph)

Sometimes I revolt against the f
whereas the foreigners can sne
supposedly because the meat is
the international diplomats and
once, what a meal in a Vietname

******

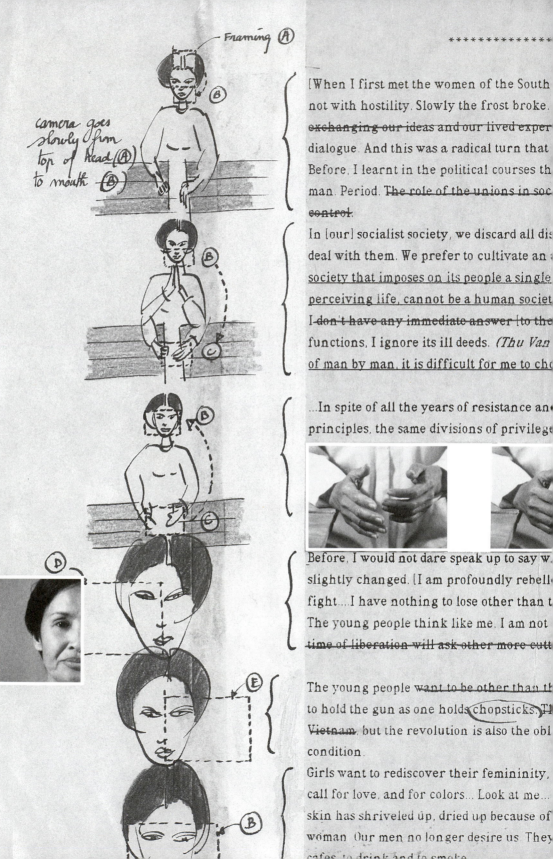

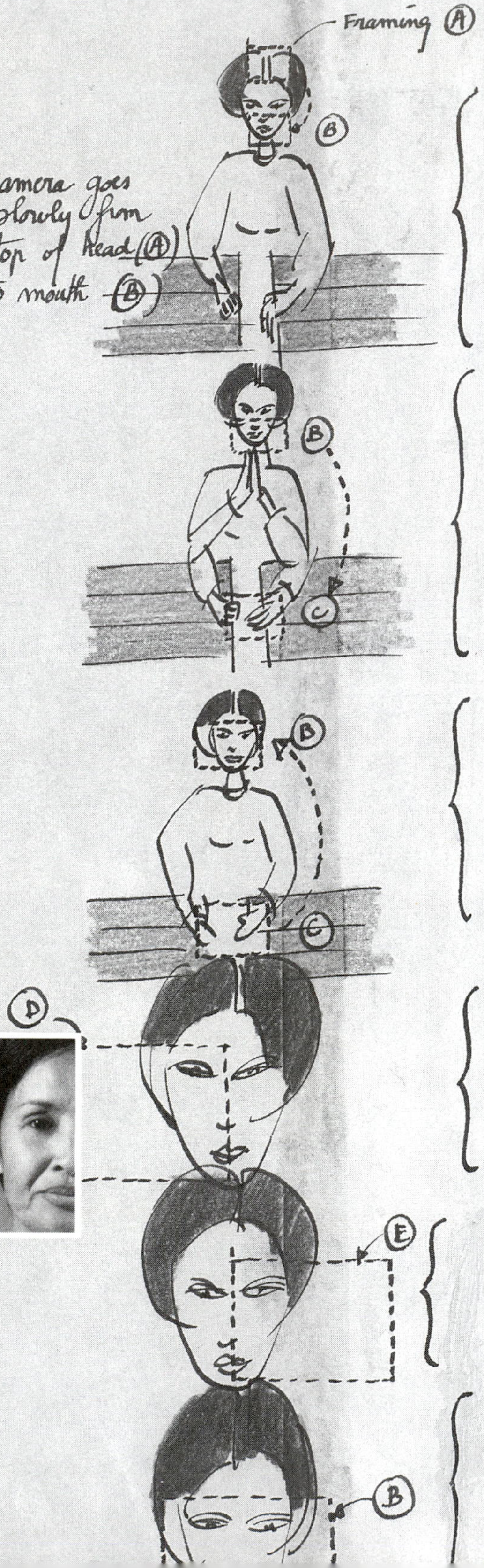

Framing (A)

(B)

camera goes slowly from top of head (A) to mouth (B)

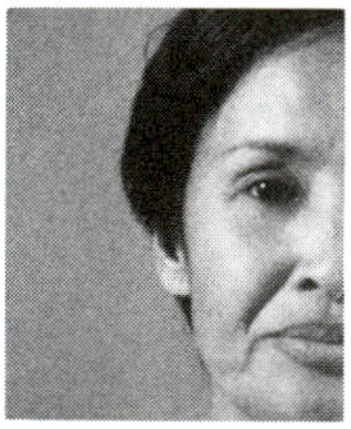

(B)

(C)

(B)

(C)

(D)

(E)

(B)

****

[When I first met the women of the South
not with hostility. Slowly the frost broke.
~~exchanging our ideas and our lived exper~~
dialogue. And this was a radical turn that
Before, I learnt in the political courses th
man. Period. ~~The role of the unions in soc~~
~~control~~.

In [our] socialist society, we discard all dis
deal with them. We prefer to cultivate an
society that imposes on its people a single
perceiving life, cannot be a human societ
I ~~don't have any immediate answer~~ [to the
functions, I ignore its ill deeds. *(Thu Van*
of man by man, it is difficult for me to ch

...In spite of all the years of resistance an
principles, the same divisions of privilege

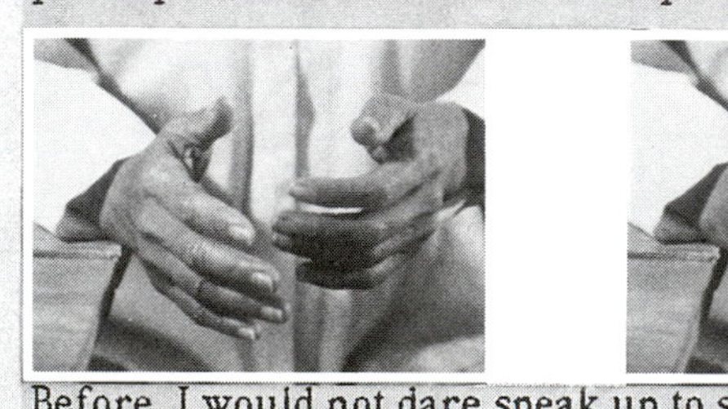

Before, I would not dare speak up to say w
slightly changed. [I am profoundly rebell
fight....I have nothing to lose other than t
The young people think like me. I am not
~~time of liberation will ask other more cutt~~

The young people ~~want to be other than th~~
to hold the gun as one holds chopsticks. Th
~~Vietnam~~, but the revolution is also the obl
condition.

Girls want to rediscover their femininity,
call for love, and for colors... Look at me...
skin has shriveled up, dried up because of
woman. Our men no longer desire us. They
cafes, to drink and to smoke.

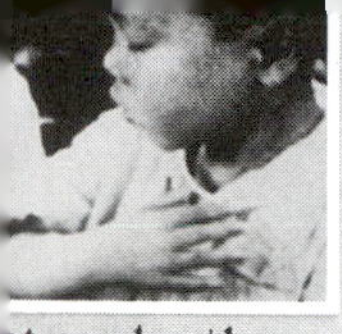

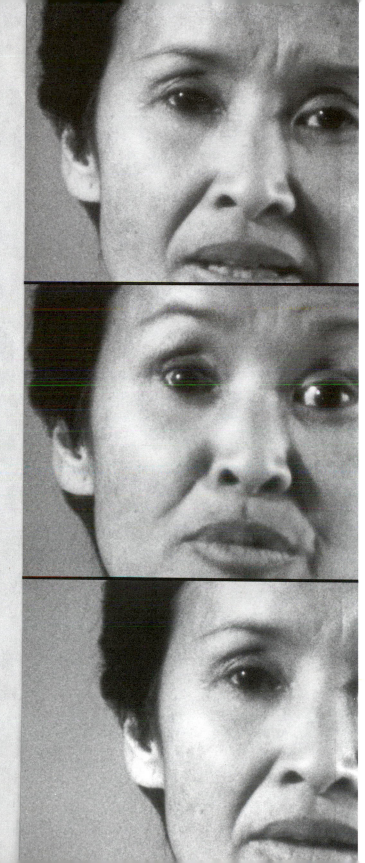

ıt each other with distrust, if
ılking to each other,
distrust, we have come to
my political understanding
was the exploitation of man by
~~is limited to an ideological~~

ıects so that we don't have to
ɔf fear and of suspicion.... A
king, a single way of

ignore how a capitalist society
ween two modes of explotation

n, the same hierachical
d. We cannot deny this
~~cy in our elders' mind~~..*and*
ss bathed in their customs
n example. One cannot kill

. But today, the situation has
awareness has turned fear into
alary and some rations tickets.
~~who were 10 years old at the~~
~~to the leaders.~~

~~oldier's cloths.~~ They are tired
~~image of heroic~~
vance human

ire, beauty. They
ave any breast, any hip... My
nment. I no longer look like a
time among themselves in

> **(Sync:)** "In [our] socialist society, we discard all disturbing subjects so that we don't have to deal with them. We prefer to cultivate fear and suspicion. . . . A society that imposes on its people a single way of thinking, a single way of perceiving life, cannot be a human society.
>
> "I ignore how a capitalist society functions, I ignore its diseases. (Thu Van smiles). . . . Between two modes of exploitation of man by man, it is difficult for me to choose! In spite of all the years of resistance and of revolution, the same hierarchical principles exist. We cannot deny what we have inherited from China. . . .
>
> "And in spite of our own divergences with China, we are nonetheless full of their customs and political conceptions. The camps of reeducation are an example. You cannot kill man's conviction by reducing him to an animal.
>
> "Before, I would not dare speak up to say what I thought. But today, the situation is different. [I have deeply rebelled,] and this awareness has turned fear into fight. . . . I have nothing to lose other than this ridiculous salary and some rations tickets.
>
> "The young people think like me, I am not alone. The young people are tired of holding the gun as one holds chopsticks. The revolution is also the obligation to live and to advance human condition. Girls want to rediscover their femininity, to please . . . to revive desire, beauty. They call for love, and for colors. . . . Look at me. . . . I no longer have any breast, any hip. . . . My skin has dried up because of undernourishment. I no longer look like a woman. Our men no longer desire us. They spend their time among themselves in cafes, drinking and smoking." (Interview with Thu Van)

There is always a tendency to identify historical breaks and to say "this begins there," "this ends here," while the scene keeps on recurring, as unchangeable as change itself.

Life seems suddenly fragile and vulnerable. . . . The past surfaces and what is almost forgotten reappears from the ruins.

Nobody knows, they say, whether Ho Xuan Huong really existed or whether she was a mere name. She wrote poems in the early 19th century, but they were notorious for the scandal they caused and they continue today to defy the principles of right speech and good manner of womanhood. So some men went as far as affirming that poems signed under her name might not be hers; they might, of course, be written by a man! Who was then, we may ask, this feminine man whose womanness was violently attacked and trashed by male poets of the time, and who wrote feminist poetry on free love, on single mothers, on *labia minora* and *labia majora* desire; who attacked polygamy and double standards of morality, who ridiculed empty male authority and religiosity, and who challenged all the norms of Confucian patriarchy?

When he claps his hands, she has entertained
When she claps her hands, he has made a significant contribution—to his village, his town, his country. The fatherland, as they call it now.

For a life to save another life
no more self-pride, no pride, no self
she kneels and begs mercy for him who is her son, her husband, her father.

(Quoted on screen:)
In the beginning, I tried to make things work* [*at the hospital*]*, but slowly, we found ourselves in an atmosphere of distrust, then of suspicion! I carried out my work in a heavy silence.
Wounds do not heal with humiliation.

Cat Tien, 50 years old, doctor, Vietnam 1982

"I am a doctor, with almost 20 years of experience. . . . My husband is also a doctor. He was assigned to the military hospital of the city. [When Saigon fell on April 30th, 1975,] we were among the most moderate. Without being communists, we are no less Vietnamese; we are nationalists. I will never erase the memory of [that day] from my mind. It was [total] panic. All our friends called us to urge us to leave. . . . My husband and I did not know what to do. . . . [He] told me: 'We have nothing to blame ourselves for, we are not criminals. We are from the South. If the country is divided into two, it is not because of us!' Of course, my husband wore the uniform, but he wore it in spite of himself. . . . Each government uses its citizens as it thinks best.

"My day began at 7:30 am and ended at 4:30 pm, with a break of one hour for lunch. Afterwards, I had to attend civil and political education courses. . . . Every other week, I had to write a resume of my past life. . . . I was smarter than them (laughs). I kept a copy of my first declaration. I recopied it exactly each time, respecting the commas and the periods. . . . In the beginning, I tried to make things work [at the hospital], but slowly, we found ourselves in an atmosphere of distrust, then of suspicion! I carried out my work in a heavy silence.

> "I stayed in the service for two years, and would probably have stayed on, had my husband not been arrested. . . . To tell the truth, we never knew the real reasons for his arrest.

(Verses below are heard voice off, simultaneous with interview:)
Nua dem an ai cung chong
Nua dem ve sang ganh gong ra di
(Loving her husband half of the night,
she spends the other half before dawn carrying her merchandise to market)

Gai cham chong me cha khac khoai
(The later she gets married, the more distressed her parents are)

Gai co chong nhu rong co vay,
Gai khong chong nhu coi xay chet ngong
(She who is married is like a dragon with wings,
She who has no husband is like a rice-mill with a broken axle)

> "Today, we suppose it was a problem of power and of competence. The patients prefer us to the [others]. There was a kind of complicity among the people of the South. . . . When the doctors of the new regime took over the hospital, all the services worked. Two years after, it was a disaster, the equipment was paralyzed, the stock of medicines emptied, the buildings dilapidated. . . . We, the older staff of the hospital, we became cumbersome. In a way, we assisted the failure of victory.

> "For a week, I didn't receive any news concerning my husband. I came up against a mixed silence around me.

(Verses heard simultaneously with interview)
. . . We are absurd petals in a puff of wind
drifting over a temporary and indifferent world.
Even the young, spring-limbed and green,
learn to stare at death through veils of white hair Nguyen Binh Khiem

Con co lan loi bo song
Ganh gao dua chong tieng khoc ni non.
Nang ve nuoi cai cung con
De anh di tray nuoc non Cao Bang.

(Exhausting herself on the riverside
while carrying rice to her husband, the stork cries dolefully,
Come back, dear, and feed our children
So I can leave for the hills and rivers of Cao Bang.)

> "My colleagues greeted me but never asked any questions about my husband's disappearance. . . . Everybody sank into silence. . . . It was terrible to live in the world of silence. I was no longer used to it. From then on, I was inhabited by a feeling of terror. I discovered fear. . . . Sometimes I did not even dare breathe, for fear of myself; I didn't want to hear my own heart beat. . . . Despair settled down within me. I had given up all form of resistance. After three months in that atmosphere, I decided to quit my job. As for my husband, I was left without news. I had to find out by myself the reasons for his arrest. . . . The question that kept on coming back in my mind was: 'Why did they wait two years before sending him to that camp of reeducation'?
>
> ". . . I prefer to forget that moment when I saw my husband in his prison clothes, looking devastated and desperate. It is a painful memory.
>
> ". . . Twenty five months! twenty five months in hell. My nerves cracked. . . . My children were neglected like orphans. The only reasonable solution was to quit that job, to accept to lose the rations tickets and to live in uncertainty. I earned 80 dong per month, a salary of destitution in a bath of humiliation." (Interview with Cat Tien)

> **(Voice off)** "Hmmm, ahem . . . I am not the ideal person [to be interviewed]. . . . I have never had a passion for politics although this does not mean that I am not interested in it." (Cat Tien)

> *"Kieu's life is very telling but it is not a singular case. I think there are hundreds, thousands of lives like hers."* (Kim, in Vietnamese)

"How tragic is women's fate," wrote Nguyen Du. In Vietnam, almost everybody, poor or rich, use verses from the *Kim Van Kieu* fluently in their daily expressions. Also known as *The Tale of Kieu,* the national epic poem recounts the misfortunes of women in the person of a beautiful talented woman, *Kieu,* whose love life has repeatedly served as a metaphor for Vietnam's destiny. The heroine, a perfect model of Confucian feminine loyalty and piety, was forced by circumstances, to sacrifice her life to save her father and brother from disgrace and humiliation, and to sell herself to become a prostitute, then a concubine, a servant, and a nun, before she was able to come back to her first lover. *Kim Van Kieu* was written in the early 19th century in the people's language *Nom*. Despite its length of 3,254 lines, it became so popular that it was widely cherished by all social strata only a few decades after it appeared. Illiterate people knew long passages of it by heart and recited it during evening gatherings. It has also been loved for its unorthodox approach to sexuality: although Kieu's destiny is meant to be sadly complicated because of the woman's beauty, she not only freely chooses her lover, but she also eagerly loves three men. Her life offers a revisionist interpretation of the Confucian principle of chastity that governed the conduct of women.

I wish to use my body as a torch
to dissipate the darkness
to awaken love among people
and bring peace to Viet Nam

Nhat Chi Mai poured gasoline over her body and lit the match

"Socialist Vietnam venerates the mothers and the wives. The woman does not exist, she is only a laborer. The liberation of women is understood here as a double exploitation.

". . . The men want to keep the better share of the cake. They hold the key positions of power, women only get the leftovers. . . . There is not a single woman at the Political Bureau. . . . The men are the only ones to discuss problems that concern us.

"[As for the Women's Union], the Mother-in-Laws' Union, they have made of us heroic workers, virtuous women. We are good mothers, good wives, heroic fighters. . . . Ghost women, with no humanity! They display us in shop-windows for foreign visitors who come to look at our lives, as if we were polite animals.

"The image of the woman is magnified like that of a saint! . . . We are only human beings. Why don't we want to admit that these women are tired of seeing their children exposed to war, deprivations, epidemics, and diseases? The very idea of heroism is monstrous!

"The woman is alone, she lives alone, she raises her children alone. She gives birth alone. It's a sea of solitude! The revolution has allowed the woman to have access to

SV

the working world. She works to deprive herself better, to eat less. She has to get used to poverty.

"Love . . . (*Thu Van smiles*). When I was young, I wanted to become a writer. My parents told me: "You have to write with your heart, but don't forget your heart belongs to the Party." How to write then? I have therefore quit writing for a more scientific profession.

"Love. . . . Personally I have crossed this word from my vocabulary, I no longer want to remember. I live in total emptiness, around me, perhaps inside me. . . .

"Yes, we have to live for love. It is an emotion that escapes men's control, that happens inside the body, a very personal intimacy. . . . I end up loving my bicycle! My old bicycle with its old tires. I have a sincere affection for it because it helps me when I am tired. It is a loyal companion. It keeps me company in my morning solitude, it takes me home in my distress in the evening. It is the only witness of my movements. . . ." (Interview with Thu Van)

(Quoted on screen:)
Socialist Vietnam venerates the mothers and the wives. The woman does not exist, she is only a laborer. The liberation of women is understood here as a double exploitation. . . .
The very idea of heroism is monstrous!

(Quoted on screen:)
. . . Life could have gone on smoothly if there had not been the liberation of the South, the reunification and my being transferred to Saigon. . . . A painful confrontation, indeed.

Thu Van, 35 years old, health technical cadre, Vietnam 1982

"I am willing to talk, but you should not have doubts about my words. There is the image of the woman and there is her reality. Sometimes the two do not go well together!

"I am 35 years old, the age of the resistance movement and the revolution! I do not know what a society of peace looks like! My childhood was that of the struggle. I am a child of the Party. My parents are high cadres. They have [fed] me with revolutionary discourses since my childhood. My childhood was secure, I was puffed up, cherished; and there were always adequate answers to my questions. I went to school

> with the red scarf around my neck, and at 16 years old, I was trusted an important role. I was leader at the [Youth Organization], of my University. . . . I was taught discipline and rigor!
>
> ". . . Life could have gone on smoothly if there had not been the liberation of the South, the reunification and my being transferred to Saigon. . . . A painful confrontation, indeed!" (Interview with Thu Van)

". . . Even you who live in the West, if you are admired and liked, it's because we, women of Vietnam, we work so that your image may be beautiful. We contribute to the respect the world has for Vietnamese women."—Ai Tran, from Vietnam

The two sisters Trung Trac and Trung Nhi of Vietnam's earliest history of resistance are proudly remembered for the uprising they led in fighting against Chinese domination. Every year in Spring time, on the sixtieth day of the second moon, young Hai Ba Trung are seen parading on their elephants in the community in L.A. It is fantasied that to conquer their female armies, the only successful strategy the Chinese soldiers finally came up with was to strip themselves to the skin and expose their "thing" shamelessly to the sight of their female opponents. The women fighters retreated in disgust and the Trung sisters committed suicide.

The stories that grew around the beloved heroines of Vietnam history tell about both the dreams of women and the fears of the men who fought or heard of such account. Popular descriptions of the physical appearance of the sisters Trung are often confusingly similar to those of Trieu Thi Trinh, another cherished figure in the memory of the Vietnamese and a young peasant woman who led thirty battles against the Chinese. She was said to be nine feet tall, with frightful breasts, three meters long, flying over her shoulders as she rode on an elephant. She too committed suicide rather than return to serfdom when her army was defeated.

"Toi muon cuoi con gio manh, dap duong song du, chem cha trang-kinh o be Dong, quet bo coi de cuu dan ra khoi noi dam duoi chu khong them bat chuoc nguoi doi cui dau cong lung lam ti-thiep cho nguoi ta . . ." (Trieu Thi Trinh)
(I only want to ride the wind and walk the waves, slay the big whales of the Eastern sea, clean up frontiers, and save the people from drowning. Why should I imitate others, bow my head, stoop over and be slave to a man?)

We call her: Trieu Thi Trinh, but also Trieu Trinh Vuong, Trieu-Trinh, Trieu-Au, Ba Trieu.

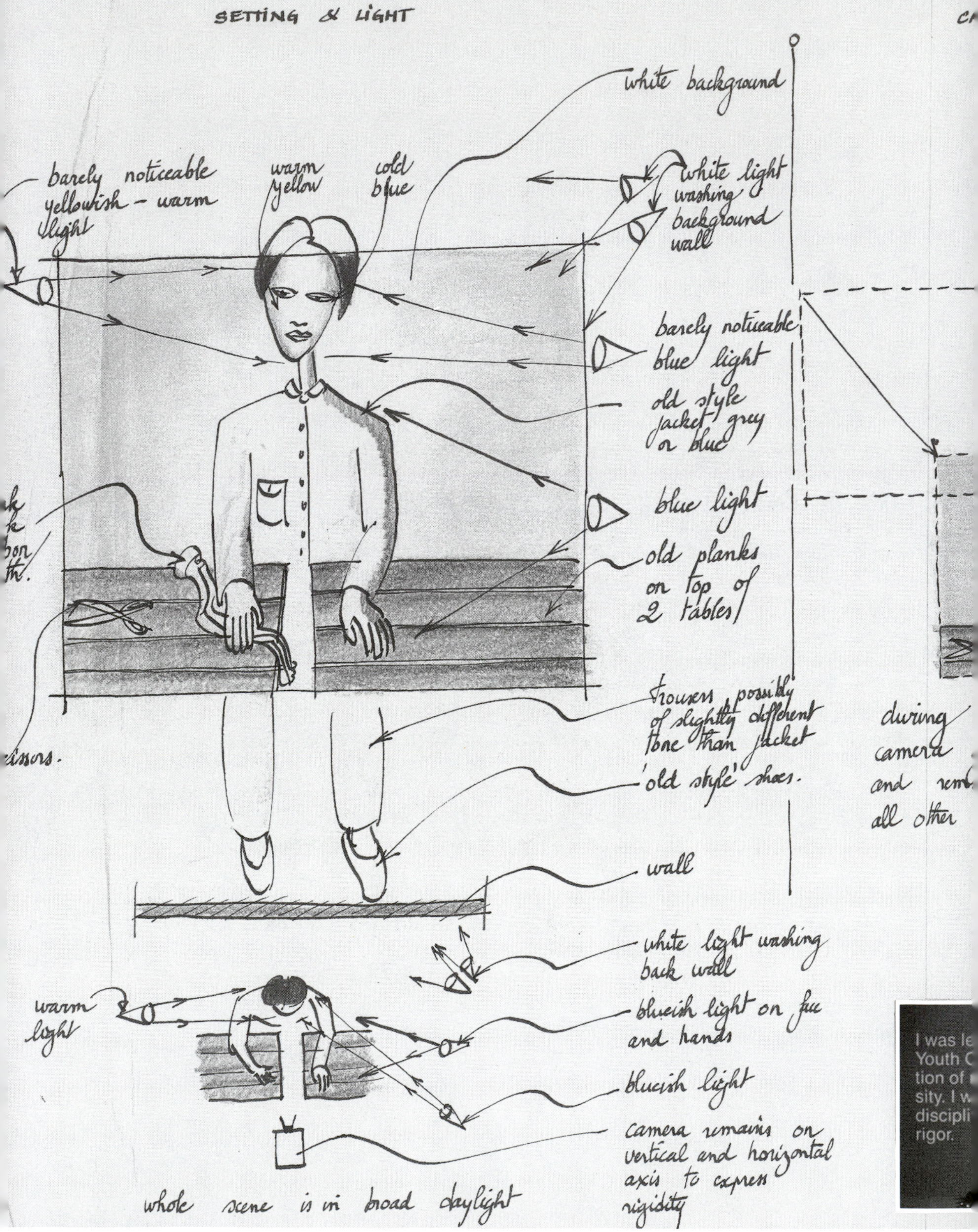

SETTING & LIGHT

white background

barely noticeable yellowish - warm light

warm yellow

cold blue

white light washing background wall

barely noticeable blue light

old style jacket grey or blue

blue light

old planks on top of 2 tables

trousers possibly of slightly different tone than jacket

'old style' shoes.

wall

during camera and remb all other

white light washing back wall

warm light

blueish light on face and hands

blueish light

camera remains on vertical and horizontal axis to express rigidity

whole scene is in broad daylight

I was le Youth C tion of sity. I w discipli rigor.

RAMING

GENERAL IDEA

North / South duality and ambivalence expressed through gaps between tables & warm and cold light on both sides of face.

Rigidity reflected in centeredness of subject and static camera

THU VAN'S GENERAL MOVEMENTS

body remains parallel to film image plane

hands and arms play freely with "red" ribbon

Thu Van looks directly at the camera

POSSIBLE SPECIFIC MOVEMENTS

camera goes from (A) to (B)

camera remains in (B)

hand slowly descending from forehead across eyes and down on table

paragraph (A) to (B) (3) during

Thu Van, 35 years

I was not born

~~I am not originally~~

1 [where I live since

experiences, that i

with the Southern

~~One can brood over~~

~~capital letters ever~~

the lives of women

1.2 ~~The Vietnamese wo~~

~~known calmness a~~

You live abroad, yo

distress. You canno

~~of Vietnamese wom~~

and mental sufferi

years.

1.3 *(Thu Van is close*

sad)

I am willing to talk

image of the woma

together!

I am 35 years old, t

know what a societ

1.4 child of the Parti. M

discourses since m

there was always a

scarf around my n

leader at the [Yout

taught discipline a

.... Life could have

the reunification a

1.6 indeed!

Our entire reason c

evolution... emerge

thought of!

The market remains women's city. "It is the heart of daily life where information is exchanged, and where rumors are spread." It is also at the market that one tastes the real popular cooking of the country.

My worthless husband gambles all day,
but if I told the world we'd both be shamed. . . .
Don't laugh, it's true, I'm the daughter
of a Confucian house. A work of art
sold to a stupid bumpkin, that's what I am.
A golden dragon bathing in a dirty pond!

They spread, on the pavements, their baskets full of merchandises and wait patiently.

Song gui nac, that gui xuong
([to her husband's family,] Alive, she entrusts her body
Dead, she entrusts her bones)

> "I will tell you the lives of women who are the misfits of history. They are by the thousands, those who live in economic distress. They sell everything that is marketable, including their bodies to support their family. They deny their dignity to survive and become prostitutes in a socialist society.
>
> **(She stares at the interviewer and says ironically:)**
> "[You're asking me if there are social services to help them?] You must be dreaming! . . . You underestimate the drama of the women of the South! We suffered the war like all our women compatriots. This war went on without our consent, we were swept along as in a tornado. Crushed by the machine, and nobody could stop it.
>
> "Today, many women must demean themselves because they have no choice at all. Some accept to live with a cadre simply because of economical necessity; they obtain thereby tickets and protection. . . . Sometimes they do it with the best intention, in the hope that their husband may be liberated. Time goes by and they see nothing happening. Sometimes a woman finds herself pregnant but goes to the camp nevertheless to visit her husband. She stands there in front of him with this belly of humiliation. The latter looks down and remains silent. I will spare you of the most sordid dramas that many women live through since the existence of the reeducation camps." (Interview with Cat Tien)

Hoa thom mat nhi di roi,
Con thom dau nua ma nguoi uoc ao?
(The fragrant flower has already lost its stamen
Why keep desiring it when it no longer bears fragrance?)

(Newsreel sound): "When the smoke clears, the inevitable roundup of prisoners, many of them seriously wounded. Among the captured a large group of women, traditionally used by the enemy as ammunition bearers, village infiltrators and informers. . . ."

Always recurring in the prisoner's mind is the fear of a time when the witnesses themselves die without witnesses, when History consists of tiny explosions of life, and of deaths without relays.

The witnesses go on living to bear witness to the unbearable.

Trong tranh nhu non khong quai
Nhu thuyen khong lai, nhu ai khong chong.
Gai co chong nhu gong deo co,
Gai khong chong nhu phan go long danh.
(Unstable like a hat without a chin-strap,
like a boat without rudder, as she is without a husband.
She who is married wears a yoke on her neck,
But she who has no husband is like a bed whose nails have come loose.)

Song bao nhieu nuoc cho vua
Trai bao nhieu vo cung chua bang long.
(There is never enough water to fill the river
There is never enough women to please a young man.)

Selling one's body remains an active trade. A Vietnamese woman journalist said: "Nothing runs in our blood except venereal disease. . . . Women do not become prostitutes for pleasure; they suffer the counter-shocks of our country's history. . . . French colonisation, American presence, long war years that have dismantled our society. . . . Today all we have left is the promise for a better society. But the sun rises every morning on anguish and uncertainty; it goes down every evening with the fear of not being able to nourish one's family."

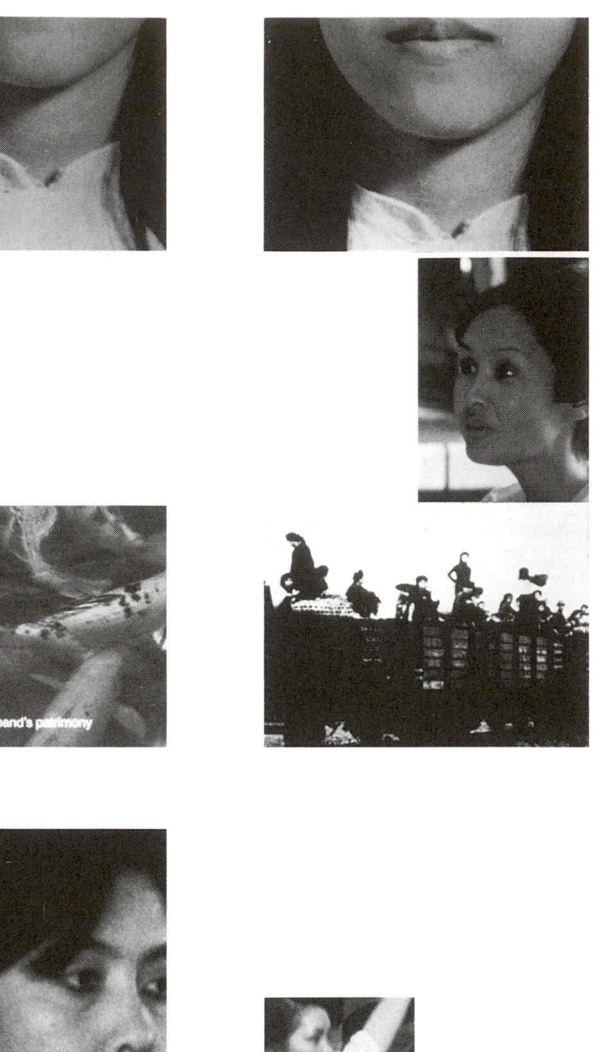
band's patrimony

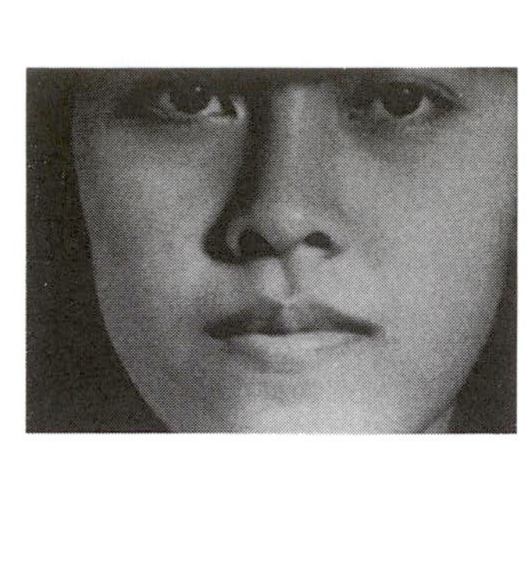

With childre
have peac

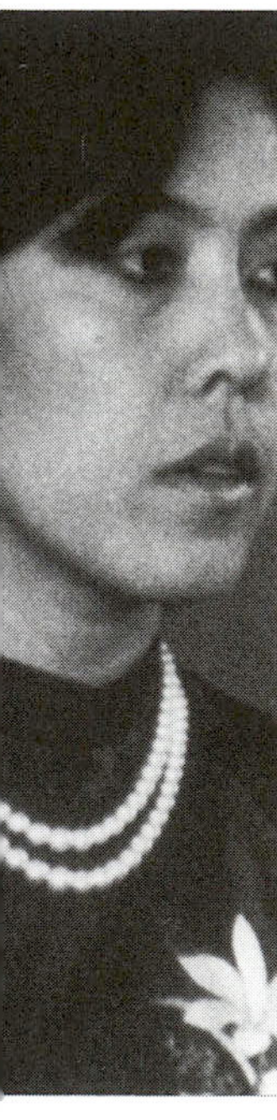

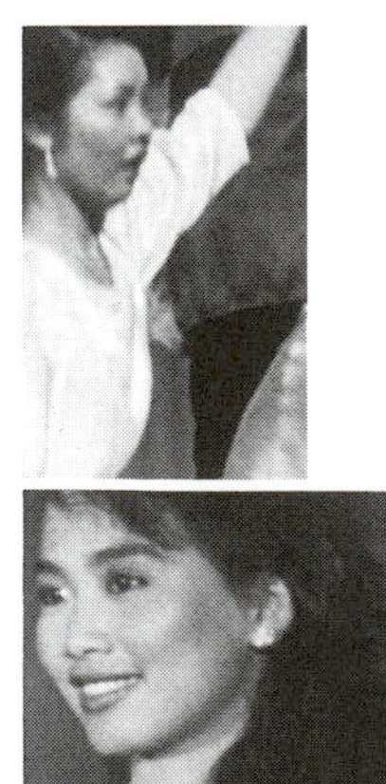
Dung Ngon Hanh
1988

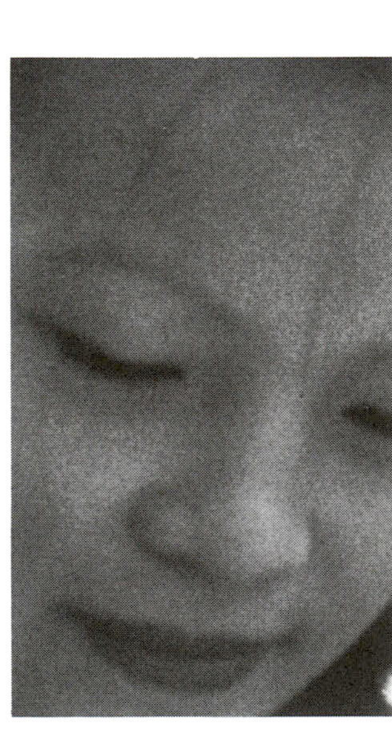

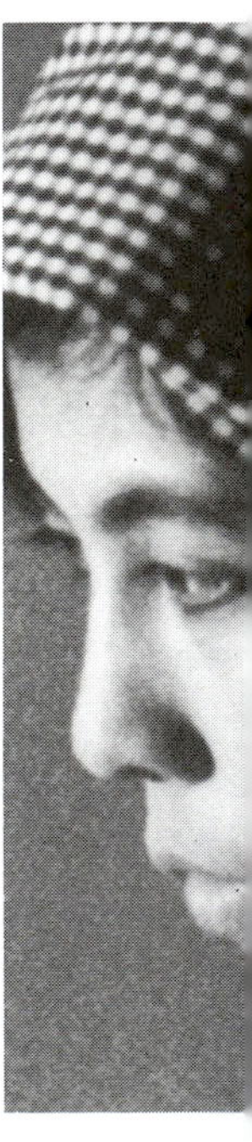

My . . . mother married me off to a child
(God knows there was no lack of young men)
and now his mauling is all the love I get. . . .
He falls asleep and snores till morning.
I ask you: What kind of spring is this?
Sisters, how many times is a flower to bloom?

Chem cha cai kiep lay chong chung,
Ke dap chan bong, ke lanh lung.
Nam thi muoi hoa nen chang cho,
Mot thang doi lan co cung khong.
Co dam an xoi, xoi lai ham,
Cam bang lam muon, muon khong cong.
Than nay vi biet duong nay nhi?
Tha truoc thoi danh o vay xong!
Ho Xuan Huong
(One rolls in warm blankets, the other freezes:
Damned this husband-sharing destiny!
You're lucky ever to have him,
He comes perhaps twice a month, or less.
Ah—to fight for—this!
Turned to a half-servant, an unpaid maid!
Had I known I would have stayed single.)

(Quoted on screen:)
I gazed at my [own image] with sustained attention and realized I wore the same clothes, the same wooden shoes, for as long as I could remember. I didn't think another world existed. I was stirred to the depth of my soul by a mad anguish, and my mind became confused. I became aware of my own existence!

Anh, 60 years old, doctor, Vietnam 1982

(Voice off, simultaneous with sync, below:) "My sister lives in the South. . . . I went to see her after the reunification. . . . More than 20 years of absence. . . . of suffering and of separation. But my sister didn't choose exile. We are too attached to our family links. We couldn't say a word. **(Sync:)** We looked at each other in silence for a long moment, full of tears and choking with emotions. More than 20 years have separated us and it was like a miracle to find ourselves there, facing each other again. . . .

> "My sister sat still. She was staring at me as if I came from another planet. I could see a glimmer of revolt in her eyes. Suddenly her cold, grave voice told me: 'You, my little sister . . . the socialist doctor! . . .' She stood up from her chair, took my hand and led me to a mirror: "Look at yourself at least once!" I had not, indeed, looked at myself in a mirror for years, and I saw an old, worn-out woman. . . . I gazed at my [own image] with sustained attention and realized I wore the same clothes, the same wooden shoes for as long as I could remember. I didn't think another world existed. I was stirred to the depth of my soul by a mad anguish and my mind became confused. I became aware of my own existence! . . .
>
> "Peace restored, our problems have increased, professional relations have deteriorated. Equality between men and women still figures on the program, but the relations between women themselves are more uncomfortable. The officer in charge is a woman, [but] she is not a doctor. Her function is above all political, she is there to control the ideological aspect of the profession. An irresolvable conflict has arisen between her and the health technicians. It's a problem of power—political power versus professional competence! . . .
>
> "We have been trained to think that a woman has to please a man to the detriment of another woman. If only woman could trust woman, then we could talk about revolution." (Interview with Anh)

(Quoted on screen:)
If only men reread their history books, they would never dare send their people killing each other for ideologies. The Vietnamese people fought to* [*throw off*] *the yoke of domination. They didn't fight for some ideological principles. One should never forget this essential point.

Anh, 60 years old, doctor, Vietnam 1982

Dear sister, what we loved most at the time my girlfriends and I, was to be able to buy little snacks to pass them on secretly to each other during class. *O mai, xi mui, che dau do, che dau trang,* how would you translate these into English? I am thrilled just at naming them! It was a real treat to savor them at one of these street-vendors' carts in front of Gia-Long School, or at Nga Sau, not far from our house, where *che sam bo luong* was their specialty! I gave some private lessons then and had some pocket-money I could spend. Since mother had always forbade us to eat on the street, I felt particularly excited to do so and to taste anything that appeared novel to me. When I think about them now, they were really nothing special, but the fact that they were forbidden made all the difference!

My friend, who was from the central region, said in Hue, girls coming back from school in hats and white *ao dai,* crowded the Truong Tien bridge every afternoon, their tunics flapping softly in the wind like butterflies. Every young man had gone through a period when he would regularly find himself standing there just to look and contemplate. If he followed her on her left, she would pull her hat down on the left side of her face, if he stepped to the right, she would pull it down on the right side to prevent him looking while she kept on glancing at him at leisure. The majority of the people there wrote and appreciated poetry, perhaps because of its unforgettable landscapes, just like those in the North about which mother and father so often told us.

Gio dua canh truc la da
Tieng chuong Thien Mu, canh ga Tho Xuong
(The wind softly rocking the bamboo blends in with
the bells of the Thien Mu Pagoda and the rooster's song of Tho Xuong
village)

"The Vietnamese woman has two qualities I've always praised: her ability to sacrifice and to endure". **(Yen, in Vietnamese)**

". . . Here, everything is public. We receive our patients in a cold, large hall, in the presence of the officer in charge. It's very difficult to establish trust. How do you want a woman to disclose her intimate sufferings when there is no intimacy to preserve professional confidences? It is impossible to feel for someone's pains and sufferings when there is no complicity between a doctor and her patient. . . .

"When a woman understood nothing about her body, about hygiene or contraception, she came to see me and shyly whispered these to me. . . . The Vietnamese woman does not unburden herself easily to someone; she is caught in prejudices, inhibitions and taboos. In the old society, the body was an unnamed place, a non-existent and not-talked-of place. If the woman's body got sick, it was immediately thought that she had had sexual relations outside the norm. . . . Even today, this mentality continues to bloom in our society. . . . Ignorance drives women to a world of silence." (Interview with Anh)

To marry and have a child, how banal!
But to be pregnant without the help of a husband, what merit! Ho Xuan Huong

Up there, a hanging panel:
The Governor's Shrine.
Oh, well, if I were turned into a man
I'd do better things than that! Ho Xuan Huong

Doctors: women who relieve other women

As in a fairy tale, "the flowers falling from my lips are changed into toads"

She helps, he directs
She directs, he reigns

> "It is a contempt for human effort to believe that we adapt ourselves, even to poverty! Our fellow people who live abroad do sometime have the same reasoning. They come back to their native land to visit their relatives, they temporarily share their promiscuity, then they go away. They can afford a small effort of heroism, and adapt themselves to the unusual surroundings.
>
> "But for those of us who remain in the country, we have to go on living this life without any joy or pride. To say that we are courageous or heroic beings is to pay a tribute to our revolution. But to glorify us is, in a way, to deny our human limits." (Interview with Anh)

Ai vo Binh Dinh ma coi
Dan ba cung biet cam roi di quon
(Come and see the women of Binh Dinh
who also know how to handle the rod and practice boxing)

The notorious double day flashes back in my memory: women work as a full unit of economic production *and* do all the unpaid housework and child care. Popular sayings qualify the three steps of her life and her victimization as that of a lady before marriage, that of a maid during marriage, and that of a monkey long after marriage.

> "One has to demystify the image of the ideal woman that has been made up and fortified for the needs of significant moments. It is only to better hide her exploitation that they flatter her conceit. Let us take the example of the street sweepers. These women are doing repellent, very repellent work. . . . They select a few of them and they put them on the platform during a congress or a meeting. They make

them read political discourses quickly put together by men, and the trick meets with success. These women forget for a while that they are sweepers, and have the illusion of being full citizens." (Interview with Thu Van)

"I am caught between two worlds. . . ." (Thu Van)

—and I would have to affirm this uncertainty: is a translated interview a written or spoken object?

"Our bosses are often men, women assist them. . . . This is what equality amounts to! We fight very tightly for our rights, but the men always succeed to win over. Sometimes they may make a few compromises because we outweigh them in number. In meetings, women never take the floor to claim or demand, they speak but only in a feminine spirit. . . . [I mean] a spirit eager to please. To please their boss. They can't simply say "we think" or "we want" . . . they only *submit* such opinion or such solicitation. They listen and they raise their little fingers. It's very difficult to speak freely when one does not have the power.

"[The cadres of the Women's Union] are our mothers-in-law. They recite texts written by men and put women on the work market. . . ." (Ly)

". . . We must fight for . . . a more equitable society. When we will have won the fight against bureaucracy, swept away the incompetent cadres, then we will have made a first step toward revolution. And this task also belongs to women." (Thu Van)

"Women have always been educated to sacrifice themselves. Women do not dare say they are being mistreated by their husbands. . . .
Meetings are the places where adverse or different ideas are minimized. They do not allow any room for confidences on our intimate lives. . . .
You have to be careful when you look at our society. There is the form and there is the content. Truth is not always found in what is visible. . . . Our reality is inhabited by silent tears and sobs. . . . Women's liberation? You are still joking, aren't you?" (Ly)

Interview: an antiquated device of documentary. Truth is selected, renewed, displaced and speech is always tactical

So how many interviews in the overall?
Whom do you choose?

SETTING

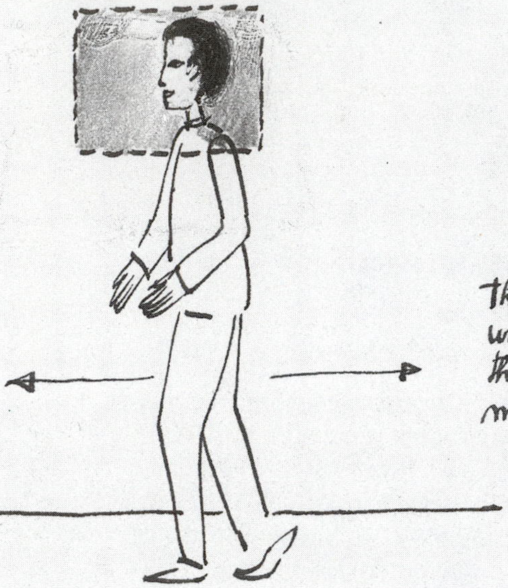

CAMERA FRAMING

camera moves right to left and vice versa but does not follow Thu Van's pacing

Example in plan:

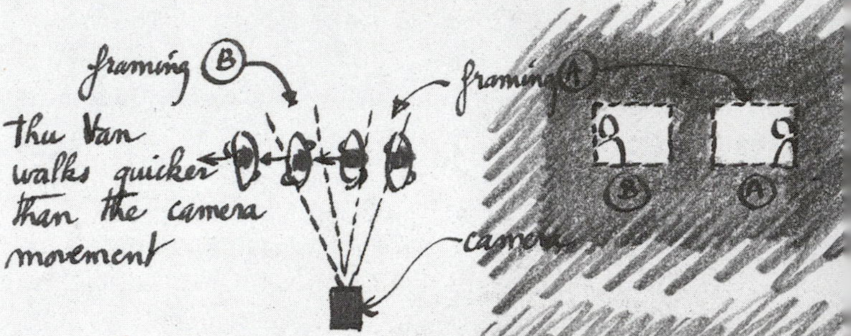

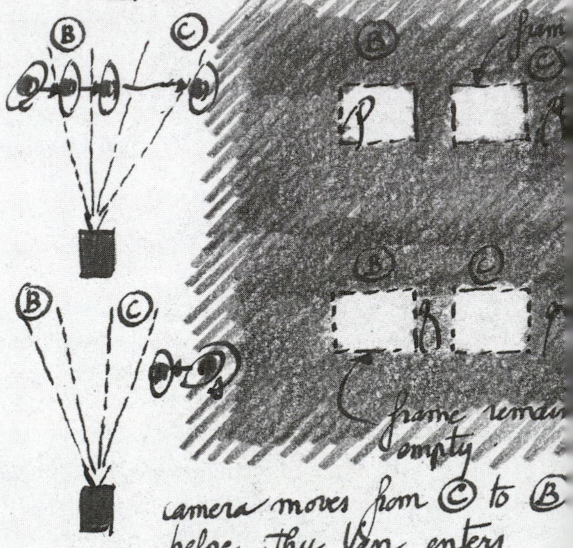

framing (B)

framing (A)

Thu Van walks quicker than the camera movement

camera

frame remain empty

camera moves from (C) to (B) before Thu Van enters the picture.

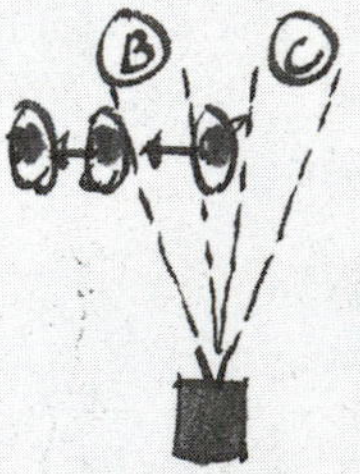

camera goes back to (C) contrary to Thu Van's main pacing direction

idea is that camera does not always on object; surrounding space is as im as object itself; empty space to engage in projecting ... etc. -

- Thu Van walks along the white wall from right to left and left to right during the entire paragraph.
- She is pacing the room as if talking to herself
- Thu Van turns her face toward the camera at: "and have the illusion"

It is only to better
exploitation that they f
conceit. Let us take the e
the street sweepers: Thes
are doing a repellent, very
job... They select a few of
they put them on the platfo
a congress or a meeting. T
them read political c

One has to demystify the image of the ideal woman ma
of significant moments. It is only to better hide her ex
conceit. Let us take the example of the street sweepers
repellent, very repellent work... They select a few of t
platform during a congress or a meeting. They make t
quickly put together by men, and the trick meets with
for a while that they are sweepers, and have the illusi

quickly put togeth
trick meets with succe
women forget for a while th
sweepers, and have the
being full citizens. I a
between two worlds: this
which I reject and the
which I do not know. I am
with no society model.

Personally, I know I will never reach the shore of soc
worlds: this socialism which I reject and the capitalism
survivor with no society model. ~~Traditional Vietnames~~
dismantled...There are too many contradictions. My mi
so as not to ask too many questions, so as not to drown

~~The politics of the arbitrary has led the best elements~~
individuals do not let themselves be impressed by ideo
....We must fight for... a more equitable society. When
against bureaucracy, swept away the incompetent cad
first step toward revolution. And this task also devolve

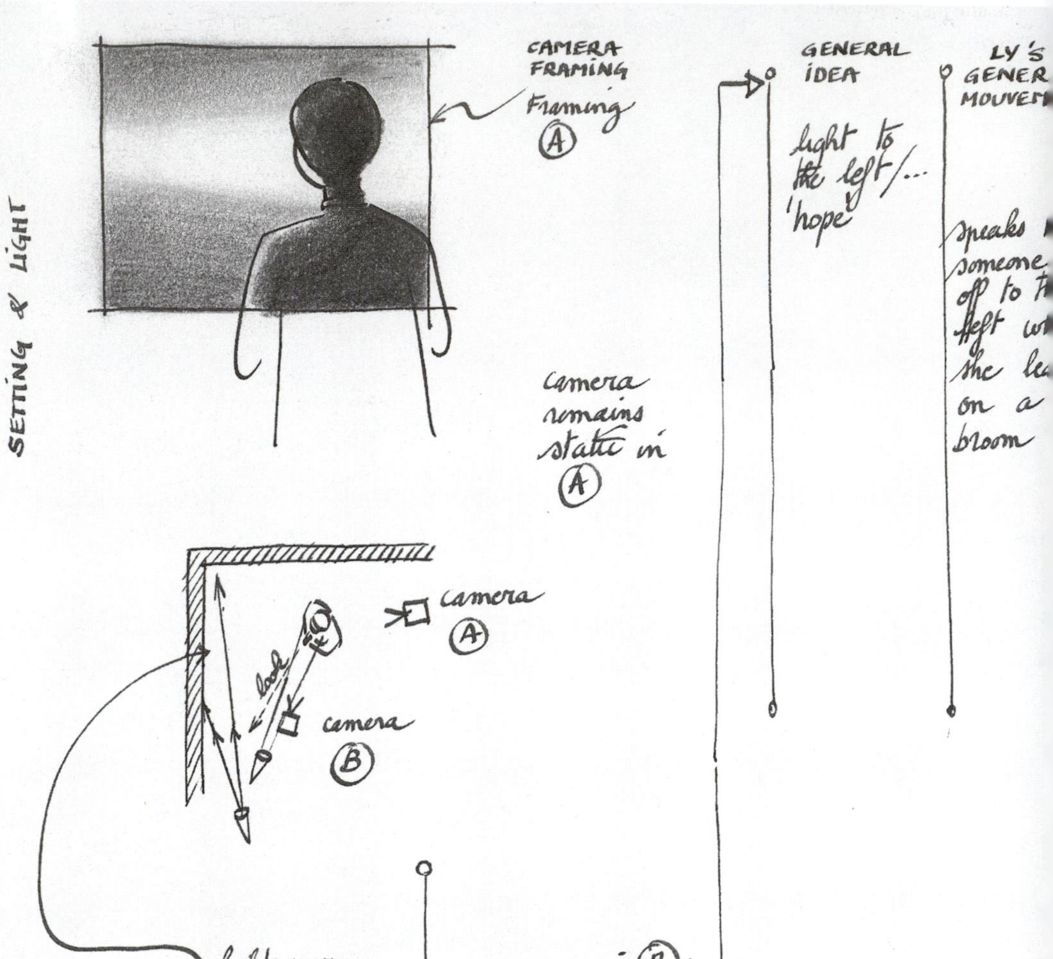

SETTING & LIGHT

CAMERA FRAMING

Framing (A)

GENERAL IDEA

light to the left/... 'hope'

LY'S GENER MOUVEM

speaks someone off to t left w she le on a broom

camera remains static in (A)

camera (A)

look

camera (B)

light warm ochre light slightly above camera field

camera in (B)!

broom

camera goes upward very slowly and stops on face at the final sentence or slightly before

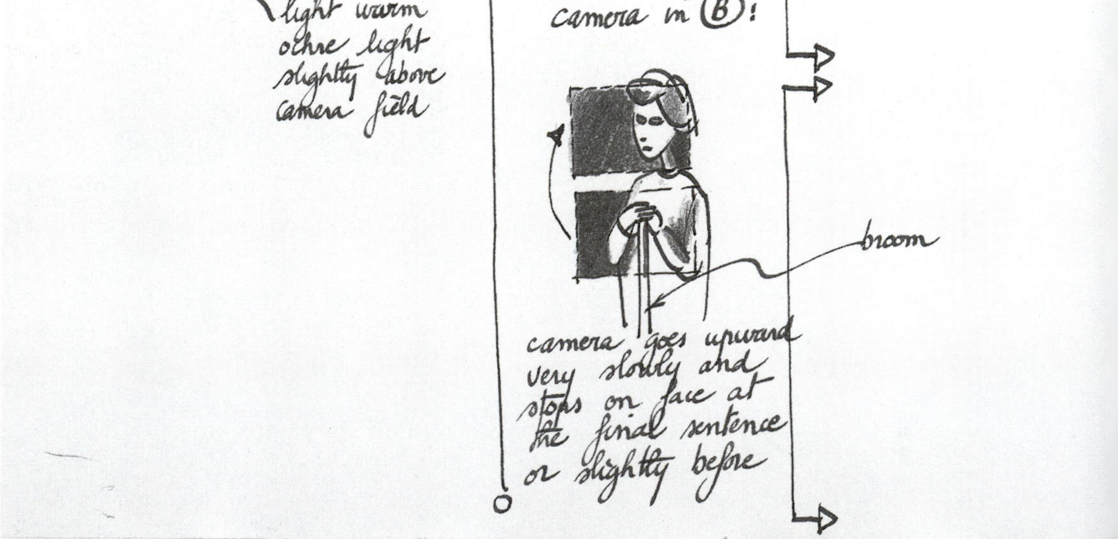

CIFIC
EMENTS

Our bosses are often men, women assi
~~not always easy~~; we fight very tightly
win over. Sometimes they may make
in number. In meetings, women neve
but only in a feminine spirit....[I mea
They can't simply say "we think" or
~~such sollicitation~~. They listen and th
speak freely when one does not have

[The cadres of the Women's Union] a
texts written by men and put women
family interests or battered women...
suffering. The old customs prevail, w
by their husbands. They are ashame

~~In meetings, first we talk about diffi~~
~~other problems encountered in daily~~
are the places where ~~adverse or~~ diff
~~room for confidences on our intimat~~

They talk a lot about equality and co
together, then the Vietnamese socie

Today we can say that the woman ha
she will speak after the men, she wi
always been educated to sacrifice th
through this....Even if the laws on se
change our ancestors' mentalities in

You have to be careful when you loo
the context. Truth is not always foun
silent tears and sobs.

[Women's Liberation!] You are still

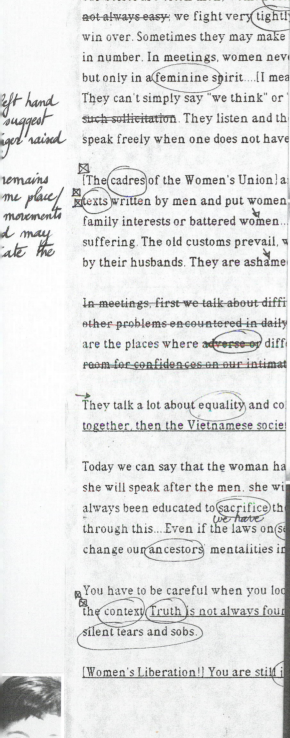

eft hand
suggest
ger raised

remains
me place/
movements
d may
ate the

we have

In one case, 150 interviews were made for the film. Five were retained in the final version.

What criteria?

age, profession, economical situation, cultural regions—North, South and Center—critical ability, personal affinity.

Spoken, transcribed and translated
From listening to recording; speech to writing
You can talk, we can cut, trim, tidy up

The game often demands a response to the content, rarely to the way that content is framed

Spoken *and* read

Between a language of inwardness and that of pure surface

Dear sister, there was something particularly pleasurable in going to an ice cream place to enjoy a drink in Vietnam. I feel no such excitement here, where ice cream shops have no ambiance. To find such pleasure again, one has to go all the way to Houston, Texas, or to Santa Ana, California, where the Vietnamese communities form their own towns and villages. It sounds like getting old and outdated.

The pose is always present, and accidents on film are known as "controlled accidents."

The more intimate the tone, the more successful the interview.

Every question she and I come up with is more or less a copy of the question we have heard before. Even if the statement is original it sounds familiar, worn, threadbare.

By choosing the most direct and spontaneous form of voicing and documenting, I find myself closer to fiction.

(Transcribed from Hien's Ao Dai presentation, in a grade school classroom):
Hien: "Good morning teacher, good morning boys and girls. I'm Hien Tran, Vin-

cent's Mom. Today I have a chance to talk to you about Vietnamese women's dress, *ao dai*. We call it *ao dai*. Vietnam has over four thousand years of history. In the beginning the Vietnamese women's dress was composed of three pieces, one in the back and two in front. The two pieces tie together. In 1744 Vietnamese King Vo, V-O, asked all Vietnamese women to dress with pants, pants like this."

(Two American children model the traditional dress)

Khien: "We would like to show you the *ao dai* designed by Madame Nhu like Mrs. Tran just told you."

(Transcribed from a conversation during lunch):
Khien: "Oh, I tell you, the first time in my life I never knew how to carry water across my shoulders. It [the pole] bites into me. But I had to do it. I act *real* good, and after 3 months they thought I had become a 'country girl,' not a Saigon person anymore. Because they were always watching us, day by day, time by time. Even at lunch. They opened the door and walked right away in my kitchen—they want to watch what I eat! But you know what, we only eat a little bit of egg (*xao xao trung*) and vegetables out of our garden."

"I speak a little English, also my husband."

". . . Yeah. I say, No, please stop, no, I don't want to escape. If I wanted to escape, I escape years ago, when Saigon first fell. I can go in the harbor—there are a lot of ships—and I can jump on a ship and escape. But no, I love our country. After my husband was reeducated by the government I love our country. So no, please don't shoot me. No. He said, 'Are you telling me the truth?' I said, I swear!"

"But you know, I read the book my husband had in the reeducation camp. So I know how to talk, So I said, I believe in the government, I believe in the chairman. We have been liberated! Why would I want to escape? I am Vietnamese. I don't even know English. I convinced him and he said, 'Hey Chi Tu'—he called me Chi Tu because I changed my name, I didn't want to be called Khien—'What is your education, what level?' I said, well—I only talk a lot—I said I have no education."

(Images of Khien at the Japanese gardens with a small boy)
Khien (voice over): "Fifteen minutes. It took me fifteen days to see him for fifteen minutes. Then I had to come back to Saigon. After I listen to my husband I came home and sold everything—the TV, the radio, the furniture, good clothes, everything goes to the fleamarket and from then I became a saleslady. On the street, in the street. I buy things, resell things, get a profit to take care of my children."

(Images of Khien and Hien sitting in a crowd, watching a show intercut with Khien at lunch)
Khien (voice off, then sync): "It was 1976. Twelve years later I work with Hills Company. They put me at the fire. They say, that one, we'll get her. And I knew about

> the fire. I talked with my supervisor, I said, no, please. He said, What's the matter? I said, everytime I look at the fire my nightmares come back and I'm thinking of the time I was in Vietnam, the bombing. And he said, Khien, be cool (he's my supervisor, and also my neighbor). He said, According to your story, you have been through a lot. What's the matter with the fire? I know you can do it. Do it Khien, don't give up! He gave me some energy, so I said, yeah, why not. Then you know what, then I do it. I was too small, then the fire goes high like this, and everytime I reached for the pole to open it I have to jump like this. And even sometimes my hair was burned, and my eyelashes burned too. I didn't know. I just tried to do the work to get the money to raise my children. Then my co-worker, she said, Khien, you burned your hair. I said, Is that right? And I touched my hair—it looks like *bun tau* and it smells. I touched my eyebrows and they were all so curly."
>
> "They couldn't give the work to someone else?"
>
> "No—that's what they hired me for. And I'm small but they know I'm very, very *strong* [**tapping her temple**] in here." (Transcribed from conversation)

Do you translate by eye or by ear?

Translation seeks faithfulness and accuracy and ends up always betraying either the letter of the text, its spirit, or its aesthetics

"The original text is always already an impossible translation that renders translation impossible" (Barbara Johnson).

Co chong chang duoc di dau,
Co con chang duoc dung dau mot gio
(With husband, she can't go anywhere,
With children, she can't even have peace for one hour)

Co con phai kho vi con,
Co chong phai ganh giang-son nha chong.
(With children, she would have to endure hardship,
With husband, she would have to bear her husband's patrimony.)

The exiled: "But if I don't have roots, why have my roots made me suffer so?"

Running mute among other survivors, your heartbeats echoing with each footstep, you were led by an American officer to a large deadly silent auditorium where suddenly upon opening the door, you found yourself in the company of thousands of voiceless presences—a soundless, densely packed mass of people awaiting their turns to be lifted off the ground.

In certain cases, the only way to enlighten one's surrounding was to burn oneself to death.

You ask me to write about what I remember most from my stay at the refugee camp in Guam. I shall never forget the day when we left. I was suffering from excruciating stomach pains and was getting ready to go and see the doctor, when an American officer showed up to tell us we had to leave in five minutes. As you knew, since father chose not to leave at that time, we were four women then, mother and daughters. Upon our arrival at the airport with our meager bundles of cloths, we were struck by the sight of people carrying suitcases of all sizes. Mother, who had had experience in fleeing war on foot, was convinced that not only we had to reduce our belongings to the minimal, but also, that the clothes we wore and carried be dark colored so as not to draw any attention on ourselves as women. The Americans were brash and coarse and they were yelling at us as if we were a bunch of cattle or pigs. At Guam, a limited number of tents and of folding beds were thrown at the flock. People panicked and everybody was shouting and crying. As the law of the jungle dictated, only the most physically brutal and aggressive succeeded to lay hand on these things; we could not compete with the men. We waited until nighttime before additional beds and tents were brought in. None of us could really sleep for weeks, especially mother, whose anguish in sharing a tent with others came not from the fear of theft, but from that of rape.
Most unbearable were the public washing and toilet facilities enclosed in some crudely assembled wooden structures. The latter were mere holes dug in the ground in which overspilling excrements could never be evacuated fast enough and could be smelled from miles and miles away. I was so obsessed by this that even today when I go to national parks, it is a real ordeal for me to be forced to use their restroom facilities; however distant the memory, I can hardly bear the sight and smell of these wooden cabins.

(Lan & Sue, day:)
Lan: ". . . sitting here thinking about my mom. I can't believe how much change she went through since we came here. . . . She went through so much transition from one culture to another, and, like, remember those spandex pants you bought me, with the snakeskin patterns? New Year's Eve I brought them home and put them on and I didn't have a matching sweater so I asked her if she had a black or grey sweater. She said, Here, and gave me this sweater and I was going to sneak out the door so she wouldn't see me but no, she comes out: Let me see those pants—"

Sue: "I can't believe it—"

Lan: "I thought she was going to be scandalized, like, they're too tight. She said, Oh, I can't believe how much that matches! She took a look at me and said, You know if you'd worn those a couple of months ago you'd have looked overweight, but you've lost just enough weight so you look good. I like that design."

Sue (laughing): "That's insane!"

Lan: "When I was looking in her closet for the sweater she had these leopardskin pattern silky shirts, something *I* could wear. I couldn't believe it—Mom's going wild. . . . But that's just one of the things. I see so much gradual change in her, her values."

Sue: "Well, you helped her a lot."

Lan: "It's not so much help—I put her through a lot!"

Sue: "Remember when you first moved out of the house after high school—that was a big drag for you."

Lan: "Yeah . . . dramatic." (Transcribed from conversation)

I am like a jackfruit on the tree.
To taste you must plug me quick, while fresh:
the skin rough, the pulp thick, yes,
but, oh, I warn you against touching—
the rich juice will gush and stain your hands. Ho Xuan Huong

Che la che lay, Con gai bay nghe:
Ngoi le la mot, / Dua cot la hai, / An khoai la ba,/
An qua la bon, / Tron viec la nam, / Hay nam la sau, /
Hay an do chau la bay.
(The seven deadly sins of a girl: one, sitting everywhere; two, leaning on pillars; three, eating sweet potatoes; four, eating treats; five, fleeing work; six, lying down too often; seven, wolfing her nephew's sweets.)

Dear Minh-ha, "Since the publication of the book, I felt like having lost a part of myself. It is very difficult for a Vietnamese woman to write about Vietnamese women. At least in France where, in spite of the Mouvement de Liberation de la Femme, maternalism remains the cornerstone of the dominant ideology. To have everything as it should be, I should have accepted a preface by Simone de Beauvoir . . . as my publisher had wished." (Mai Thu Van)

A million of Vietnamese dispersed around the globe.
It will take more than one generation for the wounds to heal

Of course, the image can neither prove what it says nor why it is worth saying it; the impotence of proofs, the impossibility of a single truth in witnessing, remembering, recording, rereading

As I was about to leave her, she reached for a magazine and asked me whether I have heard or read about the refugees, especially the mountain peoples, who had passed away in their sleep without any evidence of heart attack or any other recognizable disease. "The reporters described this as one of those mysterious, inscrutable oriental phenomena, but I think they die of acute sadness." *Buon thoi ruot*, sad to the extent that one's bowels rot, as we commonly say.

> **(In Vietnamese, from the Miss Vietnam 1988 Pageant:)** *"Candidate H——— P———, please tell us what characteristics of Vietnamese culture we should preserve in American society?" "I think that, as far as women are concerned, we should preserve our Vietnamese heritage and the four virtues Cong Dung Ngon Hanh"*

Phan gai tu duc ven tuyen,
Cong, dung, ngon, hanh, giu gin chang sai.
(Every young woman must fully practice and scrupulously conform to 4 virtues:
be skillful in her work, modest in her behavior, soft-spoken in her language,
faultless in her principles.)

Tai gia tong phu
Xuat gia tong phu
Phu tu tong tu
(Daughter, she obeys her father
Wife, she obeys her husband
Widow, she obeys her son)

Theo luan ly tam cuong ngu thuong
dan ba khi nao cung phai tuy thuoc dan ong
khi con nho thi phai theo cha
khi lay chong thi phai theo chong
khi chong chet thi phai theo con
suot doi la ke vi thanh nhan

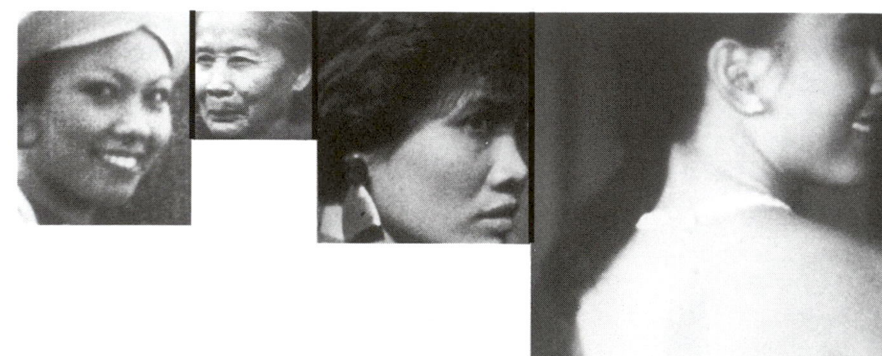

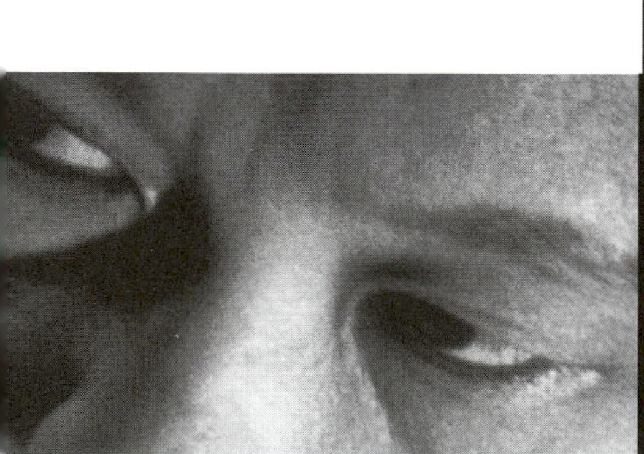

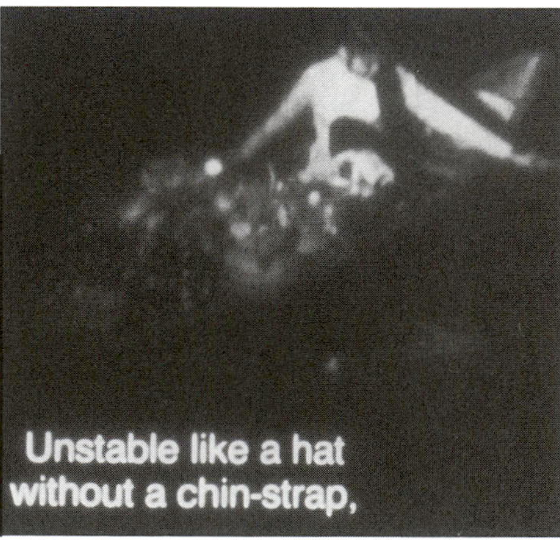
Unstable like a hat
without a chin-strap,

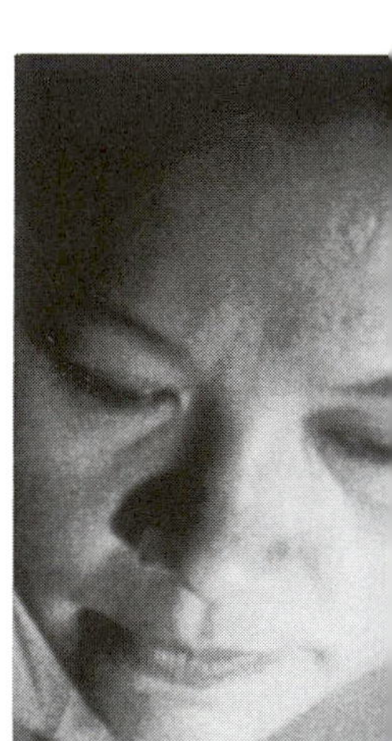

phai dua vao mot nguoi dan ong lam chu chot
chu khong bao gio duoc doc lap
(According to the moral of the three deferments and five human virtues,
women must always depend on men
Child, she must follow her father
Married, she must follow her husband
Widowed, she must follow her son
all her life she remains a minor
depending on a man as on a central axle
and can never be self-governing)

(Kim in her office and at the substation—voice off and sync voice are heard simultaneously in Vietnamese:)*"In Vietnam, when I quit school, I got married and had a child. I stayed home and didn't have an outside job. But when I came to the U.S., the sponsoring church members found a few small jobs for me. For example I babysat for a month, after that I taught French at a grade school for 3 or 4 months. Then I helped in a retirement home for half a year before I applied to work for an electric company. From 1976 until now I have been doing electrical drafting for a hydro-electric power station. I am the only woman in this job."*

(Kim, Sync:) *"At first I was very hesitant when you asked me to participate, but then I thought: why would I refuse, when I am a Vietnamese woman myself, and the role in the film speaks the truth of the Vietnamese women still in Vietnam as well as of those emigrated to the U.S.? . . . Especially since this film, unlike the commercial films is not about love stories featuring some Hollywood stars, so I didn't think there was anything excessive in my accepting to be on film. I have also read about you and your films, and am proud of your being a Vietnamese woman filmmaker."*

(Kim Voice off:) *"My son's friend who is very fond of the Vietnamese told me 'You should take that role so as to speak up the repression of your mother and sisters in Vietnam.' So, because I care about Vietnamese women in general, I want to get involved in this film.*
"I still have many friends in Vietnam. Compared with Cat Tien (my role) their condition is much worse. Some of them who were highly placed in the past are now selling treats on the street, or trying small enterprises to survive with their children."

(Kim, sync:) *I asked my husband who saw nothing wrong and encouraged me to do my best to contribute to our native country. Otherwise I would be too shy to appear on TV, not to mention film!*

(Kim, voice-over:) *Generally, every girl or woman in Vietnam must practice the four virtues. She must know how to sew, cook, speak and behave. Obviously, she is subject to the three submissions vis-à-vis her parents, her husband, although not always vis-à-vis her son.*

(Kim, sync:) *"A friend of mine opened her eyes wide when she heard I was going to be on film: 'You've never been an actress, how can you fake it?' Another friend of my husband teased me, 'They know you can act, so they have selected the right person. Who knows, maybe you'll act so well that the Americans will notice you and you'll be a Hollywood star in the future?' "*

(Kim, voice off:) *"I keep on thinking despite our emigrating to the U.S., if our surname is Viet, our given name ought to be Nam—Vietnam. For the Vietnamese woman, the family closest to her is her husband's; as for our native country, we all love it, young and old. We will always keep our last name Viet and first name Nam. Even when the women marry foreigners here, they are still Vietnamese, so I think your film title is very suggestive . . . very meaningful."*

One thing the man said he learned to let go of while in prison, is identity: this singular naming of a person, a race, a culture, a nation.

Vietnamese adjusting to their new lives: mastering elevators and escalators, learning wristwatch-type punctuality, taming vending machines, distinguishing dog's canned foods from human canned foods, and understanding that it was not permissible to wander the streets, the hotels or anywhere outside in pyjamas.

(Yen, in Vietnamese, sync:) *"When I accepted to help in this film, it was because its subject, as you told me, concerned Vietnamese women. Since I have always praised their ability to sacrifice and to endure, I thought this was an opportunity to speak out, although I was going through a lot of pressure and difficulties at the time. Once I worked on my part, I wanted to give my best because I don't think it is an individual matter but one that concerns a whole community.*

(Voice off:) *"An actress or a singer is looked down upon in traditional society. People used to say that in a respectful family, the woman cannot be involved in cinema or singing; they have many derogatory terms to qualify such a woman. But more recently, with the West's influence, cinema is considered an art and most actresses would like to play the role of a beautiful woman, so my friends were all taken aback when they heard I was acting the role of a 60 year old woman."*

(Sync:) *"Everyday I go to work before 8 am and come home around 7 pm. Then, I hurry to cook for my husband and son. Only after that am I able to rehearse my part for this film. Once the rehearsal is completed I can eat dinner and get my son and myself ready for school and work the next day."*

(Voice off:) *"I have been in the States for 16 years. I've been working for an electronics company for almost 10 years in chemical processing. The number of Vietnamese engineers* *working for technical companies grows larger everyday. Eight, nine years ago there were only 3, 4 engineers, but since then many who came in 1975 have graduated, and there are now about 300 or 400 Vietnamese engineers at my company, but only 2 of us are women . . .*

"When I started working there, I encountered lots of difficulty, first, because I am Asian, second because I am a woman. I do have to overcome these two difficulties. The Americans have always looked down on Vietnam as a second-class country. Now we Vietnamese are entering professional careers and are competing with them. So although they do not really show it, you can feel that they don't accept the fact that there are more and more Asians with Ph.Ds working in the company, especially in Research where Asians form the majority because a Ph.D is required."

(Sync:) *"Concerning my younger brother's wedding, it is in our family tradition that I, the eldest sister, be responsible for it since my father is no longer with us and my mother is advanced in age. That's why I was very divided during the filming week."*

What did your Vietnamese friends think when they heard you're going to be on film?

(Yen, in Vietnamese, sync:) *"Their reaction is very different from my reasons for accepting. They all laugh and tease me, saying that I'll become a movie star and will earn enough money so I can quit my job in the future."*

(Voice off:) *"Traditionally, the Vietnamese woman who gets married must endure many hardships. She almost never lives for herself. When she lives with her family, all decisions are made by her father. When she marries, she must obey her husband's family. All decisions belong to the husband and his family.*

"Surname Viet, given name Nam. I think when a man asks a woman whether she is married or not, by such a question perhaps she is expected to wed a Vietnamese man and to keep the Vietnamese traditions. Perhaps she expects her husband to have patriotic feelings toward his country. Every woman would want her husband to be a hero for the people.

"On TV and in newspapers, the tendency most often is to side with the North; only in a few cases the siding is with the South. But I have never come across a film or an analysis that is truthful, that stands in the middle and looks at both North and South with unbiased eyes. This is very sad, because I just want to see all the good points we need to keep, and the faults we need to change in ourselves so that we can build a new Vietnamese society. As for the foreigners, of course they look at Vietnam with their own eyes. I don't even want to see films that speak only for one side or the other. I want to find a book that speaks truthfully of Vietnam because everything I read either praises or blames, but always in an absolute, black and white

clear cut manner. And I don't think there is anything absolute; each side has its rights and wrongs."

War as a succession of special effects; the war became film well before it was shot. Cinema has remained a vast machine of special effects. If the war is the continuation of politics by other means, then media images are the continuation of war by other means. Immersed in the machinery, part of the special effect, no critical distance. Nothing separates the Vietnam war and the superfilms that were made and continue to be made about it. It is said that if the Americans lost the other, they have certainly won this one. (Inspired by Jean Baudrillard)

(Kim, in Vietnamese:) *"These images call for human compassion toward countries in war."*

There is no winner in a war.

(Yen, in Vietnamese:) *"These are images that are emotionally moving. They can change the way you think. For example if you don't like war and you see images of mothers holding their child in their arms to flee from war you'll be moved and stirred to do something to help. These images are very painful. What is often brought up is the mother's love for her child. In war the mother always protects her child's safety."*

(Lan & Sue, fireplace)
Lan: "Here in Berkeley it's not so bad—you have so many Orientals that people recognize the difference between Oriental cultures like Japanese, Chinese, Korean, Vietnamese. I don't know how many times I've run into people that, like, first of all they pretend like they're interested enough to ask you, Are you Chinese or Japanese? No, Vietnamese. Then they have the nerve to say, Oh, same difference. I find that really insulting."

Sue: "I would too. It's ridiculous"

Lan: "I wasn't so aware of it until recently, when you told me that story of—what was it?—the bus. . . . How it works both ways. What happened?"

Sue: "Oh yes. It was really funny. I was living in Taiwan and I got on the bus—the only white American—and this guy spots me from across the bus. Of course it's jammed packed and everybody's in each others' armpits and we're holding on for dear life because they're maniac drivers, and he starts making his way back. He wanted to get a little English lesson, which is fine—you like speaking English to people when they want to learn. But it happens 24 hours a day, so you're constantly speaking English."

Lan: "That gets on your nerves."

Sue: "By that time I felt pretty comfortable with Chinese. So he comes up and starts asking me questions. I told him in Chinese that I wasn't American, that I was French. And he was like, So what, you're European, you speak everything, right? So I said no, I only speak French not English. He said, That's impossible, you're all European. So finally he said okay and he just started speaking French."
[laughter]

Lan: "'Oh actually I'm German.'"

Sue: "Oh, that was embarrassing. I just had to be snobbish."

Lan: "So that's why I like this place. When I first came to visit you, I'm walking between you and Julie, you both have blonde hair, and blue eyes. Julie's speaking Japanese, you're speaking Chinese, here I am, 'Hi, Pennsylvania,' speaking English! It was a nice change of role." (Transcribed from conversation)

For years we learnt about "our ancestors, the Gauls," we learnt that" French Indochina" was situated in Asia under a hot and humid climate.

Grafting several languages, cultures and realities onto a single body. The problem of translation, after all, is a problem of reading and of identity.

Van-Lang, Nam-Viet, Hoang Viet, Dai-Viet, An-Nam (Bac Ky—Le Tonkin; Trung Ky—An Nam; Nam Ky—La Cochinchine), French Indochina, (Viet-Nam, 'Nam)

"Vietnam" (American Accent)—*they also call it 'Nam.*

Reeducation camps, rehabilitation camps, concentration camps, annihilation camps. All the distinctive features of a civilization are laid bare. The slogans continue to read: "Work liberates," "Rehabilitation through work." Here, work is a process whereby the worker no longer takes power, "for work has ceased to be his way of living and has become his way of dying" (Maurice Blanchot). Work and death are equivalents.

"In Guam I recognized a general," she said. "He [*had*] *been one of the richest men in Vietnam. . . . One morning in the camp, a mob of women came up to him. They took off their*

. . . wooden shoes and began beating him about the head, screaming: 'Because of you, my son, my brother, my husband was left behind.' " (Wendy Wilder Larsen & Tran Thi Nga)

"The world is like a butterfly," wrote a Japanese poet of the seventeenth century.

A woman discloses the content of a letter her father recently wrote in prison in Vietnam. A poet, looking desperately fragile on photo in his long silver hair, he did not write to complain about his politically condemned status, but only to weep over his eldest daughter's death on the very birthday of Buddha. Forty days after she died, he wrote, she came back in the form of a golden butterfly, encircling him insistently for an entire day.

Cong Dung Ngon Hanh. What are these four virtues persistently required of women? First, *Cong:* you'll have to be able, competent and skillful—in cooking, sewing, managing the household budget, caring for the husband, educating the children—all this to save the husband's face. Second. *Dung:* you'll have to maintain a gracious, compliant and cheerful appearance—first of all for the husband. Third, *Ngon:* you'll have to speak properly and softly and never raise your voice—particularly in front of the husband or his relatives. Then fourth, *Hanh:* you'll have to know where your place is; respect those older than you and yield to those younger or weaker than you—moreover, be faithful and sacrifice for the husband.

The boat is either a dream or a nightmare. Or rather, both. A no place. "A place without a place, that exists by itself [and] is closed on itself, and at the same time is given over to the infinity of the sea." For Western civilization the boat has not only been the great instrument of economic development, going from port to port as far as the colonies in search of treasures and slaves, but it has also been a reserve of the imagination. It is said that "in civilization without boats, dreams dry up, espionage takes the place of adventure, and the police takes the place of pirates" (Michel Foucault).

Than em nhu tam lua dao
Phat pho giua cho biet vao tay ai?
Em ngoi canh truc, em tua canh mai,
Dong dao tay lieu, biet lay ai ban cung?
(I am like a piece of silk
Floating in the midst of the market, knowing not into whose hands it will fall
Sitting on a reed, leaning against an apricot branch
Between the peach tree to the East and the willow to the West
Who shall I befriend for a lifetime?)

Hope is alive when there is a boat, even a small boat. From shore to shore small crafts are rejected and sent back to the sea. The policy of castaways has created a special class of refugees, the "beach people."

Each government has its own interpretation of *Kieu*. Each has its peculiar way of using and appropriating women's images. *Kieu* has survived in hundreds of different contexts. First appreciated for its denunciation of oppressive and corrupt feudalism, it was later read as an allegory of the tragic fate of Vietnam under colonial rule. More recently, in a celebration of its 200th anniversary, it was highly praised by the government's male official writers for its revolutionary yearning for freedom and justice in the context of the war against American imperialism. For the Vietnamese exiled, it speaks for the exodus or silent popular movement of resistance that continues to raise problems of conscience to the international community.

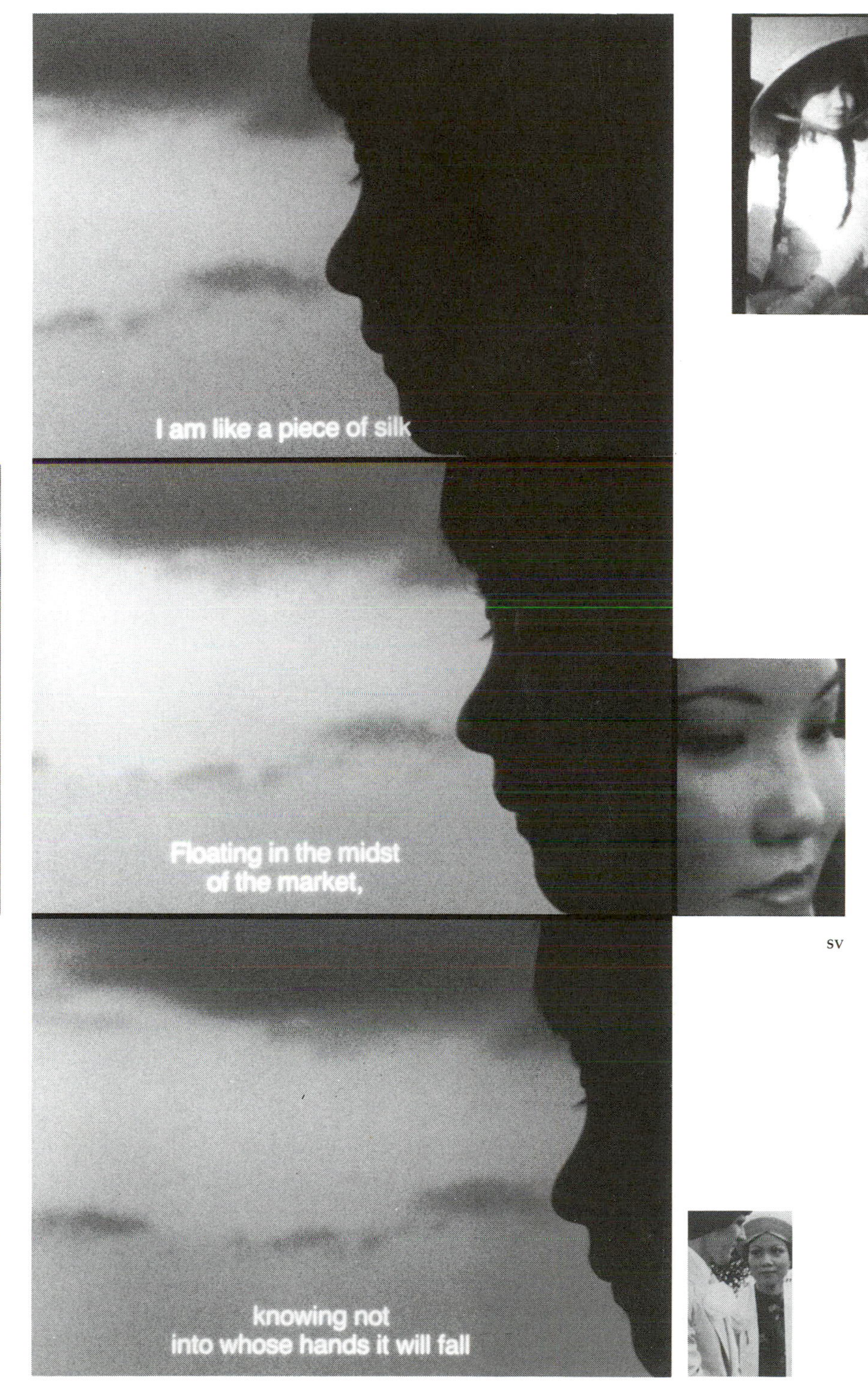
I am like a piece of silk
Floating in the midst
of the market,
knowing not
into whose hands it will fall

SV

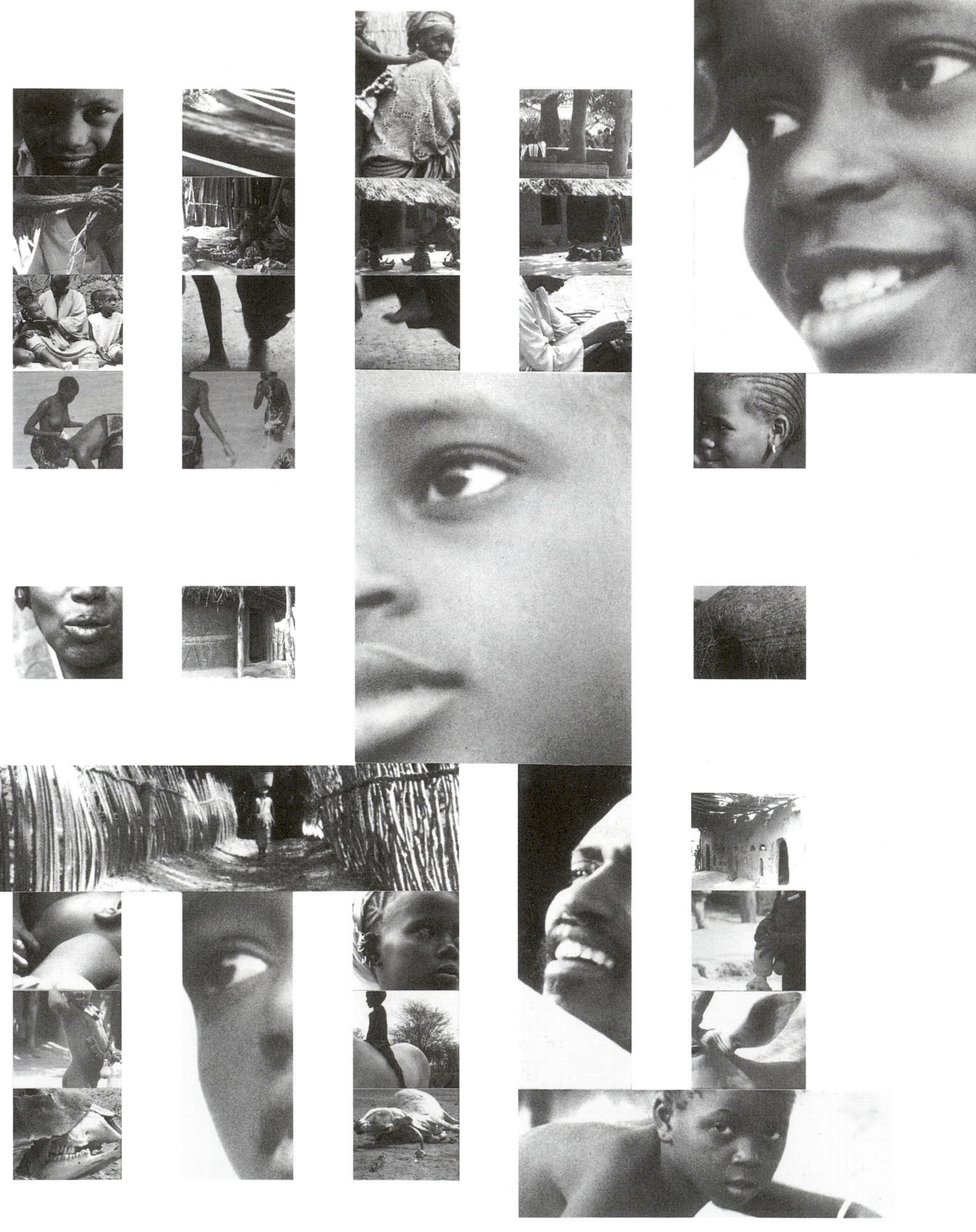

3

Reassemblage

Senegal, 1982. 40 minute color film.

Produced by: Jean-Paul Bourdier and Trinh T. Minh-ha
Directed, photographed, written and edited by: Trinh T. Minh-ha
Distributed by: Women Make Movies (New York); Third World Newsreel (New York); The Museum of Modern Art (New York); Cinenova (London); Idera (Vancouver); Lightcone (Paris); Image Forum (Tokyo); The National Library of Australia (Canberra).
First published in *Camera Obscura,* Nos 13–14, 1985.

(Music: Joola drums)
Scarcely twenty years were enough to make two billion people define themselves as underdeveloped.

I do not intend to speak about
Just speak near by

The Casamance
Sun and palms
The part of Senegal where tourist settlements flourish

A film about what? my friends ask.
A film about Senegal; but what in Senegal?

In Enampor
Andre Manga says his name is listed in the tourist information book.
Above the entry of his house is a hand-written sign which says
"Three hundred and fifty francs"
A flat anthropological fact

In numerous tales
Woman is depicted as the one who possessed the fire
Only she knew how to make fire
She kept it in diverse places
At the end of the stick she used to dig the ground with, for example
In her nails or in her fingers

Reality is delicate
My irreality and imagination are otherwise dull

The habit of imposing a meaning to every single sign

She kept it in diverse places
At the end of the stick she used to dig the ground with, for example

First create needs, then, help
Sitting underneath the thatched roof which projects well beyond the front wall of his newly built house, a Peace-Corps Volunteer nods at several villagers who stop by to chat with him. While they stoop down beside him and start talking, he smiles

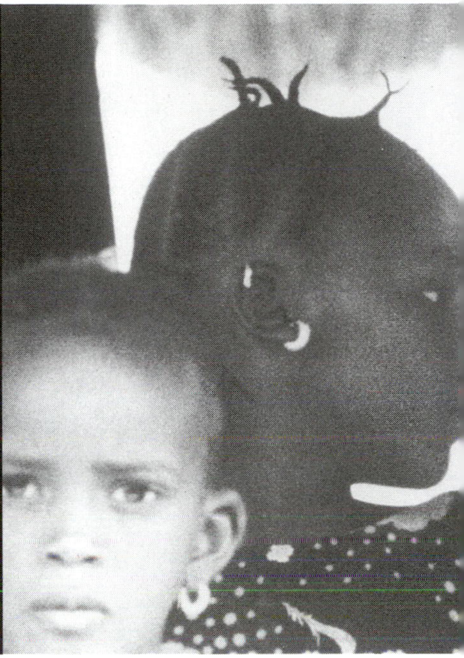

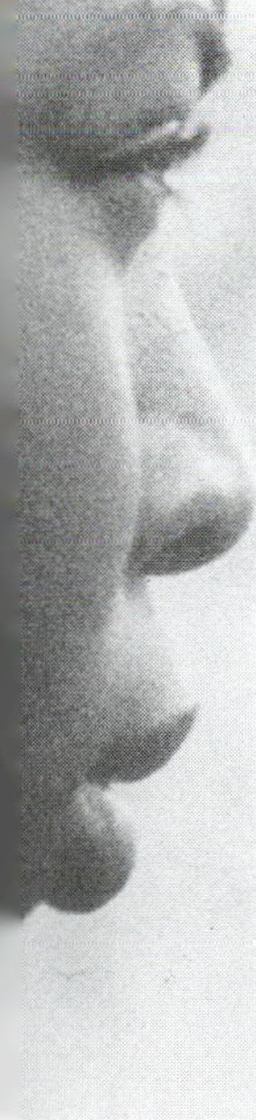

R

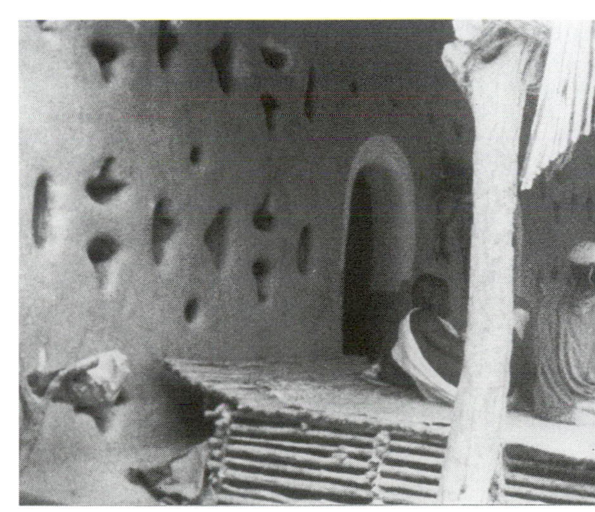

blankly, a pair of headphones over his ears and a Walkman Sony cassette player in his lap

"I teach the women how to grow vegetables in their yard; this will allow them to have an income" he says and hesitates before he concludes: "I am not always successful, but it's the first time this has been introduced into the village."

The first time this has been introduced into the village
Woman is depicted as the one who possessed the fire. Only she knew how to make fire

What can we expect from ethnology?

(Voices: Sereer language; excerpts of conversation and voice of Djumalog, *femme savante* of the village of Boucoum)

The land of the Sereer people

(Women pounding: sound of pestle against mortar and laughter)

The land of the Manding and the Peul peoples

A film about what? my friends ask.
A film about Senegal, but what in Senegal?

I feel less and less the need to express myself
Is that something else I've lost?
Something else I've lost?

(Voices: same conversation in Sereer language)

Filming in Africa means for many of us
Colorful images, naked breast women, exotic dances and fearful rites.
The unusual

First create needs, then, help
Ethnologists handle the camera the way they handle words
Recuperated collected preserved
The Bamun the Bassari the Bobo
What are *your* people called again? an ethnologist asks a fellow of his

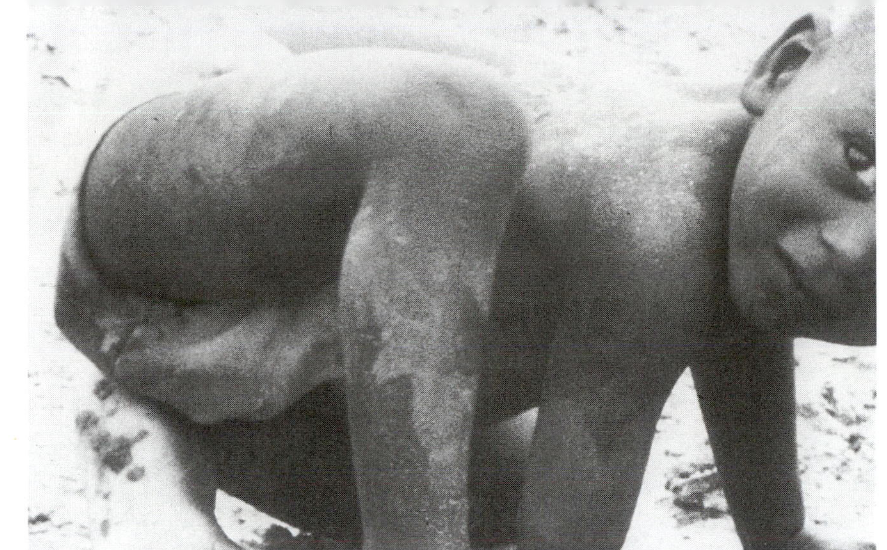

R

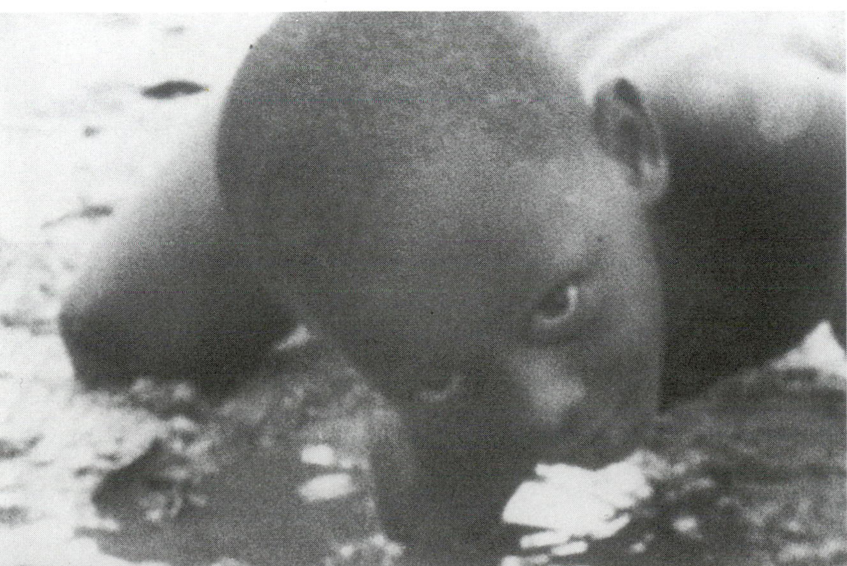

R

In numerous tales

Diversification at all costs
Oral traditions thus gain the rank of written heritage

Fire place and woman's face
The pot is known as a universal symbol for the Mother, the GrandMother
the Goddess

Nudity does not reveal
The hidden
It is its absence

A man attending a slide show on Africa turns to his wife and says with guilt in his voice: "I have seen some pornography tonight."

Documentary because reality is organized into an explanation of itself

Every single detail is to be recorded. The man on the screen smiles at us while the necklace he wears, the design of the cloth he puts on, the stool he sits on are objectively commented upon

It has no eye it records

(Cicada sound)

"A fine layer of dust covers us from head to toe. When the sandstorm comes," says a child, "we lay on our mat with our mother's headscarf on our face and wait until it goes away"

The omnipresent eye. Scratching my hair or washing my face become a very special act

Watching her through the lens. I look at her becoming me becoming mine

Entering into the only reality of signs where I myself am a sign

(Music: Bassari. Repeated hootings of a woman; drum beats; men's chanting)

The land of the Bassari and the Peul peoples

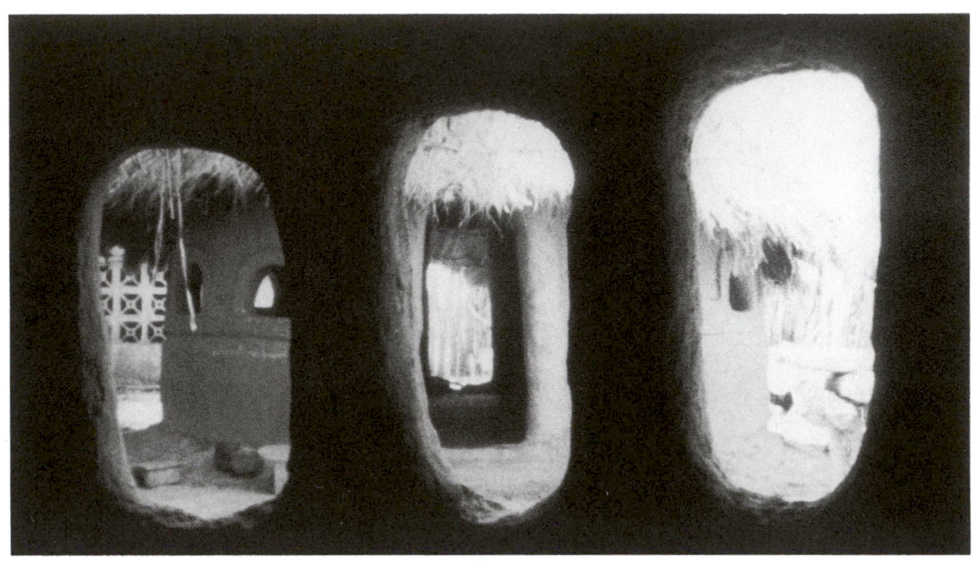

R

Early in the morning. A man is sitting with his little girl on his lap next to the circular stone hut built after the model of a Bassari house. A catholic white sister comes up to him and blurts out: "It's only 7 am. Your little girl is not that sick. How many times have I told you our dispensary is closed on Sunday? Come back on Monday"

An ethnologist and his wife gynecologist come back for two weeks to the village where they have done research in the past. He defines himself as a person who stays long, long enough, in a village to study the culture of an ethnic group. Time, knowledge, and security. "If you haven't stayed long enough in a place, you are not an ethnologist" he says
Late in the evening, a circle of men gathers in front of the house where the ethnologist and his wife gynecologist stay

One of the villagers is telling a story, another is playing music on his improvised lute, the ethnologist is sleeping next to his switched-on cassette recorder

He thinks he excludes personal values. He tries or believes so but how can he be a Fulani? That's objectivity

Along the Senegal River, the land of the Sarakhole and the Peul peoples

(Sound used in this section: women's pounding; cicada sound; hooting of Bassari women)

I come with the idea that I would seize the unusual by catching the person unawares. There are better ways to steal I guess. With the other's consent. After seeing me laboring with the camera, women invite me to their place and ask me to film them

The habit of imposing
Every single sign

For many of us the best way to be neutral and objective is to copy reality meticulously

Speak about
K-about

The eternal commentary that escorts images

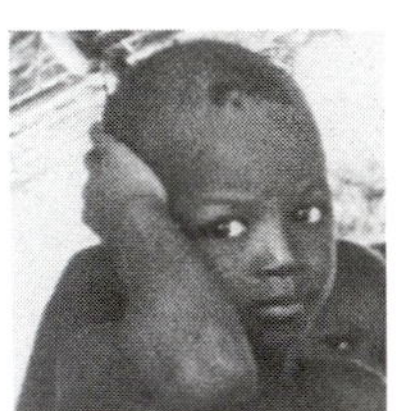

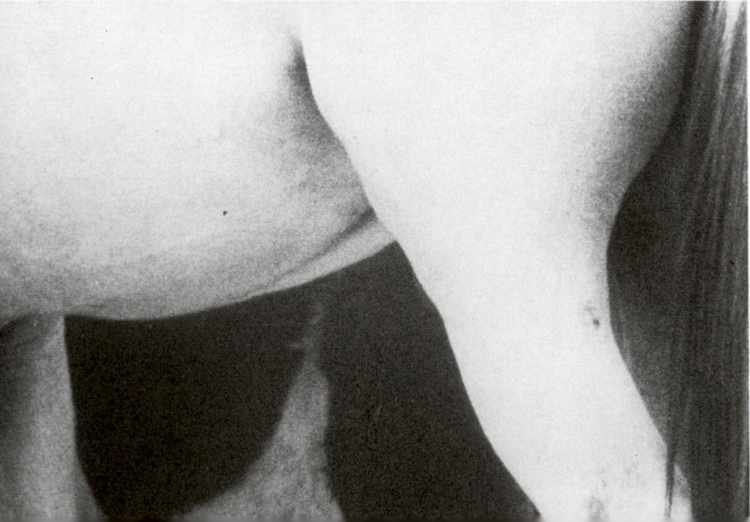

R

Stressing the observer's objectivity
Circles round the object of curiosity
Different views from different angles

The a, b, c . . . of photography

Creativity and objectivity seem to run into conflict. The eager observer collects samples and has no time to reflect upon the media used

Scarcely twenty years were enough to make two billion people define themselves as underdeveloped

What I see is life looking at me

I am looking through a circle in a circle of looks

115 degrees Farenheit. I put on a hat while laughter bursts out behind me. I haven't seen any woman wearing a hat

Children, women and men come up to me claiming for gifts
A van drives in the dust road, greeted by another boisterous wave of children.
"Gift, gift" they all yell while the car stops under the shade of a tree.
A group of tourists step out and immediately start distributing cheap candies

Just speak near by

A woman comments on polygamy: "It's good for men . . . not for us. We accept it owing to the force of circumstances. What about you? Do you have a husband all for yourself?"

(Same passage of Joola music as in the beginning of the film)

R

R

Interviews

4

Film as Translation

A Net With No Fisherman*

with Scott MacDonald

MacDonald: You grew up in Vietnam during the American presence there. This may be a strange question to ask about that period, but I'm curious about whether you were a moviegoer and what films you saw in those years.

Trinh: I was not at all a moviegoer. To go to the movies then was a real feast. A new film in town was always an overcrowded, exciting event. The number of films I got to see before coming to the States was rather limited, and I was barely introduced to TV before I left the country in 1970. Actually, it was only when the first television programs came to Vietnam that I learned to listen to English. Here also the experience was a collective one since you had to line up in the streets with everyone else to look at one of the TVs made available to the neighborhood. I had studied English at school, but to be able to follow the actual pace of spoken English was quite a different matter.

Interview conducted by Scott MacDonald in November 1989, when *Surname Viet Given Name Nam* was screened at Utica College of Syracuse University.

* Except for the interview with Jayamanne and Rutherford, all titles have been added by myself for this book—T Mh.

M: Did you see French films in school?

T: No. A number of them were commercially shown, but during the last few years I was in Vietnam, there were more American than French films. My introduction to film culture is quite recent.

M: Reassemblage *seems to critique traditional ethnographic movies*—Nanook of the North, The Ax Fight, The Hunters . . . *I assume you made a conscious decision to take on the whole male-centered history of ethnographic moviemaking. At what point did you become familiar with that tradition? Did you have specific films in mind when you made* Reassemblage?

T: No. I didn't. You don't have to be a connoisseur in film to be aware of the problems that permeate anthropology, although these problems do differ with the specific tools and the medium that one uses. The question of limit in writing, for example, is very different from that in filmmaking. But the way one relates to the material that makes one a writer-anthropologist or an anthropological filmmaker needs to be radically questioned. A Zen proverb says "A grain of sand contains all land and sea," and I think that whether you look at a film, attend a slide show, listen to a lecture, witness the fieldwork by either an expert anthropologist or by any person subjected to the authority of anthropological discourse, the problems of subject and of power relationship are all there. They saturate the entire field of anthropological activity.

I made *Reassemblage* after having lived in Senegal for three years (1977–80) and taught music at the Institut National des Arts in Dakar; in other words, after having time and again been made aware of the hegemony of anthropological discourse in every attempt by both local outsiders and by insiders to identify the culture observed. *Reassemblage* was shot in 1981 well after my stay there. Although I had by then seen quite a number of films and was familiar with the history of Western cinema, I can't say this was a determining factor. I had done a number of super-8 films on diverse subjects before, but *Reassemblage* was my first 16 mm.

M: You mentioned you were looking at films before you went to Senegal. Were you looking at the way in which Senegal or other African cultures were portrayed in film?

T: No, not at all. Despite my having been exposed to a number of non-mainstream films from Europe and the States at the time, I must say I was then one of the more passive consumers of the film industry. It was when I started making films myself that I really came to realize how obscene the question of power and production of meaning is in filmic representation. I don't really work in terms of influence. I've never been able to recognize anything in my background that would allow me neatly to trace—even momentarily—my itinerary back to a single point of origin. Influences in my life have always happened in the most odd, disorderly way. Everything I've done comes from all kinds of direction, certainly not just from film. It seems rather clear to me that *Reassemblage* did not come from the films I looked at, but from what I had learned in Senegal. The film was not realized as a reaction to anything in particular, but more I would now say, as a desire not to simply mean. What seems most important to me was to expose the transformations that occurred with the attempt to materialize on film and between the frames the impossible experience of "what" constituted Senegalese cultures. The resistance to anthropology was not a motivation to the making of the film. It came alongside with other strong feelings, such as the love that one has for one's subject(s) of inquiry.

M: So the fact that you found a film form different from what has become conventional as a means of imaging culture was accidental. . . .

T: Not quite accidental, because there were a number of things I did not want to reproduce in my work: the kind of omniscience that pervades many films, not just through the way the narration is being told, but more generally, in their structure, editing and cinematography, as well as in the effacement of the filmmakers, or the invisibility of their politics of non-location. But what I rejected and did not want to carry on came also *with* the making of *Reassemblage*. While I was filming, for example, I realized that I often proceeded in conformity with anthropological preoccupations, and the challenge was to depart from these without merely resorting to self-censorship.

M: Often in Reassemblage *there'll be an abrupt movement of the camera or a sudden cut in the middle of a motion that in a normal film would be allowed to have a sense of completion. Coming to the films from the arena of experimental moviemaking, I felt familiar with those kinds of tactics. Had you seen much of what in this country is called "avant-garde film" or "experimental film?" I'm sorry to be so persistent in trying to relate you to film! I can see it troubles you.*

T: [Laughter] I think it's an interesting problem because your attempt is to situate me somewhere in relation to a film tradition, whereas I feel the experimentation is an attitude that develops with the making process when one is plunged into a film. As one advances, one explores the different ways that one can do things without having to lug about heavy belongings. The term "experimental" becomes questionable when it refers to techniques and vocabularies that allow one to classify a film as "belonging" to the "avant-garde" category. Your observation that the film foregrounds certain strategies not foreign to experimental filmmakers is accurate, although I would add that when *Reassemblage* first came out, the experimental/avant-garde film world had as many problems with it as any other film milieus. A man who has been active in experimental filmmaking for decades said for example, "She doesn't know what she's doing."

So, while the techniques are not surprising to avant-garde filmmakers, the film still does not quite belong to that world of filmmaking. It differs perhaps because it exposes its politics of representation instead of seeking to transcend representation in favor of visionary presence and spontaneity which often constitute the prime criteria for what the avant-garde considers to be Art. But it also differs because all the strategies I came up with in *Reassemblage* were directly generated by the material and the context that define the work. One example is the use of repetition as a transforming, as well as rhythmic and structural, device. Since the making of the film, I have seen many more experimental films and have sat on a number of grant panels. Hence I have had many opportunities to recognize how difficult it is to reinvent anew or to defamiliarize what has become common practice among filmmakers. It was very sad to see, for example, how conventional the use of repetition proved to be in the realm of "experimental" filmmaking. This does not mean that one can no longer use it, but rather that the challenge in using it is more critical.

I still think that repetition in *Reassemblage* functions very differently than in many of the films I have seen. For me, it's not just a technique that one introduces for fragmenting or emphasizing effects. Very often people tend to repeat mechanically three or four times something said on the soundtrack. This technique of looping is also very common in experimental music. But looping is not of any particular interest to me. What interests me is the way certain rhythms came back to me while I was traveling and filming across Senegal, and how the intonation and inflection of each of the diverse local languages inform me of where I was. For example, the film brought out the musical quality of the Sereer language through untranslated snatches of a conversation among villagers and the varying repetition of certain sentences. Each language has its own music and its practice need not be reduced to the mere function of communicating meaning. The repetition I made use of has, accordingly, nuances and differences built within it, so that repetition here is not just the automatic reproduction of the same, but rather the production of the same with and in differences.

M: *When I had seen* Reassemblage *enough to see it in detail, rather than just letting it flow by, I noticed something that strikes me as very unusual. When you focus on a subject, you don't see it from a single plane. Instead, you move to different positions near and far and from side to side. You don't try to choose a view of the subject; you explore various ways of seeing it.*

T: This is a great description of what is happening with the *look* in *Reassemblage,* but I'll have to expand on it a little more. It is common practice among filmmakers and photographers to shoot the same thing more than once and to select only one shot—the "best" one—in the editing process. Otherwise, to show the subject from a more varied view, the favored formula is that of utilizing the all-powerful zoom or curvilinear travelling shot whose totalizing effect is assured by the smooth operation of the camera.

Whereas in my case, the limits of the looker and of the camera are clearly exposed, not only through the repeated inclusion of a plurality of shots of the same subject from very slightly different distances or angles (hence the numerous jump-cut effects), but also through a visibly hesitant, or as you mentioned earlier, an incomplete, sudden and unstable camera work. (The zoom is avoided in both *Reassemblage* and *Naked Spaces,* and diversely acknowledged in the more recent films I have been making.) The exploratory movements of the camera—or structurally speaking, of the film itself—which some viewers have qualified as "disquieting," and others as "sloppy," is neither intentional nor unconscious. It does not result from an (avant-garde) anti-aesthetic stance, but occurs, in my context, as a form of reflexive body writing. Its erratic and unassuming moves materialize those of the filming subject caught in a situation of trial, where the desire to capture on celluloid grows in a state of non-knowingness and with the understanding that no reality can be "captured" without trans-forming.

M: The subject stays in its world and you try to figure out what your relationship to it is. It's exactly the opposite of "taking a position": it's seeing what different *positions reveal.*

T: That's a useful distinction.

M: Your interest in living spaces is obvious in Reassemblage *and more obvious in* Naked Spaces. *You also did a book on living spaces.*

T: In Burkina Faso, yes. And in collaboration with Jean-Paul Bourdier.

M: Did your interest in living spaces precede making the films or did it develop by making them?

T: The interest in the poetics of dwelling preceded *Reassemblage.* It was very much inspired by Jean-Paul, who loves vernacular architecture and has been doing relentless research on rural houses across several Western and non-Western cultures. We have worked together as a team on many projects.

Reassemblage evolves around an "empty" subject. I did not have any preconceived idea for the film and was certainly not looking for a particularized subject that would allow me to speak *about* Senegal. In other words, there is no single center in the film—whether it is an event, a representative individual or number of individuals in a community, or a unifying theme and area of interest. And there is no single process of centering either. This does not mean that the experience of the film is not specific to Senegal. It is *entirely* related to Senegal. A viewer once asked me, "Can you do the same film in San Francisco?" And I said, "Sure, but it would be a totally different film." The strategies are, in a way, dictated by the materials that constitute the film. They are bound to the circumstances and the contexts unique to each situation and cultural frame.

In the processes of emptying out positions of authority linked to knowledge, competence and qualifications, it was important for me in the film to constantly keep alive the question people usually ask when someone sets out to write a book or in this case, to make a film: "A film about Senegal, but what in Senegal?" By "keeping alive" I mean, refusing to package [a] culture, hence not settling down with any single answer; even when you know that each work generates its own constraints and limits. So what you see in *Reassemblage* are people's daily activities: nothing out of the ordinary; nothing "exotic"; and nothing that constitutes the usual focal points of observation for anthropology's fetishistic approach to culture, such as the so-called objects of rites, figures of worship and artifacts, or in the narrow sense of the terms, the ritualistic events and religious practices. This negation of certain institutionalized cultural markings is just one way of facing the issues that such markings raise. There are other ways. And while shooting *Reassemblage,* I was both moved by the richness of the villagers' living spaces, and made aware of the difficulty of bringing on screen the different attitudes of dwelling implied without confronting again and differently what I have radically rejected in this film. This was how the idea of making another film first appealed to me. *Naked Spaces* was shot three years later across six countries of West Africa, while *Reassemblage* involved five regions across Senegal.

M: Reassemblage *takes individual subjects—people, actions, objects—and provides various perspectives on them;* Naked spaces *enlarges the scope but uses an analogous procedure. You deal with the same general topic—domestic living spaces—and explore its particular manifestations in one geographic area after another. And the scope of the view of particular spaces is enlarged too: you pan across a given space from different distances and angles (in* Reassemblage *the camera is generally still, though you filmed from different still positions). There's a tendency to move back and forth across the space in different directions to rediscover it over and over in new contexts.*

T: The last description is very astute and very close to how I felt in making *Naked Spaces.* Although I would say that the procedure is somewhat adverse (even while keeping a multiplicity of perspectives) rather than analogous to the one in *Reassemblage,* the immediate perception is certainly that of an enlarged scope; physically speaking, not only because of the way the film works on duration and of the variety of cultural terrains it traverses, but also because, as you point out, of its visual treatment. In *Reassemblage,* I avoided going from one precise point to another in the cinematography. I was dealing with places and was not preoccupied with depicting space. But when you shoot architecture and the spaces involved, you are even more acutely aware of the limit of your camera and how inadequate the fleeting pans and fractured still images used in *Reassemblage* are, in terms of showing spatial relationships.

One of the choices I made was to have many pans; but *not* smooth pans, and none that could give you the illusion that you're not looking through a frame. Each pan sets into relief the rectangular delineation of the frame. It never moves obliquely, for example.

M: It's always horizontal. . . .

T: Or vertical.

M: And it's always referring back to you as an individual filmmaker behind the camera. It never becomes this sort of Hitchcock motion through space that makes the camera feel so powerful.

T: In someone else's space I cannot just roam about as I may like to. Roaming about with the camera is not value-free; on the contrary, it tells us much about the ideology of such a technique.

M: It's interesting too that the way you pan makes clear that the only thing that we're going to find out about you personally is that you're interested in this place. Much hand-held camerawork is implicitly autobiographical, emotionally self-expressive. In your films camera movement is not *autobiographical except in the sense that it reveals you were in this place with these people for a period of time and were interested in* them, *rather than in what they mean to your culture.*

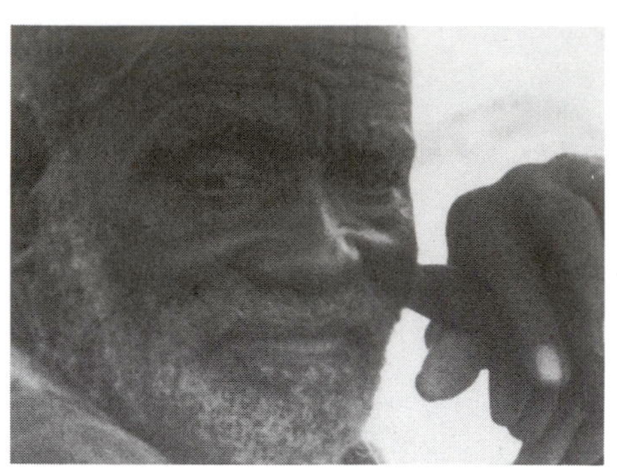

NS

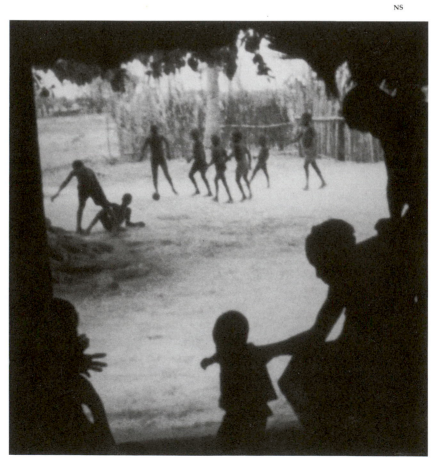

T: There are many ways to treat the autobiographical. What is autobiographical can often be very political, but not everything is political in the autobiographical. One can do many things with elements of autobiography. However, I appreciate the distinction you make because in the realm of generalized media colonization, my films have too often been described as a "personal film," as "personal documentary" or "subjective documentary." Although I accept these terms, I think they really need to be problematized, redefined and expanded. Because personal in the context of my films does *not* mean an individual standpoint or the foregrounding of a self. I am not interested in using film to "express myself," but rather to expose the social self (and selves) which necessarily mediates the making as well as the viewing of the film.

M: "Personal," "subjective," suggests that something else is impersonal and objective, which is ludicrous.

T: Right. Too often a binary opposition between subjectivity and objectivity is perpetrated in the claim that one makes subjective documentary—as if anyone can produce such a thing as objective documentary. There is nothing objective and truly impersonal in filmmaking, although there can be a formulary, cliched approach to film. What you often have is a mere abidance by the conventions of documentary practice, which is put forward as *the* "objective" way to document other cultures. It is as if the acknowledgment of the politics of the documentation and the documenting subject disturbs because the interests at stake are too high for the guardians of norms.

M: In Naked Spaces *we're inside the dwellings as much as we're outside. In fact, the movement from outside to inside, and vice versa, seems central to the film.*

T: Yes. When you walk from outside to the inside of most rural African houses, you come from a very bright sunlight to a very dark space where for a moment, you are totally blind. It takes some time to get adjusted to the darkness inside. This experience is one of the conceptual bases of *Naked Spaces*. To move inside oneself, one has to be willing to go intermittently blind. Similarly, to move toward other people, one has to accept to take the jump and move ahead blindly at certain moments of inquiry. If one is not even momentarily blind, if one remains as one is from the outside or from the inside, then it is unlikely that one would be able to break through that moment where suddenly everything stops; one's luggages are emptied out; and one fares in a state of non-knowingness, where the destabilizing encounters with the "unfamiliar" or "unknown" are multiplied and experienced anew.

M: *Since as a technology, film captures light, the traditional assumption has been that anything that's dark is not worth looking at. At most, darkness is a context for romance and for danger. Even in a documentary, we'd either never see the types of dimly lit spaces you reveal, or they'd be lit artificially, which would allow the technology to record them, but in a way that would distort the real experience of such spaces. The technology determines what one can see about other cultures. You depart from this not only by recording indoor spaces in their own natural low light conditions, but by revealing the beauty of these spaces.*

T: You can imagine these houses being shot with a light inside. What would totally be damaged are the quality of solid darkness and the shafts of light that penetrate the inside spaces.

M: *Instead of intimate—if that's the right word—the spaces would become bare, empty.*

T: Yes, yes. . . . The question of cinema and light is pivotal in *Naked Spaces*. Dwelling is both material and immaterial; it invites volume and shape as well as it reflects a cosmology and a way of living creativity. In other words, to deal with architecture is to deal with the notion of light in space. To deal with the notion of light in space is to deal with color, and to deal with color is to deal with music, because the question of light in film is also, among others, a question of timing and rhythm. Such mutual accord of elements of daily existence is particularly striking in the built environments filmed and the way these materialize the multiple oneness of life.

There are a number of direct statements on color and color timing in *Naked Spaces*. ("Color is life / Light becoming music"; "Orange and blue; warmer or colder; more luminosity, more presence. Timing acts as a link between natural and artificial light.") The look of a film and how people are represented depends so vitally on color timing. For me, it has always been crucial to work closely with the color timer, even more so in *Naked Spaces*. Very often, when films shot in Africa reach the lab, they are treated the same way as with films shot in Western cultures; that is, they are timed more on the blue side of the color chart for people with fair skin. Hence, the African people often come out with a skin color that is dull charcoal black. This is not the vibrant skin color that I saw and retained, so I devoted much of my energy at the lab learning from and cooperating with the timer on "color correcting"; insisting, whenever appropriate, on the orange and warmer colors to obtain the missing vibrant quality.

The relationship I worked on between color and light was also the link I conspicuously drew between architecture, music and film. The connections that determine the structure of the film are those that I have experienced in the living spaces of the different peoples involved. The roundness of life is not only literally manifested in the round shape of many of the houses. It is also recognizable in all spheres of socio-cultural activities, such as the various dances shown or even the way women work together. "The house opens onto the sky in a perfect circle," a voice states in *Naked Spaces,* while the subtitle of the film reads "Living Is Round."

M: *You were talking about music and architecture. Certainly one of the things that's very unusual about both African films is the soundtracks: the movement back and forth between music, other everyday sounds, the various narratives and silences. I know nothing about your music composition, but I assume this interweaving of different strands of sound and silence derives from your interest in music.*

T: I guess now I can come back to your earlier question about the film background I don't really have, by relating the way I work with film to my musical background. I fare with ease in the world of experimental music, perhaps because of the cultural hybridity of both its instrumentation and its deterritorialized space—the way it questions the boundaries of what is music and what is not. I really admired, for example, John Cage, whose Zen-inspired compositions and readings have effected radical change in all fields of the arts. I was very attracted to his work because it touched on something I was similarly groping for but had not articulated. The fact that Cage brought silence and the sounds of life both into the consecrated realm of concert halls and out onto the domain of public debate, was very liberating. "Experimental music" in this context is a constant exploration of sound as sound, rather than as a substitute for something else: a personal feeling or a psychological state. Narrative music is thus exposed in its ideology, its closures and its link with power and knowledge.

Many viewers have, indeed, thought of my films as operating more like a musical score than like any structure found in film traditions. And I also tend to think of film montage and music composition as being very much alike, although one can also argue further that in poetry, a very similar process happens in the play of words. (With the understanding here that montage is not reduced to the editing stage, but can occur in the conception and shooting stage[s] of the film as well.) For me, the exploration of new complex subjectivities and the problematizing of the subject in contemporary theory can be best carried out through poetical language—as long as poetical language is not equated with a mere aestheticizing tool nor practiced as a place to consolidate a "subjective" self. In poetry, the "I" can *never* be said to simply personify an individual. It's amusing that the feedback I often get from my relatives or close friends on my book of poems tends to be something like: "We are far from suspecting that you could be what you are in your poetry!" For them all the feelings and situations depicted in poetry are *personally* true. They immediately associate you with the "I" who speaks in your poetry and assume it's "real," which is not wrong, but it's not accurate either. In poetical language, there is no "I" that just stands for *my*self. The "I" is there; it has to be there, but it is there as the site where all other "I's" can enter and cut across one another. This is an example of the very strength and vitality of poetical language and of how it can radically contribute to the questioning of the relationship of subjects to power, language and meaning in theory. Theory as practiced by many is often caught in a positioning where the theorist continues to stand in a "safe place" to theorize about others.

M: *I've often felt that way about the little I know of theoretical film writing. Part of the reason I write articles is to consolidate a position for myself within an institution, to give myself a certain amount of economic and psychic security. Theorists talk about how the artist is situated within an economic system, but I rarely hear of any discussion of writing theory as a marketable activity.*

T: Exactly, and vice versa.

M: *If I show* Nanook of the North *and* Ax Fight, *and then* Reassemblage, *it's like film theory in action. Anybody who sees those three films, one after the other, is discovering all sorts of things about all of them. Language has such a hard time grasping what's on the screen that it's just easier to put the films next to one another and let the audience discover what they reveal about each other.*

T: There is a tendency in theorizing *about* film to see theorizing as one activity and filmmaking as another, which you can point to in theory. This is an important question for me because I teach theory partly to people who come to school—in a university department of cinema—primarily for film production. There's an antitheory tradition that runs deep among some of the "production people." The way I try to teach it by promoting "bridge" courses and by emphasizing the indispensability of their mutual challenge can actually be summarized in an old statement by Marx: that theory cannot thrive without being rooted in practice, and that practice cannot liberate itself without theory. When one starts theorizing *about* film, one starts shutting in the field; it becomes a field of experts whose access is gained through authoritative knowledge of a demarcated body of "classical" films and of legitimized ways of reading and speaking about films. That's the part I find most sterile in theory. It is necessary for me always to keep in mind that one cannot really theorize about film, but only *with* film. This is how the field can remain open.

M: *The thing I find frustrating about the whole theory/practice issue as it has played itself out in the last 10 or 12 years is that to make a film one has to take a chance with one's life and* *one's resources. It's true in Hollywood films and in independent film, where, if you're going to try to come up with $35,000 to make a movie, you have to restructure your life. You have to take a direct and dangerous part in whatever the national economy is that you live in. When I write about films—and I don't write theory, but I think it's also true there—you don't have to reorganize anything: you can remain within an institutional framework where you have a salary: you can critique without changing your lifestyle. I go to independent film to see what those people who are willing to put their lives on the line are able to discover. Theory can be brilliant and enlightening, but I don't feel people's lives on the line in the same way.*

T: Well, I think there's such a resistance to theory because theory is often deployed from a very safe place. And I am not even talking here about the other resistance which is found within the academic system itself, where theory can threaten the status quo and a distinction could be made between intellectual activities and academicizing pursuits. But I, myself, think of theory as a practice that changes your life entirely, because it acts on your conscience. Of course, theory becomes a mere accessory to practice when it speaks from a safe place, while practice merely illustrates theory when the relationship between the two remains one of domination-submission and of totalization. I see theory as a constant questioning of the framing of consciousness—a practice capable of informing another practice, such as film production, in a reciprocal challenge. Hence theory always has the possibility, even the probability, of leading the other practice to "dangerous" places, and vice versa. I can't separate the two. The kind of film I make requires that economically, as you point out, I readjust my life; but because of the film, I am constantly questioned in who I am, as its making also transforms the way I see the world around me. You know, history is full of people who die for theory.

M: When I'm making these statements, I guess I'm thinking of those in academe who call themselves theorists, but who merely use the real theorists for their own academic ends.

Can we go back to Naked Spaces? *How did you decide on the order of the sections? Until I went to the atlas, I thought perhaps you travelled in a circle.*

T: Except for the end of the film, which, as you just suggest, leads us back to its opening sequences, *Naked Spaces* is organized in the geographical order of my itinerary: from one country, one region, to another. Each location is indicated by having the names of the people and the country appear briefly on the screen, more as a footnote than as a nametag or a validating marker. The soundtrack is however more playful: a statement made by a member of a specific group may be repeated in geographical contexts that are different. Needless to say, this strategy has not failed to provoke hostility among "experts" of African cultures, "liberal" media specialists, and other cultural documentarians.

Apparently, some "professional" viewers cannot distinguish between a signpost whose presence only tells you where you are, and one whose visual arrangement suggests either a different function or certainly more than one function at work. Depending on how one uses them, letters on an image have many functions, and viewers who abide by media formulas are often insensitive to this. For me, the footnotes or the names that appear on screen allow precisely the non-expert viewer to recognize that a few selected statements issued by one source or heard in one group are repeated across borderlines of ethnic specificities. Thus, the names also function as acknowledgment of the strategical play of the film—what one may more easily call the filmmaker's manipulations.

Such deliberate act of taking, for example, a Dogon (Mali) statement on adornment and desire or on the house as a woman, and juxtaposing it with specific images of dwellings among the Kabye (Togo) and then again, among the Birifor (Burkina Faso) is a taboo among experts. Because what one ethnic group says can absolutely not be reproduced in another group. Yet this is also applicable in the film to quotes from Westerners such as Paul Eluard's "The earth is blue like an orange," which appears among the Oualatans (Mauritania) as well as the Fon (Benin). And I use a similar strategy in music: in both *Naked Spaces* and *Reassemblage,* music from one group is first heard with that very group and then varingly repeated afterwards in other groups. The viewer is diversely made aware of such "violation" of borders.

There is a very interesting issue involved here. The peoples of Third World countries used to be lumped together in their undifferentiated otherness. And this is reflected pervasively in Western media discourses—radio, books, photos, films, television. You might have a program on Vietnam, for example, but you hear persistent Chinese music in the background. Even today, in many mainstream films on the Vietnam experience, the people cast for the Vietnamese roles are the neighboring Southeast Asians who can hardly speak a word of Vietnamese. Of course, for many American viewers, it doesn't matter. Asians are Asians, and you can even take someone from the Philippines or from Korea to fill in the roles. Well, it's certainly the perpetuation of such attitude that the cultural experts and anthropologists work against. And they should. But to rectify the Master's colonialist mistakes, they have come up with disciplinarian guidelines and rules. One of them, for example, is that you always show the source of the music heard, hence more generally speaking, the music of one group should not be erroneously used in the context of another group. However, such rationalization also connotes a preoccupation with authenticity; one that supposes culture can be objectified and reified through "data" and "evidences." Here the use of sync sound becomes binding, and its validation as the most truthful way of documenting is taken for granted.

It is fine for me if the Master's heirs are now correcting his errors to raise their own consciousness of other cultures. But when circumstantial and history-bound methods and techniques become validated as the norms for *all* films no matter who the (ahistorical) subject is, then they prove to be very dangerous: once more an established frame of thinking, a prevailing system of representation is naturalized and seen as the only truthful and "correct" way. Surely enough, these "rules" are particularly binding when it is a question of Third World people: films made on white American culture, for example, can use classical music from any European source and this hardly bothers any viewer. In *Naked Spaces,* I can neither reproduce the Master's mistakes nor abide by his disciplinarian criteria of correct representation, hence the importance of the naming of the peoples to acknowledge the deliberate gesture of carrying certain cultural statements across ethnic boundaries.

M: So the imagery is a kind of grid against which the spectator can consider your manipulations of sound.

T: Yes. One could certainly have a more restrained soundtrack, and let the images move back and forth in their transcultural signs, but the choice here was to have that transgressive fluidity in the sound. The visuals, as we discussed earlier, have their own critical strategies. After all, boundaries are extremely arbitrary. Boundaries between nations are a more recent phenomenon. The village people themselves refer to kinship boundaries, which are usually also the boundaries between different ethnic groups. And ethnic grouping cuts across geo-political borderlines.

M: One activity that certainly confirms this idea is the pounding of grain, which we see in culture after culture.

T: At five o'clock in the morning, I would wake up and listen to that sound in most villages, and it would go on late into the evening. The day begins and ends with women pounding to prepare the meals. And yes, it is a collective background sound that you'll recognize in villages across Africa.

M: At times you can't tell whether what you're hearing is daily labor or music.

T: More than the music of labor, you also have the body rhythm of collective work. In the film, the way women bodily relate to each other while working is very rhythmic and musical. In other words, daily interactions among the people are music. You mentioned earlier the various aspects of the soundtrack: the silence, the commentary, the environmental, vocal and instrumental music. All these elements form the musical dimension of the film, but the relationship between and within the visuals is also rhythmically determined. The way an old woman spins cotton; the way a daughter and her mother move in syncopation while they pound or beat

NS

the grain together; the way a group of women chant and dance while plastering the floor of the front court in a house; or the way the different cultures counteract or harmonize with one another; these are the everyday rhythms and music of life. In such an environment one realizes how much modern society is based on compartmentalization—the mentality colonialism has brought in with its spread.

M: On the soundtrack, the statements about Africa are presented in such a way that the deepest voice seems to speak from within the cultures being discussed, the highest voice speaks—as you said in the introduction to the text published in Cinematograph *(Vol. 3, 1988, pp. 65–78)—"according to Western logic and mainly quotes Western thinkers"; and the medium-range voice (yours) speaks in the first person "and relates personal feelings and observations." But while the speakers vary their statements often overlap. Were you suggesting that what you heard about any given culture, or within any culture, is a combination of what it says about itself and what it knows is said about it by others?*

T: One can see it that way, certainly. Some viewers have told me, "If you had fictionalized these voices a little bit more" (which probably means they want the voices to be more in opposition rather than simply be "different"), "it'd be easier to understand the role of these voices." But I find it informative that a number of people have difficulty hearing the difference between the voices, even though their tone ranges, their accents and their discursive modes are so distinct. On the media we are used to consume one, unitary, narrating voice-over. It is not surprising then, that it may take some viewers more than one viewing to hear them in their differences. A viewer thought the difficulty comes from the fact that the voices are "disembodied" (meaning thereby that the narrators do not appear on screen), which may be true. But I think there are also other factors involved, because this same viewer may have no difficulty whatsoever listening to a "disembodied" omniscient voice-over on one of the TV programs. This is all a question of: "How does one speak?"

Any person who has had prolonged interactions with country people and villagers—whether from their own culture or from another culture—know that you have to learn to speak differently in order to be heard in their context. So if you listen carefully to your own speech in your interactions with them, you would recognize that even though you may both speak the same language—the case is further complicated when you don't—you speak differently. This sounds like a very banal statement until you find yourself in a situation where you wish to relate again what the villagers say to your audience—in other words, to translate them. Translation, which is interpellated by ideology and can never be objective or neutral, should here be understood in the wider sense of the term—as a politics of constructing meaning. Whether you translate one language into another language, whether you narrate in your own words what you have understood from the other person, or whether you use this person directly on screen as a piece of "oral testimony" to serve the direction of your film, you are dealing with cultural translation.

To give an example: a villager may say, while pointing toward the front court of her dwelling: "Calabash, we call it the vault of heaven." The local interpreter may translate: "The calabash is the vault of heaven." But when outsiders to the culture try to translate this to their audience back home, it might come out, "The calabash is like the vault of heaven," or "stands for the vault of heaven." There are all these little devices in language that "explain" instead of stating "this, this" or "this *is* this" with no explanation added. When you translate, you automatically rationalize what people say according to the logic and habits of your own language or mode of speaking. This tendency, which seems to me to be particularly naturalized in the media, is dealt with in *Naked Spaces* by assigning the explanatory logic and its ensuing linguistic devices to the voice of the woman whose English accent (actually South African) is easily detectable (Linda Peckham's). It was a real challenge for me to try to bring out these subtleties of translation and to remain consistent in the distinction of the three discursive modes. Moreover, the only voice in the film that can afford to have some kind of authority (not media or academic institutionalized authority, but rather a form of insider's assertion) is the mediated voice of the people, the low voice that quotes the villagers' sayings and other statements by African writers. My voice gives little anecdotes and personal feelings.

The distinction made between the voices is not a rigid one, and the latter do at times overlap in what they say and how they speak. The moment when the three are joined together is in the last third of the film, when the viewers see images of the Fon's lake-dwellings. The two voices that often speak in agreement then—as contrasted to the third one—are those of the two women of color: Barbara Christian and myself. We haven't really met in our statements until then, but here the issue in the village, whose people's income thrive on touristic trade, concerns the controversy of giving and taking. As it is fairly well known, in the First World–Third World relationship, what may assert itself in appearance as "giving" very often turns out to be nothing but a form of taking and taking again. The problematics of donor and acceptor is thus played out in that part in the soundtrack. This can be said to be the only place in the film where the First World and Third World voices work in opposition. Most of the time, it was important for me that the voices meet or not meet, but that they are not just set up in opposition to one another.

The voice of Western logic quotes a number of Western writers, including Cixous, Bachelard and Eluard. For me, these quotations are very relevant to the context of dwelling I was in. I don't situate myself in opposition to them just because the writers are Westerners. Actually, in a public debate, a white man resentfully asked me why I quoted Heidegger and added: "Why not let *us* quote him?" This is like saying that I have encroached on some occupied territory and that the exclusive right to use Heidegger belongs to Euro-Americans. Such ethnocentric rationale is hard to believe (although not the least surprising) when you take as examples, figures of modernity such as Picasso or Brecht (to mention just two names): what would their works be like without their being exposed to African sculpture or to Japanese and Chinese theaters? History constantly needs to be rewritten. In fact, whether I like it or not, Heidegger is also part of my hybrid culture.

M: In effect the soundtrack is a nexus for all *these voices. And all these voices meet in you; you're not only a first-person observer, you have internalized many voices.*

T: Exactly. The place of hybridity is also the place of my identity.

M: Actually, different forms of culture are present in Africa; there's no point in pretending that African peoples live in isolation from the world.

T: Sometimes you can never win. On the one hand, I encounter reactions such as "Why don't you show more of the trucks and the bicycles we see all the time in African villages?" When I hear similar questions, I can tell the type of villages the questioner is familiar with; he may have been to rural Africa, but he seems to have no idea of the villages I went to, which are fairly remote and difficult of access. On the other hand, some viewers also ask, "Why show all the signs of industrial society in these villages?" (referring here to the way the camera lingers on, for example, the white doll a child was playing with in *Reassemblage,* a red plastic cup, or a woman's pink plastic shoe in *Naked Spaces*).

At the same time as it is reassuring for certain Western viewers to see evidence of their own industrial society spreading over Third World rural landscapes (what one can call the marks of the West in its economical dominance), it is also irritating for others to see the camera explicitly looking at some of these industrialized objects, or gazing at them a few seconds too long. Since the shooting of *Reassemblage* has informed me of the potentials of a notion of cultural difference whose manifestations neither oppose nor depend on the West—in other words, neither succumbs to assimilation nor remains entirely pristine in its traditions—the decision was precisely to work in the remote countryside where circulation was mainly either on foot, by bicycle, or by pirogue. As a result of this choice, whenever any element of industrial society was found in such context, it became very visible. And the camera reproduced accordingly such visibility when an opportunity presented itself.

M: One thing that's been said about anthropologists is that, essentially, by going into "primitive" cultures and gathering information, they are "scouts" for the dominant culture, leading the way toward the destruction of indigenous people.

T: There is some truth to that metaphor, although it is a dangerous one because none of us who have gone to the cultures in question can claim to be free of it. I would use another metaphor: sometimes anthropologists act as if they were fishermen. They select a location, position themselves as observers and then throw a net, thinking that they can thereby catch what they look for. I think the very premise of such an approach is illusory. If I pick up that metaphor again and apply it to myself, I would have to be the net myself, a net with no fisherman; for I'm caught in it as much as what I try to catch. And I am caught with everything that I try to bring out in my films.

M: You were saying yesterday that some people who like the African films were unpleasantly surprised by Surname Viet Given Name Nam. *There are common elements in all three films, but your decision to explore what we might consider your own experience, your own heritage, requires you to more obviously distance yourself, to more overtly question your own position of authority with regard to your culture. One of the centers of the film is the set of interviews that were originally recorded in Vietnamese by someone else, and then translated into French, and are finally reenacted in your film by women who have come to the United States from Vietnam. In at least one sense, the film is as much about the process of translating meaning from one culture to another, as it is about Vietnam.*

T: You raise several questions. That some people are reacting differently to my last film is true, but I would not say this is only due to a difference between my African films and this film. There has already been a split reaction between *Reassemblage* and *Naked Spaces.* A number of people who really loved *Reassemblage* had problems with *Naked Spaces* when it first came out. I guess everything has its own time. When *Reassemblage* was released, I had to wait a whole year before the film really started circulating and before I got any positive feedback from viewers. It was such a hopeless situation, for I was piling up, one after the other, rejections from film festivals and numerous other film programs. In their own words, people "didn't know what to do with such a film"; it was totally misunderstood. Then unexpectedly, the film started being picked up simultaneously from diverse places. Viewers were bewildered but very enthusiastic; different venues opened up, and the unanticipated circulation of the film continues to grow since then. A somewhat similar process happened with *Naked Spaces.* Although the film got to be shown almost immediately to some packed audiences, the disappointment from those who came expecting another *Reassemblage* was quite apparent. Most of the praise and positive reactions I obtained in the first few months were from people who had not seen *Reassemblage*. One of the sympathizing viewers at a festival told me that when she shared with others her admiration for the film, she was told that she had to see *Reassemblage* first before offering any comment. *Reassemblage* was then often referred to by these viewers as a model. And yet, since then, I have had very, very moving and elating feedback on *Naked Spaces*—sometimes well beyond any expectations I had for that film.

M: *Was the objection some people had to* Naked Spaces *the fact that it is less overtly feminist than* Reassemblage, *that it doesn't foreground the role of women in African cultures as obviously as the earlier film?*

T: I don't think so. The most obvious problem people have with *Naked Spaces* is the length of the film. The notion of time and of duration are worked on in a way that makes the experience quite excruciating for some. Time not only as the result of editing, but time made apparent within the frame itself: by the gaze of the camera; by its slow unstable movement across people and their spaces; by the quiescence and contemplative quality of many of the scenes shown; and moreover by the lack of a central storyline or guiding message. Moviegoers do not mind sitting a couple of hours for a narrative feature. But to go through two hours and fifteen minutes of non-action film with no love story, no violence and "no sex" (as a viewer reminded me) is a real trial for many and a "far out," unforgettable experience for others. It was important for me on the one hand, to bring back a notion of time in Africa that never failed to frustrate foreigners eager to consume the culture at a time-is-money pace. (One of them, for example, warned a newcomer: "You need immense, un-limit-ed patience here! *Nothing is happening!*"). On the other hand, it was also critical to bring about a different way of experiencing film as well as of relating to our environment.

Some of the objections to *Naked Spaces* also have to do with the fact that certain viewers prefer the overt politics of *Reassemblage*. But *Reassemblage* cannot be repeated, and the audiences for the two films sometimes overlap, other times remain quite distinct. *Naked Spaces* seems to appeal strongly to people who are aware of the predicament of dwelling in modern society and are tuned to the inseparable questions of aesthetics, spirituality, sociality and environment. I have had, for example, intense and exalted feedback from a few Native American viewers. I could never anticipate this when I made the film.

For a while, I didn't quite know how to locate some of the hostilities toward *Surname Viet Given Name Nam*, although in making it, I was well aware of the risks that it was taking and the kind of difficulties it might encounter. Now that I have participated in more public debates on the film than I ever wish to, I can at least identify two kinds of viewers who have problems with it. Actually, they are the same, since the problems are fundamentally related. These are the viewers who either feel antagonistic, maintain a competitive attitude toward the feminist struggle, or are simply unaware of its complexities in relation to other struggles of liberation. Many of these viewers may think of themselves as pro-feminist, but they are not really into the feminist struggle, and this slips out in the questions they raise, in the lack of concern they show for any earnest inquiry into gender politics.

There are also other viewers who identify themselves as belonging to the anti-war movement and who do not really see *women* in *Surname Viet* (just like many male radicals in the sixties could not take seriously their female co-workers and the feminist struggle that was burgeoning independently right in the midst of their struggle for freedom of speech). These viewers tend to deny, or worse, to *obscure* entirely the question of gender by constantly casting the Vietnam reality back into the binary mold of communism and anti-communism. They also seem to be more preoccupied with what they militated for, or more eager to preserve an idealized image of Vietnam they supported, than they are willing to look at the actual situation of post-revolutionary Vietnam. As with many libertarian movements, there are people who are genuinely fighting for change, hence they remain sensitive to the complexities of the feminist struggle; and there are those who only work to consolidate a position of authority, hence they feel threatened by any form of resistance other than the one they are familiar with—here feminist. Right now in Vietnam, the leaders are acknowledging some of the failures of the system and are raising questions pertaining to the transformation of socialist society. So even when the people who are directly involved see the necessity for change, you have people from the outside still holding fast to a past image of Vietnam, where for example, all the women involved in the revolution are upheld as "heroines." The work of critical inquiry cannot be content with fixed anti-positions, which were, in their own time, necessary in regards to the war in Vietnam, but need to be problematized in the context of contemporary histories of political migration.

The struggle will never end, and we women still have a long way to go. The more I discuss these questions, the more I realize how little is known of the historical debates within the feminist struggle, not to mention the Sisyphean efforts of women of color across nations to expose the politics of gender within revolutionary movements. After this long detour to respond to your question, let me end it by linking it briefly to the initial point you made on the fact that *Surname Viet* is as much about the process of translating as it is about Vietnam. To unravel the "name" of Vietnam in the context of translation is to confront the much debated politics of identity—female identity, ethnic identity, nation identity. For translation, as I suggest earlier, implies questions of language, power and meaning; or more precisely in this film, of women's resistance vis-à-vis the socio-symbolic contract—as mothers, wives, prostitutes, nurses, doctors, state employees, official cadres, heroines of the revolution. In the politics of constructing identity and meaning, language as translation and/or film as translation is necessarily a process whereby the self loses its fixed boundaries—a disturbing yet potentially empowering practice of difference. For me, it is precisely in fighting on more than one front at a time—that is, in fighting not only against forms of domination and exploitation but also against less easily locatable forms of subjection or of binarist subjectivity—that the feminist struggle and other protest movements can continue, as discussed earlier, to resist falling back into the consolidation of conformism.

NS

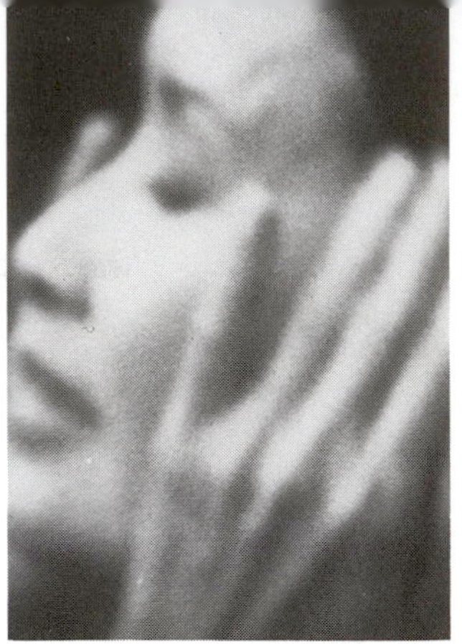

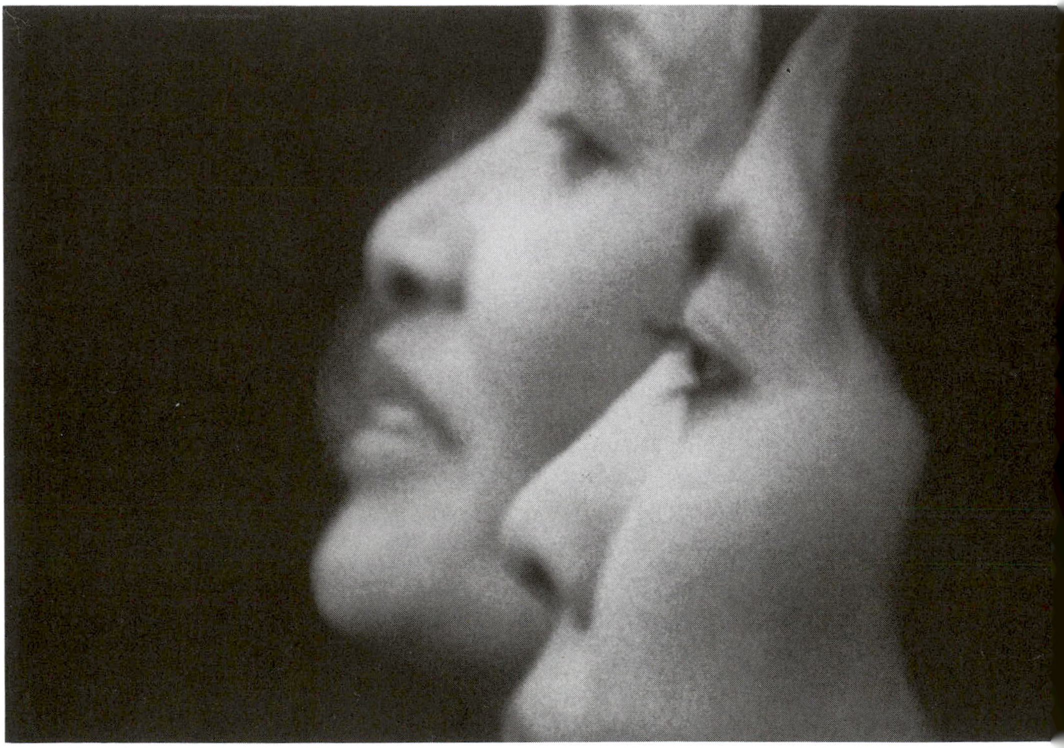

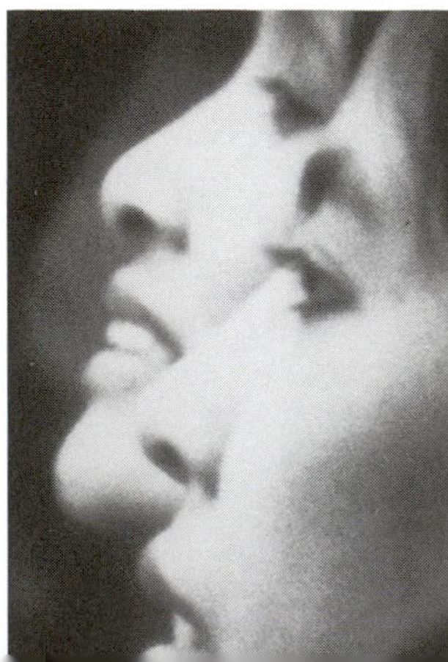

5

From a Hybrid Place

with Judith Mayne

Mayne: One of the things I admire about your work—your films as well as your book Woman, Native, Other*—is that it resists any easy categories. Your book is a work of theory, but it is very poetic: the reader has a different relationship to it than is usually the case in theoretical writing. Your films are obviously not documentaries in any classic sense, and it's not accurate to call them "commentaries" on the documentary genre either. Could you talk about this resistance to categorization that seems to be a crucial part of your work?*

Trinh: I am always working at the borderlines of several shifting categories, stretching out to the limits of things, learning about my own limits and how to modify them. The book, for example, was completed in 1983. It took me that long to find a publisher. Ironically enough (although not surprisingly), what I went through in submitting it for publication seemed to be sadly consistent with certain repressed realities of women's writing and publishing, which I discussed in its very first chapter. The book was rejected by no less than thirty-three presses. The kind

---

Interview conducted by Judith Mayne in May 1990, when *Surname Viet Given Name Nam* was screened at the Wexner Center for the Arts. First published as "Feminism, Filmmaking and Postcolonialism: An Interview with Trinh T. Minh-ha," in *Feminisms*, September–October (part I) and November–December (part II) 1990; and in *Afterimage* 18, no. 5, December 1990.

of problems it repeatedly encountered had precisely to do with marketable categories and disciplinary regulations; in other words, with conformist borders. Not only was the focus on postcolonial positionings and on women of color as a subject and as subjects of little interest to publishers then, but what bothered them most was the writing itself.

For academics, "scholarly" is a normative territory that they own all for themselves, hence theory is no theory if it is not dispensed in a way recognizable to and validated by them. The mixing of different modes of writing; the mutual challenge of theoretical and poetical, discursive and "non-discursive" languages; the strategic use of stereotyped expressions in exposing stereotypical thinking; all these attempts at introducing a break into the fixed norms of the Master's confident prevailing discourses are easily misread, dismissed, or obscured in the name of "good writing," of "theory," or of "scholarly work." I was continually sent back and forth from one publisher to another—commercial, academic, and small presses—each one equally convinced in its kind suggestions that the book would fit better in the other marketing context. What transpired through all the comments I received was mainly that the work never quite corresponded to what these diverse publishers were "looking for." Obviously, as they said, they were very interested in writings "from the Third World," but this one "would not fit in the series" they had or were in the process of establishing. An editor of a small press specializing in creative writing seriously felt he was being helpful when he decreed "it's not good writing because it's too impure."

It was a depressing experience. But I accept it as part of the struggle that this book is carrying on. I have to find a place for myself since I am at odds with all these categories of writings and modes of theorizing. A straight counterdiscourse is no longer threatening. It ultimately contributes to things remaining in place, because it tends more often than not to block critical thinking; it is unable to do much but repeat itself through the same anti-repressive rhetoric of modernist ideology. Let's take the example of a notion in vogue like "interdisciplinary." This notion is usually carried out in practice as the mere juxtaposition of a number of different disciplines. In such a politics of pluralist exchange and dialogue the concept of "inter-" (trans)formation and growth is typically reduced to a question of proper accumulation and acquisition. The disciplines are simply added, put next to one another with their boundaries kept intact; the participants continue happily to speak within their expertise, from a position of authority. It is rare to see such a notion stretched to the limits, so that the fences between disciplines are pulled down. Borderlines remain then strategic and contingent, as they constantly cancel themselves out. This "new" ground, always in the making, is what interests me most in everything I do. It constitutes the site where the very idea of a discipline, a specialization, and an expertise is challenged. No single field, profession, or creator can "own" it.

I never think of my films as specifically documentary or fictional, except when I send them off to festivals. Then I have to choose my jury. It is with this jury in mind that I place the film in a category. For years, no matter which one I chose, it seemed as if I constantly made the "wrong" selection. When I chose "documentary," I knew the problem would have to do with what people expect from a documentary and the ensuing rigidity of criteria. Most of these specialized jurors not only had difficulty in accepting my films as documentaries but also hardly considered them befitting the social, educational, or ethnographic categories. The same problem occurred when I opted for "film art" or "experimental," because jurors of such a category tend to see "experimental" as a genre on its own rather than as a critical venture working upon "genre" itself. Many still hold on to a mystical concept of "visionary art," and any preoccupation with or attempt at exposing ideology is rejected as "corrupt"—lacking pure vision, hence being no real Art. Now it seems that as my work is getting better known the categories become less important. But these used to be something that completely limited the ground on which the films could circulate.

M: You mention the word "borderline" several times, and the immediate connection that comes to mind is Gloria Anzaldua's Borderlands/La Frontera. *That notion of a space in between conventional opposing pairs has been very important to the work of many women of color. I wonder how you see your own work in relation to that of other women writers of color?*

T: I really like Anzaldua's works, and I often quote her in my own writings. I don't want to collapse all fights into one, however. I do realize the question of borderlines is particularly exigent in the Latina/Latino community because for many it remains physically an acute, everyday experience. This being said, and without forgetting the specificities of each context, I also recognize the commonalities between that border fight and the ones carried out, literally as well as figuratively, by women of color across ethnicities and cultures.

As in all struggles there are divergences among us; mostly in terms of strategy and location, I would say, but sometimes also in terms of objective and direction. What I understand of the struggle of women of color, however, is that our voices and silences across difference are so many attempts at articulating this always-emerging-already-distorted place that remains so difficult, on the one hand, for the First World even to recognize, and on the other, for our own communities to accept to venture into, for fear of losing what has been a costly gain through past struggles.

To unlearn the reactive language that promotes separatism and self-enclosure by essentializing a denied identity requires more than willingness and self-criticism. I don't mean simply to reject this language (a reactive front is at times necessary for consciousness to emerge) but rather to displace it and play with it, or to play it out like a musical score.

Many of the younger diasporic generation who come forth today, on the artistic as well as the theoretical scene, have voiced their discomfort with any safeguarding of boundaries on either side of the border. This is precisely because the repressed complexities of the politics of identity have been fully exposed. "Identity" has now become more a point of departure than an end point in the struggle. So although we understand the necessity of acknowledging this notion of identity in politicizing the personal, we also don't want to be limited to it. Dominated and marginalized people have been socialized to see always more than their own point of view. In the complex reality of postcoloniality it is therefore vital to assume one's radical "impurity" and to recognize the necessity of speaking from a hybrid place, hence of saying at least two, three things at a time.

M: *What's loosely called "French theory" has obviously influenced you.*

T: France colonized Vietnam for a long time. Despite having fiercely resisted the French colonials, someone like Ho Chi Minh would admit that he preferred the French mentality to the American one. Colonialism really has a grip on its people. At a recent conference on African cinema in San Francisco, the Mauritanian filmmaker Med Hondo started out saying a few lines in perfect English, but he immediately ruptured his speech by saying that he was colonized *first* by the French, and he went on in French for the rest of the session! "French theory" is certainly part of my hybrid reality, although I would say it is only one part among others.

M: *At one point in your book, commenting on the work of Helene Cixous, you say, "The One is the All and the All is the One; and yet the One remains the One and the All the All. Not two, not One either. This is what Zen has been repeating for centuries." I think there is something very contemplative about your films and your writing, a meditative quality. So-called "high theorists" never want to talk about a spiritual element in the text, but I sense that element very strongly in your work—specifically in the references to Zen, but more generally in your approach to representation.*

T: This is a point hardly ever discussed. Since it took so long to find a publisher for the book, I had to resort to other publishing venues. Hence, some parts excerpted for this purpose had appeared here and there, in different journals. Now people confidently talk about earlier versions that "were later elaborated in the book," but in fact the book was written in its entirety long before any of these "articles" came out. After submitting these "excerpts" to journals, I received detailed comments from academic readers whose advice was sought by the concerned editors. Some of the readers, indeed, had a major problem with the Zen materials included, which they considered to be useless in a theoretical context. They reacted most scornfully, focusing on the "what" and turning a blind eye to the "how"—the way the materials are used and the inter-links created (as with Cixous's feminism in the example you mentioned).

I can understand such a reaction, especially living in California. I think that Zen—as it has spread in the West, especially in the 60s, with prominent names like John Cage, Alan Watts, Allen Ginsburg—has been mystified in its very demystifying practices. (This despite and *not* because of the works of the individuals mentioned.) Zen was recuperated into a dualistic and compartmentalized worldview. Speaking again of classifications and borders, you are here either "holistic" or "analytical," but you can't possibly be both, because the two are made into absolute antithetical stances. Zen has the gift to frustrate and infuriate the rational mind, which hurriedly dismisses it as simply one more form of mystification. So Zen's tenets are a real problem for a number of academics; but I myself do not operate within such divisions, and I don't see why I have to be bound to them. Spirituality cannot be reified. It's difficult to talk about it, not only because it escapes the principles of logic but also because "spiritual" itself is an impossible term: disinherited and vacated in this society of reification, hence not easy to use without exacting negotiations. The first book I wrote in 1976–77, *Un Art sans oeuvre* (An art without masterpiece, published in 1981), includes a chapter relating the works of Jacques Derrida and Antonin Artaud to those of Krishnamurti and Zen Buddhism. For me many of Derrida's theories, including the critique of the metaphysics of presence, are forces that have been active in Zen and in other forms of Buddhism for centuries. So what he says is not really "new," but the way he puts them into discourse, the links he makes, *are*. The weaving of Zen in my text is therefore not a "return to my roots" but a grafting of several cultures onto a single body—an acknowledgment of the heterogeneity of my own cultural background.

M: This connects to one of the issues you discussed at the screening last night, the notion of "negative space."

T: In my films the notion of negative space has always been crucial. The "object-oriented camera"—a camera that focuses only on catching the object and is eager to objectify—obscures the role of negative space. I don't mean the ground behind the filmed subject or the field surrounding it, but rather the space that makes both composition and framing possible, that characterizes the way an image breathes. To see negative space as intensely as the figure and the field, instead of subjecting it to the latter in cinematography, mise-en-scene, and narrativity, implies a whole different way of looking at and of relating to things. This is not far from the notion of the Void in Asian philosophies. People often don't even know what you are talking about when you mention the vitality of the Void in the relationships between object and non-object, or between I and non-I. Again, they may think it's a form of mystification. This is a problem with reifying, binarist thinking: emptiness here is not merely opposed to fullness or objecthood; it is the very site that makes forms and contents possible—that is, also inseparable.

M: I'm curious how you see your most recent film in relationship to your two previous films, both of which depict the women of Africa and your relationship, as an Asian woman, to Africa. I'm thinking here especially of the term "hybridization" that you used last night to describe your approach to filmmaking.

T: The title of the film—*Surname Viet Given Name Nam*—is taken from recent socialist tradition. When a man encounters a woman, feels drawn to her, and wants to flirt with her, he teasingly asks, "Young woman, are you married yet?" If the answer is negative, instead of saying no, she will reciprocate, "Yes, his surname is Viet and his given name is Nam." In this apparently benign reply the nation-gender relationship immediately raises questions. One of the recurring motifs in the film is the *wedd*-ing, women being married: to a little boy or to a polygamous husband through family arrangements; to the cause, the fatherland, the state; to a foreigner bowing *a la* Vietnamese; then to a native man in Western outfit. The predicament of married women, which is woven here with the condition of single women insinuated or directly commented upon in poetry, proverbs, and popular stories, is unfolded in contexts of Vietnam that cut across the times before, during and after the revolution, including the periods of Chinese and French dominations, as well as the shift to life in the Vietnamese community in the United States. As one interviewee affirms toward the end of the film, whether a woman marries a foreigner or a Vietnamese, her surname will always remain "Viet" and her given name "Nam." A slight mutation of meaning occurs in that affirmation as it gets transferred from one context to another.

The question of nation and gender is opened up in a multiply layered way. The inquiry into identity provides another example. The latter can be said to develop in the film through a (re)appropriation of the inappropriate(d) body—the relations indirectly built up between the problematics of translation; the multiple (re)naming

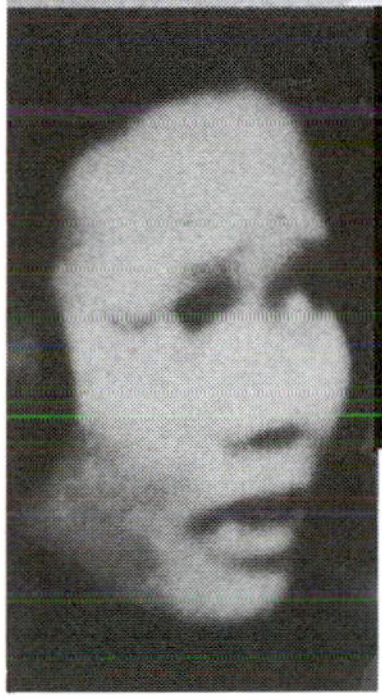

SV

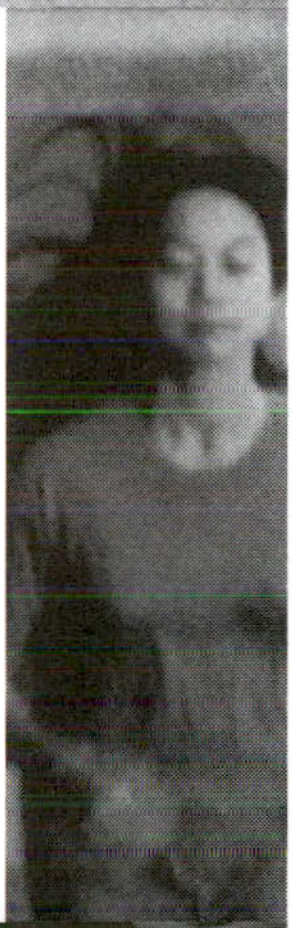

of a country; and the plural expropriation (owning, selling, humiliating, burning, exposing, glorifying) of women's bodies. Translation, like identity, is a question of grafting several cultures onto a single body. For example, the name of Trieu Thi Trinh, one of the historical heroines who resisted Chinese domination, has at least five variations (heard and seen on screen); each of these is a different reading, a different emphasis of her attributes—her lineage (by her last name), her gender and age status, her leadership, or merely her simplicity. Similarly, each of the numerous names used to designate Vietnam (also heard and seen on screen) relates to a historical period of the nation, thereby to the diverse outside and inside influences that have contributed to what is viewed as the Vietnamese culture. So hybridization here refers to a negotiation of the difference not merely between cultures, between First World and Third World, but more importantly within the culture. This plural singularity and the problematization of the insider-outsider position are precisely what I have explored at length in my previous films, although in a way that is hardly comparable since it is so differently contextualized.

M: One of the most striking features of Surname Viet Given Name Nam *is your exploration of different modes of storytelling, or what you described last evening as two different kinds of truth.*

T: Storytelling is an ongoing field of exploration in all of my works, hence a vast subject to discuss. I'm afraid I can only cover a few aspects of it here. The interviews originally carried out by Mai Thu Van in Vietnam were published in the book *Vietnam: un peuple, des voix* (Paris: Pierre Horay, 1983. Vietnam: one people, many voices). I ran across this book while browsing in a small bookstore in France some years ago. It was certainly a discovery. I was very moved, both by the stories of the women interviewed and by the personal story of the author herself. Born in New Caledonia, she is a second-generation exile, her mother having been sent there by force to work in nickel mines because her village was among those that rose in rebellion against the French colonials. Mai came to Paris at the age of twenty-three to work and study and went to Vietnam in 1978 to research Vietnamese women, which resulted in the book mentioned. Being a Marxist, she landed in Hanoi with "a plethora of images of liberated women who have disturbed old concepts to meet socialism," and her stay there, as she puts it, "had profoundly shaken [her] preconceived ideas as well as pulverized the stereotypes of [Vietnamese] women made up by the press." It took her tenacity and an almost morbid care for the truth to wait for the ice to melt, to develop trust in an atmosphere of fear and suspicion, to take the blows, and to accept the eye-opening realities of women who refused to let themselves be mystified as heroines in postrevolutionary times. In brief, it took her five years to collect the interviews in question.

So in using some of the interviews in my film, the question for me is: Which truth does one want to offer to the viewer? The truth that Mai spent five years to approach, or the truth that we can easily claim by setting up an interview situation, directing a microphone at a person (like myself right now!), and trying to skim the cream off the answers afterwards? The point at issue is somewhat different here, however, because when an interview is recorded and transcribed for publication you can work on it, and the length of the interviewee's replies is usually respected. But in film the problem of editing is much more acute, because you can't reword to condense, nor can you add to clarify; you can only cut. And you cut what you want people to be saying: you cut only the statement that will help you to make your point. So there are certain kinds of unintended surface truths that may emerge as unique to the filmed interview situation, but there are also other kinds that can never be accessible through this antiquated device of documentary—unless the element of realism is worked on.

Perhaps one can find an example in a film like *Chronique d'un été* (Chronicle of a Summer, 1961, by Jean Rouch), where an interviewer just pointed a microphone at people in the street, asking, "Are you happy?" The shallow answers might have been a reaction to such a question, but they also implied the shallowness of such an interview setup. The director must then "work on" this shallowness, that is, deliberately acknowledge it in order to further the film's inquiries. As spectators, our attitude toward interviews often proves to be naive. We tend to forget how tactical speech always is, no matter how naturally it seems to come out. To assume that testimonies filmed on the site are de jure more truthful than those reconstructed off the site is to forget how films are made. Every representation of truth involves elements of fiction, and the difference between so-called documentary and fiction in their depiction of reality is a question of degrees of fictitiousness. The more one tries to clarify the line dividing the two, the deeper one gets entangled in the artifice of boundaries.

The making of *Surname Viet* allows the practice of interviews to enter into the play of the true and the false, the real and the staged. In the first part of the film, the interviews were selected, cut, and blueprinted for reenactment. A certain length of the speech and the image was deliberately kept to preserve the autonomy of each story as it unfolded and, paradoxically, to render perceptible the play on traditional realism. The latter becomes more and more manifest as the film progresses, until further on the viewer is presented with a series of "real" interviews with the same women as in the first part, but in the explicit context of the U.S. The editing of these last interviews comes closer to the conventions of documentary as the statements are chopped up, redistributed, and woven in the filmic text with footage of the women's "real" life-activities. By using both reenacted interviews and on-site interviews and by demarcating some of their differences (in the duration, mode of address, use of English, camera work), in other words, by presenting them to the viewer together, what is visibly addressed is the invisibility of the politics of interviews and, more generally, the relations of representation.

I am not really interested in judging which truth is better than the other, but rather in working with both together to open a critical space in the viewing of the film. Whether the viewer is knowledgeable enough in cinema to attribute some of the strategies to a questioning of the conventions of documentary authority is also not the point. The viewing situation created is such that it is likely to provoke questions and reactions. By playing with the false and the true at work in the two kinds of truth, what is usually taken for granted in interviews suddenly becomes very prominent. As a bewildered Vietnamese viewer told me: "Your film is different. I can't yet tell exactly how, but I know it's different from the documentary films I am used to seeing." The recognition that the early interviews in the film are reenactments comes at different places and stages for different viewers. This is deliberately planned, as I previously suggested. Of course, as you probably noticed at yesterday's screening, some viewers were furious because they expected to be told about it at the outset of the film (as the norms dictate). But other viewers felt that to reveal the reenactment from the start would be to give away the "plot" of the film; they were uncomfortable with the lingering uncertainty, but retroactively they loved the challenge and the intermittent discomfort. I obviously do not intend to "hide" the reenactment—on the contrary—only to delay or grade its visibility for strategic purposes. Nor do I feel compelled to flatten out the film to facilitate its consumption. Instead of being a mere illustration of a point that is evident from the beginning, a film could be a constant discovery process. Much of filmmaking and storytelling relies on an ability to withhold information as well as to let go of knowledge and intention.

M: The process of "recognition" in the film is very unsettling.

T: The distance between the written texts and the images is necessary. The women are asked both to embody other selves, other voices, and to drift back to their own selves, which are not really their "natural" selves but the selves they want to present or the images they want to project in front of the camera.

M: *Another kind of distance is the discrepancy between written text and voice, sometimes small—suggesting that the text is being performed.*

T: If it is unsettling, it's because the line between performance and nonperformance in these interviews is not so evident. You can't tell right away that they are staged—you do ask the question, but you can't tell for sure until you get enough "cues."

M: *In conclusion, could you say something about the kind of work that has most influenced you?*

T: It's very difficult for me to talk about influence. Even with someone like Ho Xuan Huong, the early nineteenth-century poet quoted in the film: I knew of her, but she was hardly taught in school. I remember how perversely excited we (the students) were whenever a teacher announced that a poem of hers would be read in class. Not only because her poetry is known for its forbidden sexuality and explicit defiance of Confucian (male-chauvinist) mores, but mainly because she is a poet whose work we are never truly exposed to. All this to say that on the side of women you always have to do more; you have to be committed to reach out to nonmainstream works and to the writings of other women. This is one of the constraints that you necessarily assume as a feminist. The writing of *Woman, Native, Other* touches upon this specific issue. For example, the only chapter that deals exclusively with the world of white males is the chapter on anthropology. This chapter is also one, however, in which all the names of the representative famous men are replaced in the text by impersonal, stereotyped appellations ("The Great Master," "The modern anthropologist," "the wise man"). Their proper names, their "true" names, are "buried" in the footnotes.

For me there is no such thing as a one-way influence. In (re)reading women's works—actually any work—I am not sure who influences whom, for I have the feeling that I've contributed as much as I've learned. And if I take the example of a few Western writers with whom I have affinities, such as Roland Barthes, Walter Benjamin, Maurice Blanchot, or Derrida, sure, I find their writings uplifting and penetrating. But our actualities are undeniably different. They have their own house to empty out, their own obsessions to pursue. However, their works do provide tools of resistance that we can use on our terms. Tools that also allow me independently to rediscover, let's say, Zen Buddhism or other Asian philosophies as if I were reading them for the first time; *and* vice versa. What has become more evident to me is that I can't settle down with any single name, any single work. The only times I felt that something could strongly inspire me, and in ways that were both moving and baffling, was when I was staying in the villages in Africa. The richness of the diverse oral traditions is humbling. Again this may seem romantic to many—although in the context of other cultures it is rather "realistic." As a Yoruba song of divination says, "Anybody who meets beauty and does not look at it will soon be poor." Stories, songs, music, proverbs, as well as people's daily interactions, certainly constitute for me the most moving sources of inspiration.

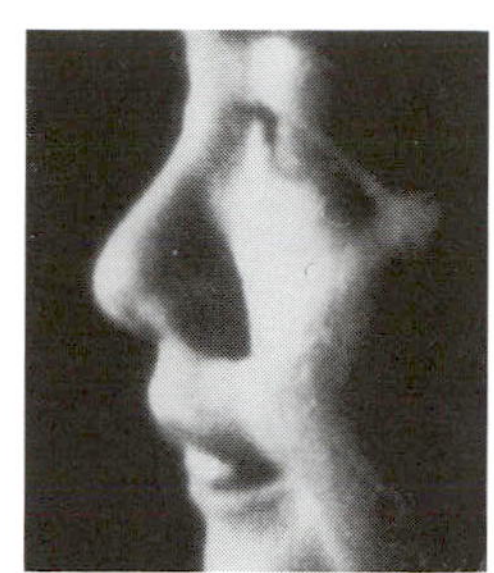

SV

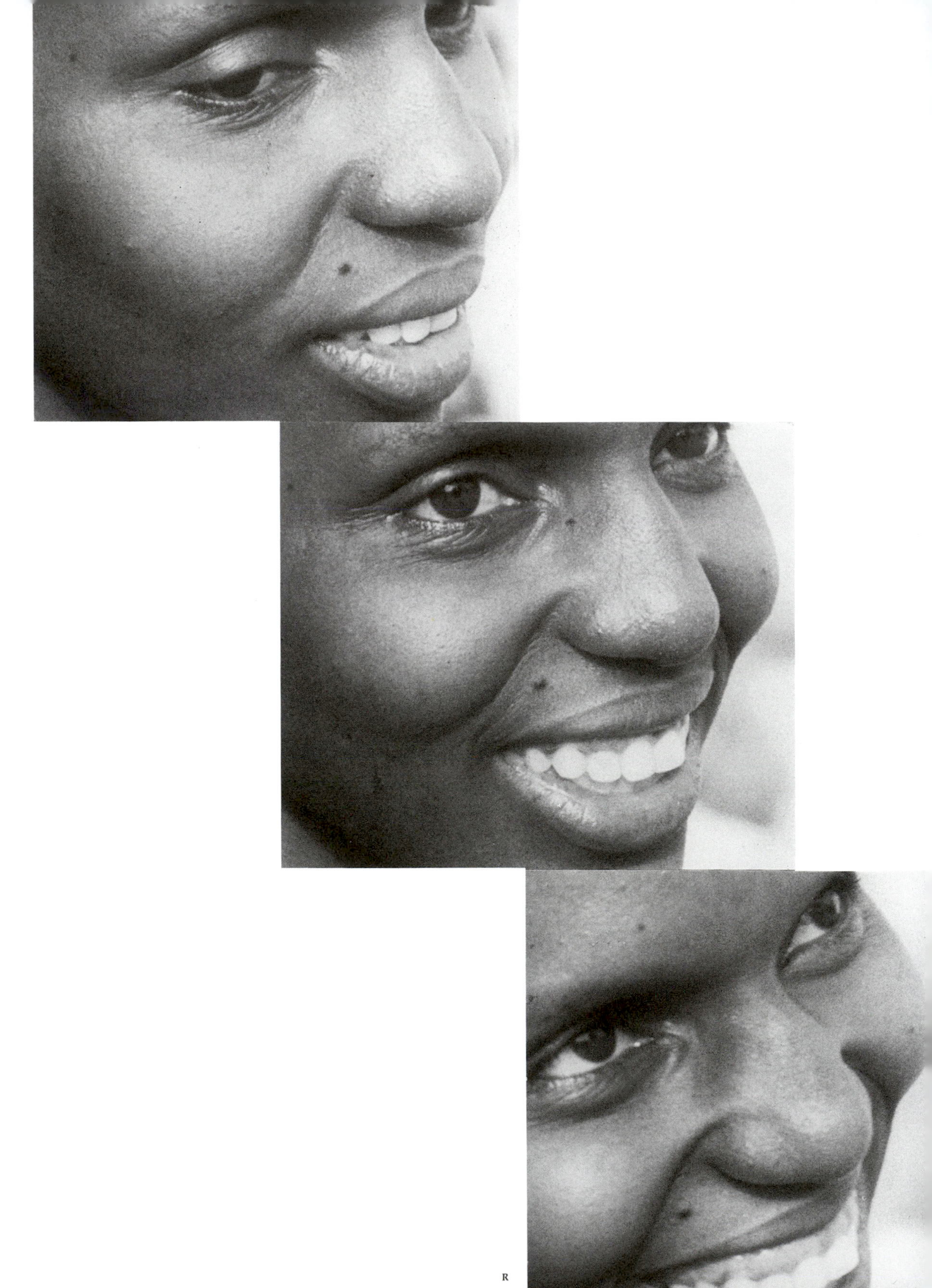

6

Between Theory and Poetry

with Pratibha Parmar

Parmar: I would like to start by asking you how you place yourself as a "Third World Woman" vis-à-vis the women's movement.

Trinh: Well, it took me many pages in the book to develop this. The fact is that we are standing on a very precarious line. I see the women's movement as being necessarily heterogeneous in its origin, even though it may be claimed more readily by certain groups and remains largely white in its visibility. On the one hand, I readily acknowledge my debt to the movement in all the reflections advanced on the oppression of women of color. On the other hand I also feel that a critical space of differentiation needs to be maintained since issues specifically raised by Third World women have less to do with questions of cultural difference than with a different notion of feminism itself—how it is lived and how it is practiced. Naming yourself a feminist is not without problem, even among feminists. In a context of marginalization, at the same time as you feel the necessity to call yourself a feminist while fighting for the situation of women, you also have to keep a certain latitude

---

First published as "Woman, Native, Other: Pratibha Parmar Interviews Trinh T. Minh-ha," *Feminist Review,* no. 36 (Autumn 1990).

and to refuse that label when feminism tends to become an occupied territory. Here, you refuse, not because you don't want to side with other feminists, but simply because it is crucial to keep open the space of naming in feminism.

P: *The back-cover blurb on the book jacket of* Woman, Native, Other *describes the book as "post-feminist." I find this term problematic, because my understanding of it within the context of England is that it is a term used by the mainstream media as a way of denigrating current feminist practices. Furthermore, it also carries with it the notion that feminism is dead and is no longer a viable or necessary social movement. Can you say what you think about this and how you use the term?*

T: Actually, I don't know how the word popped upon the back cover of the book, except that the first subtitle I thought of included it as well as the word "Third World," which reviewers also strongly rejected. Its reappearance here is the publisher's choice, not mine. I took it out at an early stage, not so much because I distrust its use as because, precisely as you said, it raises a number of confusing interpretations. I fear that one does not even need to go to the context of England to see how it can be condemned by certain feminists. Within feminism, there are, as in all movements, women whose questioning of the dominant system constantly pushes to the outer limits of what feminism is and what it is not. But you also have others who just hop in the wagon and are likely to turn feminism into a rigidly prescriptive practice, perpetuating thereby the same power relations as those established in the patriarchal system. Feminism is thus weakened in its political undertaking as it is reduced to something as simplistic as man-hating.

Sure, the mainstream is always very quick to appropriate subversive strands to their own conservative end, but one need not fall prey to this. For me, the notion of postfeminism is as problematic, but also as interesting, as is the notion of postmodernism through which, for example, the definition of modernism keeps on being displaced in its certainties. Therefore, postmodernism cannot be reduced to something that merely comes *after* modernism or to a simple rejection of modernism. As some theorists argue, it can point back to a nascent stage of modernism, a dawning stage before the closure, in other words, a stage in between closures. Postfeminism in this context is both a return to a nascent stage of feminism where the movement is at its most subversive, and a move forward to a stage in which we have learned from the many difficulties we've encountered that, in spite of all the refinements of sexist ideology, the fight is far from being over. It has, on the contrary, become so much more complex now that the movement has reached an impasse on the issue of essentialism, whether this idea of an innate "womanness" is defined by men or championed by women.

P: In your book as in your films you critically engage with the "problem" of how to represent a Third World female Other. This critical engagement with certain "master discourses" leads you to interrogate anthropology, deconstructionist philosophy, postcolonial literary criticism and feminist theory. In relation to feminist theory it is quite clear that Black women and "women of color" have shifted the frameworks of what was once the dominant trajectory of the euro-centric, middle class and white women's movement both in the U.S. and in Europe. Would you agree that we have instigated these shifts through our interventions, our writings, our political practices?

T: As I mentioned earlier, I don't believe the movement to be otherwise than heterogeneous in its origins. In fact, this is the condition of *any* socio-political or esthetic movement. That's why history and culture keep on having to be rewritten. Because of their more privileged status, white feminists have been taking up this task more extensively, but the women's movement resulted from the works of both white women and women of color around the world. Now that more women of color have access to education, there will be more and more rewriting work to be done on our side. (This is not an easy situation to be in, since as I wrote in the book, writing is always practiced at the cost of other women's labor.) Moreover, the influence has always been mutual: if women of color had at times taken their cue from white women's sexual politics, their fight has consistently contributed to radicalize the feminist struggle. As you put it, it continues to shift the framework of Euro-American feminism and, depending on how the work is carried out, the refocus on women of color in white feminist discourse lately can be seen as a simultaneous form of appropriation and expropriation, or as an acknowledgment of intercultural enrichment and of interdependency in the fighting-learning process. The precarious line we walk on is one that allows us to challenge the West as authoritative subject of feminist knowledge, while also resisting the terms of a binarist discourse that would concede feminism to the West all over again.

P: What I find very exciting about your book was the fact that there's a seamless quality between your subjective perceptions of fragmentation, your questioning of language and of identity as a post-colonial subject, and the more structured processes of how you give those experiences a theoretical coherence. In other words, organic to your theoretical project is your very personal voice which is integrated poignantly and often self-reflectively.

What is also quite unique is the way you use poetical language and engage with writings of women of color, be they prose, poetry, autobiography, as philosophical and theoretical texts. Can you talk more about this?

T: You put it very nicely. This will help to give another dimension to what I am about to discuss. What you find exciting in this "theoretical project," to use your own terms, seems precisely to be the source of problems I have repeatedly encountered while seeking publication of the book. Aside from the fact that its subject appeared to be of little interest and relevance to publishers in general, what was widely rejected both by publishers and readers to whom they sent the book for review reports was the way I chose to write. Never had I experienced so extensively, at least in intellectual matters, the dilemma of crossing borderlines. Academics, infatuated with their own normalization of what constitutes a "scholarly" work, abhor any form of writing that exceeds academic language and whose mode of theorizing is not recognizable, hence not classifiable as "theory" according to their standard of judgement. Likewise, the militant presses also reject it because it does not square with the rhetoric of militancy and its insistence on liberal thinking; while the feminist presses refuse it because either it is "too speculative to be a useful textbook for institutions" or it is simply "not quite what we are looking for." Last, but not least, the small presses focusing on creative writing condemn the book for being too "impure." In other words, what bothers all these presses is its "impurity": the irrespectful mixing of theoretical, militant and poetical modes of writing.

Part of the fight carried on in the book is to show how theory can relate intimately to poetry; how they interact when meaning is prevented from becoming dogma or from ending with what is said, thereby unsettling the identity of the speaking/writing/reading subject in the signifying process. Theorists tend to react strongly against poetry today because for them, poetry is nothing else but a place where a subjectivity is consolidated and where language is estheticized (such as building vocabulary and rhyming beautiful lines). Whereas poetry is also the place from which many people of color voice their struggle. Consider Cuban and African poetry, for example. And if you look into Asian, Hispanic, African and Native American literatures here in the U.S., poetry is no doubt the major voice of the poor and of people of color. So poetical language does become stale and self-indulgent when it serves an art-for-art's-sake purpose, but it can also be the site where language is at its most radical in its refusal to take itself for granted.

As feminists have insistently pointed out, women are not only oppressed economically, but also culturally and politically, in the very forms of signifying and reasoning. Language is therefore an extremely important site of struggle. Meaning has to retain its complexities, otherwise it will just be a pawn in the game of power. Even theorists like Julia Kristeva who only write prose, recognize that only in poetical language lies the possibility of revolution. For me, the political responsibility here is to offer meaning in such a way that each reader, going through the same statements and the same text, would find tools for herself (or himself) to carry on the fight in her (or his) own terms.

P: At the core of the book lies a questioning of the languages and discourses of the grand narratives of the human sciences which seek to universalize and homogenize. What is inter-

esting here is that rather than constructing an oppositional discourse you move in and out of these languages, challenging, deconstructing and reformulating their suppositions and ideological underpinnings.

You say, "From jagged transitions between the analytical and the poetical to the disruptive, always shifting fluidity of a headless and bottomless storytelling, what is exposed in this text is the transcription and the de-scription of a non-unitary female subject of color through her engagement, therefore also disengagement, with master discourses."

In many ways, I think it is women of color who are often best placed to engage and also disengage with master discourses, since our entry into the "master's house" continues to be a forced entry rather than a polite invitation. Also, we don't hold "white, male, Christian masters" as voices of authority and legitimation. What do you think are the consequences for you as an individual who traverses so many theoretical and personal boundaries?

T: Perhaps I can answer this question by coming back to an important part which I left out in my earlier response: the role of theory. The situation is not unlike what we said earlier about feminism. You have people who practice theory in a very deadening way, so theory keeps on aiming for closures and building up boundaries rather than voiding them. What is constituted are areas of expertise and specialization the fortification and expansion of which need a whole network of disciplinarians. I find this particularly true with film theory, for example. It certainly seems to be heading toward a dead end as it tends to become a mere form of administrative inquisition. In reflecting on language(s) as a crucial site for social change, theory should precisely challenge such a compartmentalized view of the world and render perceptible the (linguistic) cracks existing in every argument while questioning the nature of oppression and its diverse manifestations.

This is where disrupting "the grand narratives of the human sciences" becomes a means of survival, and where a straight oppositional discourse is no longer sufficient. In the book, I came back, for example, to the age-old division between the instinct and the intellect, and briefly discussed theory in relation to how women conceive the "abstract." The way I dealt with a non-unitary notion of subjectivity in my film *Naked Spaces—Living Is Round* may also contribute further to questioning reductive oppositions. The film has three female voice-overs which constitute, broadly speaking, three ways of informing. One of the voices quotes African writers and villagers' sayings, while another reasons according to writings from the West, and the third tells personal anecdotes and feelings. This analytical differentiation is useful here, but it is certainly not adequate, since the three voices often overlap in their functions. The first voice is perhaps the most concrete, yet it has a pervasive abstract quality to it. Because it does not inform with a rationale recognizable to the West, Western viewers often either classify it as being "symbolic" or they decide that it is simply part of an abstract "intellectualizing" process. I would say that this is not false, but it's not true either. It is not false because representation is here visibly and audibly shown as being mediated by my own background and rationalization of the culture. It is not quite true, because this eagerness to equate the abstract with "intellectualization" is an impoverishment due to the dominance of the literal mind. When you hear the conversations of these village women, you can never separate the abstract from the concrete, and the level at which signs and symbols operate leads us directly into the very details of their daily existence. This, I believe, is where the power of the poetry of our environment lies. And this is also what theory can achieve when it comes closest to poetry in its signifying operation.

The above example of simultaneous engagement and disengagement with master discourses can indeed, as you point out, be heightened by the fact that our entry into the "master's house" continues to be a forced entry. Even and especially when I visibly walk in the "center" with all spotlights on, I feel how utterly inappropriate(d)ly "other" I remain—not so much by choice nor by lack of choice, as by a mixture of survival instinct and critical necessity. Here, the fact that one is always marginalized in one's own language and areas of strength, is something that one has to learn to live with. I can't help noticing this in every single realm of my activities: how I am sent off from one disciplinary border, one classification to another in academic milieus (never "quite corresponding to what they are looking for"); how I am categorized in conferences; how I am introduced in diverse public events; how I am viewed and read through my work; how I am rejected and retrieved by different communities; the kind of job I am expected to take on, the institutional territories I am allowed or not allowed to step into; and so on. Impurity and marginalization have always had strong bonds; the more one strengthens these, the more one's position proves to be fragile. It's nothing new.

P: *I would like to move on to a question about definitions and identities that comes up quite frequently amongst radical post-colonial intellectuals: "Are we victims of fragmentation or, precisely because of our cultural hybridity and post-colonial experiences of displacement and marginality, are we a synthesis placed very much in the center?"*

T: For me it's not a question of fragmentation versus synthesis, but rather, of how one understands what happens within the notion of fragmentation itself. If one sees a fragment as being the opposite of a whole, then I have no affinities with the term, since it carries with it the compartmentalized worldview I questioned earlier. But if the fragment stands on its own and cannot be recuperated by the notion of totalizing whole, then fragmentation is a way of living with differences without turning them into opposites, nor trying to assimilate them out of insecurity. Fragmentation is here a useful term because it always points to one's limits. Since the self, like the work you produce, is not so much a core as a process, one finds oneself, in the context of cultural hybridity, always pushing one's questioning of oneself to the limit of what one is and what one is not. When am I Vietnamese? When am I American? When am I Asian and when am I Asian-American or Asian-European? Which language should I speak, which is closest to myself, and when is that language more adequate than another? By working on one's limits, one has the potential to modify them. Fragmentation is therefore a way of living at the borders.

P: So how would you look at questions of identity as a woman, as a woman of color, as a writer, as a filmmaker?

T: Again, if it is a point of redeparture for those of us whose ethnicity and gender were historically debased, then identity remains necessary as a political/personal strategy of survival and resistance. But if it is essentialized as an end point, a point of "authentic" arrival, then it only narrows the struggle down to a question of "alternatives"—that is, a perpetuation, albeit with a reversed focus, of the notion of "otherness" as defined by the master, rather than a radical challenge of patriarchal power relations. The claim of identity is often a *strategic* claim. It is a process which enables me to question my condition anew, and one by which I intimately come to understand how the personal is cultural, historical or political. The reflexive question asked, as I mentioned earlier, is no longer: *Who* am I? but *When, where, how* am I (so and so)? This is why I remain skeptical of strategies of reversal when they are not intricately woven with strategies of displacement. Here the notion of displacement is also a place of identity: there is no real me to return to, no whole self that synthesizes the woman, the woman of color and the writer; there are instead, diverses recognitions of self through difference, and unfinished, contingent, arbitrary closures that make possible both politics and identity.

P: I wanted to move on to talk about your films more specifically. What would you say is your agenda in terms of your filmmaking practice? Partly, I'm asking this as a way of going back to what we were saying earlier about the dominant culture being in many ways a mainstream fiction. I think the kind of work you are engaging with in your films and through your writings is actually changing the cultural topography of whole areas of visual discourses.

T: It is difficult to talk about a single agenda in my filmmaking. Each work engenders its own agenda. I can try, however, to trace some of the preoccupations that run through the different works produced. For example, I wrote *Woman, Native, Other* approximately at the same time as when I made my earlier films, and yet I was committed to not mentioning film in this book because I was dealing with writing rather than filmmaking. But in both filmic and written works, the attempt is to reflect on the tools and the relations of production that define us, whether as a filmmaker or as a writer. By doing so, what I hope for is to provide myself and others with tools not only to beat the master at his own game, but also to transform the terms of our consciousness. Since my films are not materializations of ideas or visions that precede them, the way they take shape entirely depends on what happens during and in between the process(es) of producing them. Therefore, what it is about can never be separated from how it is made.

Let's take the example of my latest film, *Surname Viet Given Name Nam*. It is a work in which a number of questions tightly intersect: identity, popular memory, culture(s). In focusing on Vietnamese women in Vietnam and in the States, I was interested in exploring how we project ourselves through our own stories and analyses as well as how we are constituted through the image-repertoire that insiders and outsiders to the culture have historically fashioned and retained of us. Here the role of popular memory and of oral tradition remains pivotal in the film as it allows me to offer the viewer, not some "factual" information on the condition of women and on the history of their resistance, but songs, proverbs, stories that bring to the fore their oppression, their struggle, and highlight how and what people remember of them. While breaching the question of plural identity for example, the film works simultaneously at different levels on the intersection of nation and gender; on the problems of translation within a culture as well as between several cultures; on the politics of interviews with its emphasis on oral testimonies and its "voice-giving" claims; and finally on the fictions of documentary.

All this being said, I feel that in trying to respond to your statement, hence to look for a specific agenda, to explain, contain, or justify it, I am simply led to this banal question: Why write? Why make film? there is obviously no single answer to this. Perhaps it is not so much a question of "making" as that of allowing things to be (or not to be) and to take form on their own. Perhaps resistance in this context is not to go against, but to assume a difficult "freedom," one that also refutes itself as freedom.

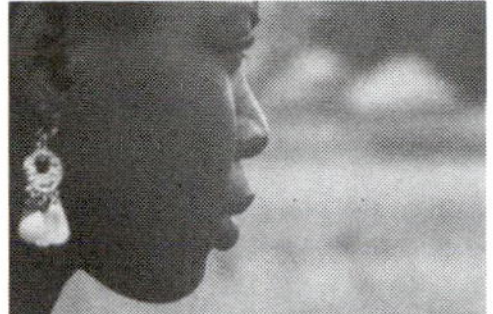

R

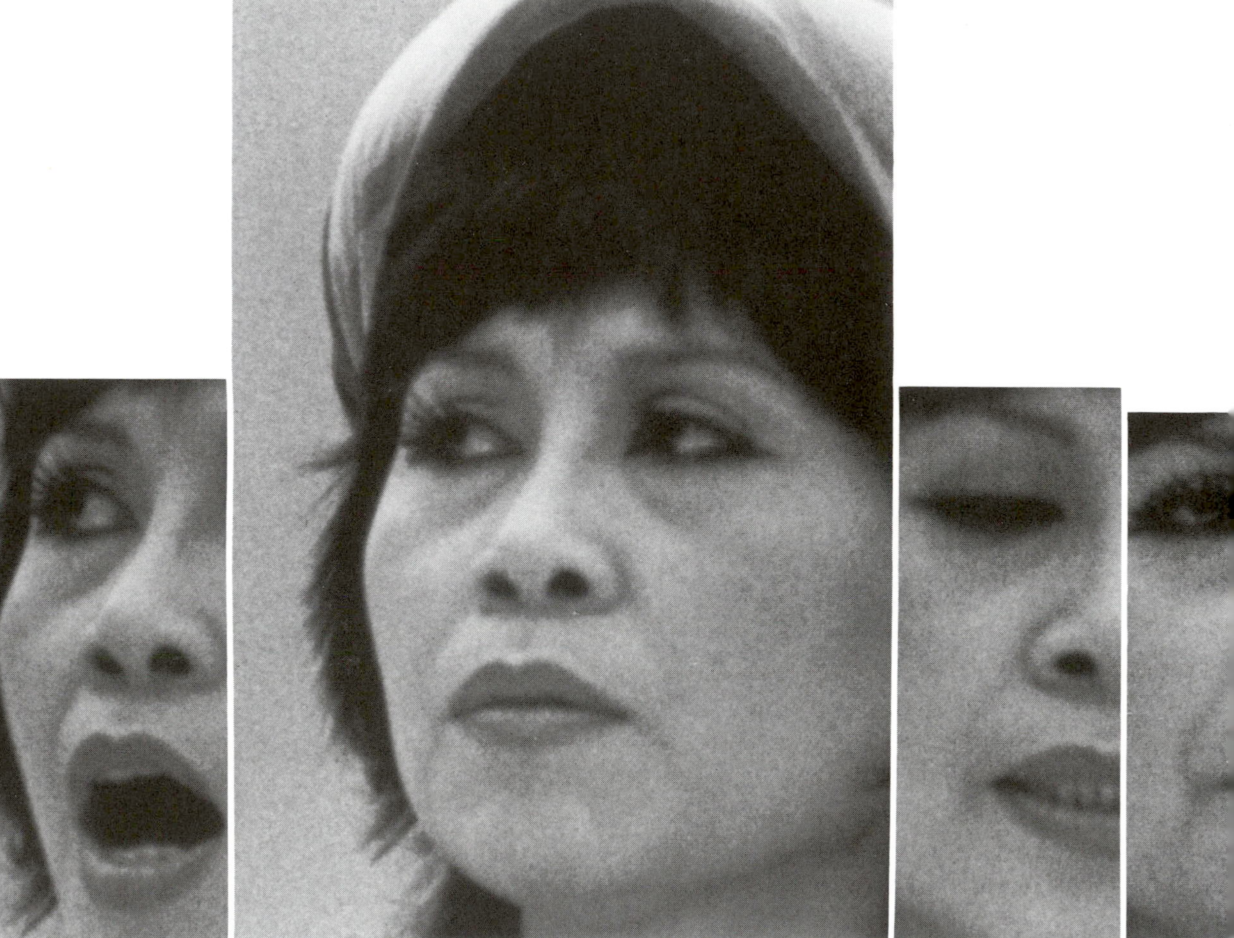

7

"Why A Fish Pond?"

Fiction at The Heart of Documentation

with Laleen Jayamane and Anne Rutherford

Laleen Jayamane: *You've said and I quote you, "to cut across boundaries and borderlines is to leave the maze of categories and labels. It is to resist simplistic attempts at classifying, to resist the comfort of belonging to a classification and of producing classifiable works." In this context how appropriate is it to position your work as documentary? Especially because you undo some of the canonical forms of this genre.*

Trinh: In other words why such a category at all in film? Although I myself would never categorize my own films, it's difficult to ignore how they are being shown and received. The question remains entangled in the vicissitudes of history, and to develop it one would have to take into account both the way the history of cinema has been made and the way we tend to take it for granted in our consumption of the media. Why for example the convenient split set up between Lumière and Méliès? Or between Eisenstein and Vertov, to mention just a few? How can one justify the logic of classification in film programming today? The answers to these questions are multiple. They involve not only the material conditions of filmmaking and film-

---

Interview conducted by Laleen Jayamane and Anne Rutherford in June 1990, when Trinh T. Minh-ha was guest at the Sydney and Melbourne International Film Festivals, where her film *Surname Viet Given Name Nam* was screened. First published in *Filmnews* (Sydney) 20, no. 10 (November 1990).

viewing in relation to a highly commercialized production system, but also the praxis of a politics of difference that enables one to challenge rather than to fortify the territorial mind in every imposition of well-defined boundaries. To simplify a complex situation, let's say that when people come to see a fiction film, they usually expect a good story, whereas when they come to see a documentary film, they expect information and truth. Since these are the very notions I work with in my films, it is not incorrect to position my work as documentary because that is where the "battleground" has been situated. However, I see my films more as cutting across several boundaries—boundaries of fiction, documentary, as well as experimental films, for example (for many, the word "experimental" means only the adoption of an avant-garde vocabulary, hence only another category in film, albeit an "alternative" one). The work of modifying and expanding frontiers operates in more than one direction at a time, so these films question both their own interiority and their own exteriority to the categories mentioned.

Anne Rutherford: A lot of the way your work has been taken up and written about is in terms of its deconstruction of documentary—as if all of the techniques that you use are specifically working against standard devices of documentary form. To me, that seems a fairly inappropriate way of talking about those devices.

T: Well, there was a time when my films were only talked about in terms of ethnographic filmmaking—because of the subject that I chose to film and also because of certain issues of anthropology that I raised. At that time I strongly felt that such a location was used more as a form of escapism than as an attempt to understand what was at stake in these films. It was a convenient means to confine their critical scope to a specific practice of filmmaking, hence to deny the full implications of their strategic choices. Now, people talk about them more in terms of documentary because of the last film I made. But the issues of representation raised do not just pertain to ethnographic and documentary filmmaking. What I bring into question in connection with anthropology obviously does not just concern anthropology, but the whole of the human and social sciences. So for me, all the questions broached in my films have a much wider scope than the frames they are often confined to, although they remain specific and context-bound in their materializations.

AR: *Taking up the question of the relation to ethnographic film: In, for example,* Reassemblage, *it seems to me that one of the ways you are attempting to challenge the position of knowledge which derives from anthropology or ethnography is to work with elements of visual fascination—fascination and pleasure in looking as an attempt to induce a different form of spectatorship than one that expects an access to knowledge. Is that how you see what you are doing in* Reassemblage? *It seems that* Surname Viet Given Name Nam *has shifted quite a lot away from that strategy. What's happened in that shift?*

T: It's always interesting to hear how other people see the different films. I myself didn't see that much of a jump on this question in the last film. I see it more as taking up similar issues but from a different angle, and in a different context of knowledge production. Coming back to the first part of the question, I think you have put your finger on an aspect of my work that is not always easy to talk about; namely, the resistance to the packaging of knowledge through a certain insistence on visual fascination and pleasure, or as I would put it, on the non-verbal dimension of film, which includes the silences, the music and the environmental sound as well. Instead of talking about visual pleasure in *Reassemblage,* I would rather say that, without being acquainted with the feminist works on film at the time, I was mainly working with the look. How the West has been looking at other cultures, how these cultures look at themselves being looked at, and how my own story as onlooker looked at is enmeshed in such a reflection. When you see an object, you are not seeing the look. Or in other words, you can't see the look when you look at the eye and vice versa. That's why for many people it was impossible to understand the film because they were looking for the object and hence expecting some kind of packaging of the culture.

I remember how in the first Robert Flaherty Seminar I attended, a man was so exasperated at the end of the debate after the screening of *Reassemblage,* that he just said, "Could you please tell us what the film is about?" And the only thing I could tell him was that I can't summarize what the film is about after having refused to do so on film. What the film is and is not about has been hotly debated among members of the audience for over an hour and I didn't feel that I should wrap it up or have the last word. The question of the look is at the same time so tangible and intangible that one cannot just summarize it. Who is looking at whom and from what place the look is offered—all this keeps on shifting. Perhaps the point is also to take the risk and to let a certain look, a certain hearing and voice emerge while one is looking at or listening to something not quite tangible nor intangible—like culture.

LJ: At the Third Cinema Event at the Edinburgh Festival, one or two black Americans questioned the validity of you as a non-black making films about Africa—referring to Naked Spaces: Living Is Round *and* Reassemblage.

T: I understand that anger, especially coming from African Americans rather than from Africans for example, because of the history of African Americans—why not them, rather than an Asian woman, making films on Africa? I do feel that it is legitimate to be suspicious in this case, and that's what I answered to the person who raised the question. The difference suggested in my work is here crucial, but difference does not easily lend itself to commodification, hence it is always less recognizable as a political stance than straight opposition. So such generalized anger can also denote something very narrow: a short-sightedness in terms of new complex forms of resistance and an uncritical acceptance of the very territorial mind that has kept all marginal groups in a definable place. We have been herded as people of color to mind only our own cultures. Hence, Asians will continue to make films on Asia, Africans on Africa, and Euro-Americans on . . . the world. Every time you hear similar reactions to your films, you are bound to realize how small the limits and the territory remain in which you are allowed to work. And such reactions come as much from your community or from the communities of people of color as it comes from the dominant groups.

LJ: I just want to go back to the question about the undoing or deconstruction of a set of conventions. With regard to an undoing of the conventions of the interview, it seems that your staged interviews are conducted as performances, lit in a particular theatrical manner, posed as it were by the voice and performed by the camera, whose rhetoric varies with each interview. In all of this you are simultaneously undoing the convention and creating a scene where what is spoken has almost a ritual charge. It is as you say neither a matter of simply parodying the cliche or the set of conventions or of correcting it, but doing something else altogether. Can you speak about what this something else is for you as director and then as subsequent viewer of your film?

T: To come back to the choice of staging these interviews, usually in documentary films re-enactments are used mainly when people want to break away from the monotony of talking heads. Most of the time, re-enactment has to do with the desire for action or for a story to develop. But here re-enactment is used precisely for the part that usually people would not think of re-enacting, which is interviews. It is used to deal with the notion of inter-viewing itself and with the interview as a cinematic frame, thereby refusing to reduce its role to that of a mere device to authenticate the message advanced. The latter reductive approach to interviews is precisely what makes talking heads boring, not the talking in itself nor the heads. The more one abides by the norm of having story and action as "remedy" to the common prose of life—or to one's own dullness—the more one contributes to the denigration of what Hollywood calls "issues films," hence to the limitation of film language in general.

In *Surname Viet,* I worked with both the re-enacted and the so-called natural interviews. Thanks to their co-existence and the play between them, I was able to open a critically creative space for myself as director and viewer, and hopefully for the audiences as well. By having the staged and the real together, what is brought out is the element of fiction in representation—the fictions of film caught in the fictions of life. Of course, the point here is not to blur the line between fiction and fact so as to render invisible the artifice of re-enactments. These were acknowledged throughout the film in a wide range of cues, but when exactly the cues were picked up depends on each viewer.

Some viewers would realize the re-enacting somewhere right in the beginning, either by the way the women speak, by the uncut length of the monologues, or perhaps by the lighting and minimal setting. A number of other viewers also become aware of the re-enactments because of the progression in the presentation of the interviews. Towards the beginning you have interviews that seem rather "discreet" in their staging, then after more than an hour or so, the staging becomes more and more obvious as you see a woman pacing back and forth, in and out of the camera frame while speaking, which is somewhat unusual in an interview situation. Then you move onto another woman who even turns her back to the camera, speaking while gazing at a flare of light in front of her, and that is even more unnatural. This is also the place in the film where you are confronted with both the interviewees' words and the filmmaker's reflections on interview as a device of documentary. But for other viewers yet, it's even further into the film that they are finally conscious of the re-enactments: at the most explicit part, when the women, in the "real" interviews in Vietnamese, shared the reasons for which they accepted to play a role on screen, and the comments their friends and relatives gave on their being "film actresses."

So there are different entries into the film. To have the staged and the real together is to call attention to the politics of interviews, and to set into relief the manipulations that tend to be taken for granted in documentary. With the more conventional editing of the "real" interviews in the latter part of the film, the frequent cutting and montage of the selected statements as well as other elements of manipulation become much more visible, and what one thinks of as being more natural or closer to the conventions of documentary, is actually just as (if not more) fictionalized as in the earlier parts of the film.

Moreover, if I was very much a director in the re-enacted part of the film, I was more a coordinator in the "real-life" part, because I asked the women to choose how they wanted to be presented as we moved to their own stories. The choices they came up with were often disturbing to me. I was expecting something that relates intimately to their daily existence and instead, they chose something that was . . . I wouldn't say nonexistent, but almost. For example, one woman wanted to be seen at a fish pond and she had no fish pond at home so the whole crew had to go

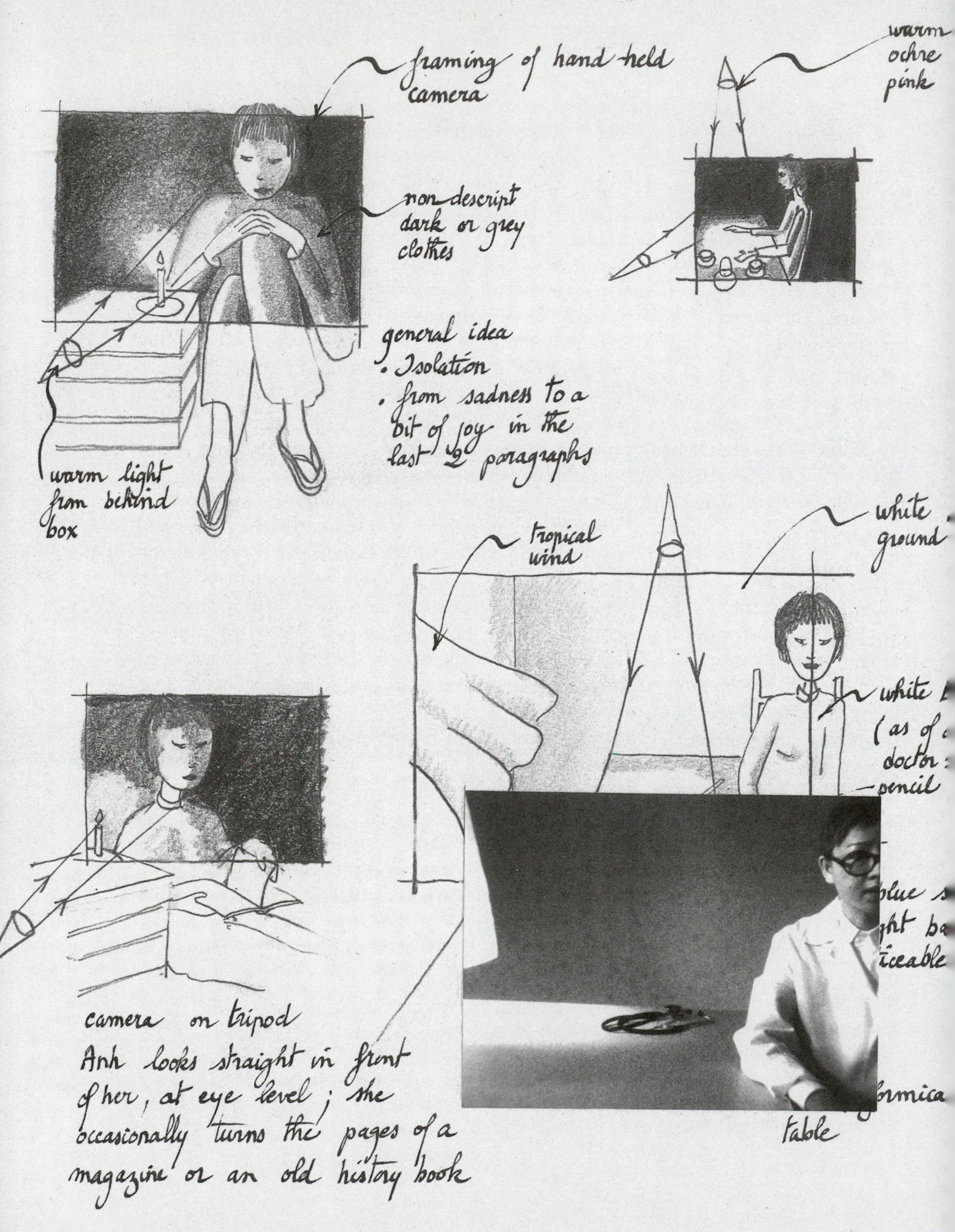
framing of hand held camera
non descript dark or grey clothes
general idea
• Isolation
• from sadness to a bit of joy in the last 2 paragraphs
warm light from behind box
warm ochre pink
tropical wind
white ground
doctor
pencil
camera on tripod
Anh looks straight in front of her, at eye level; she occasionally turns the pages of a magazine or an old history book
table

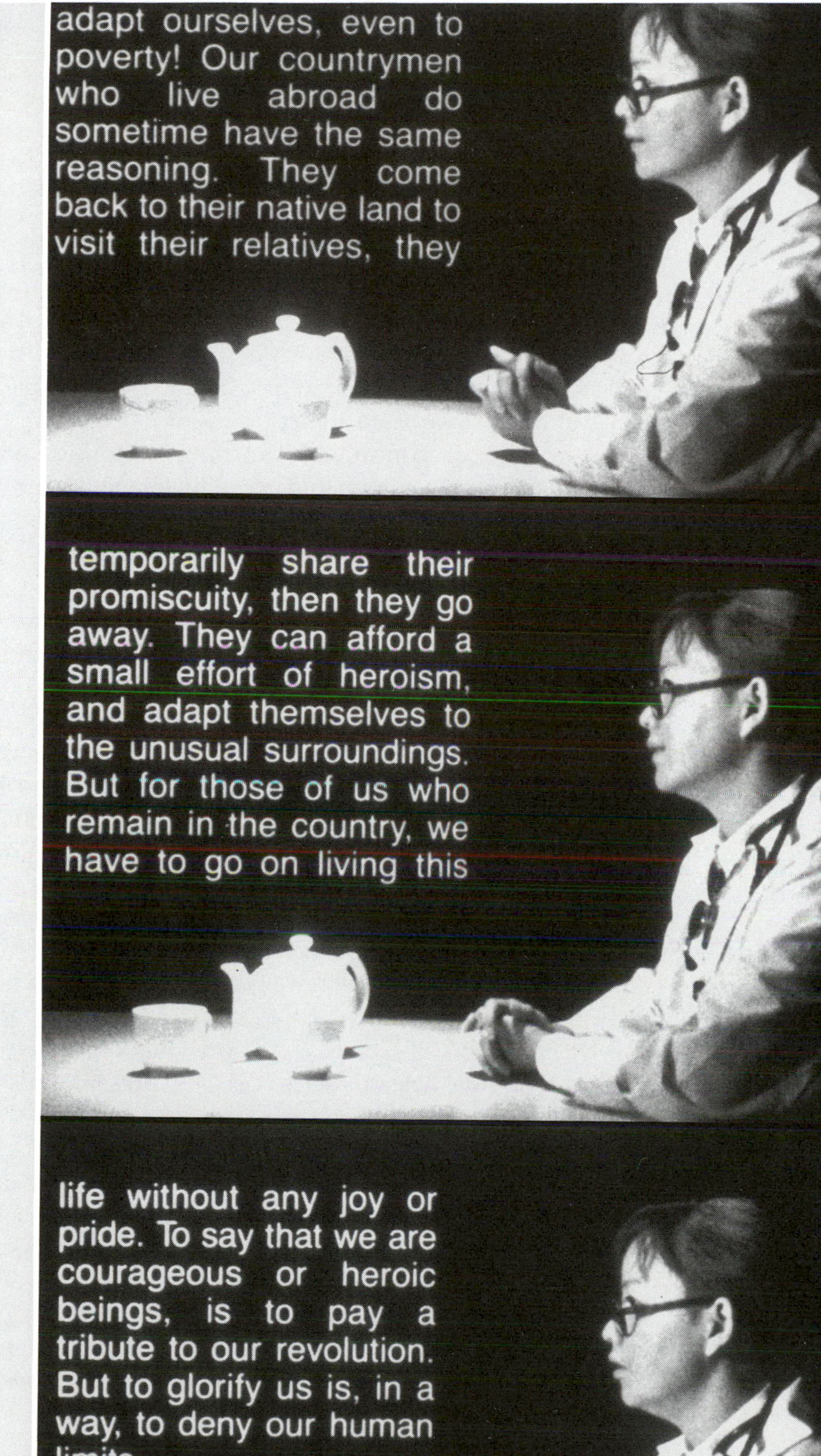
adapt ourselves, even to poverty! Our countrymen who live abroad do sometime have the same reasoning. They come back to their native land to visit their relatives, they
temporarily share their promiscuity, then they go away. They can afford a small effort of heroism, and adapt themselves to the unusual surroundings. But for those of us who remain in the country, we have to go on living this
life without any joy or pride. To say that we are courageous or heroic beings, is to pay a tribute to our revolution. But to glorify us is, in a way, to deny our human limits.

through this ordeal of finding a fish pond for her. Why a fish pond? Why not choose something you really like in your daily situations? She said no, it is a fish pond that I really like to be shot with, and I realized afterwards looking at the footage (when asked why, the only answer she kept on giving me was "I love fish ponds") how important this fish pond is, both for her personally and for the film. She is a working-class woman living at the time in a very small apartment with a large family, and having always been such a richly significative symbol in Asian cultures, the fish pond seems to point here to a dream space, a space of meditation where you can rest and retreat from the pressure of daily work. The fact that she made that choice was not only meaningful with regard to her own situation, it also tells you how, when you want something true to someone's life, what you get usually goes much further than the mere details of that person's daily existence.

The same applies to the way they chose to dress. I know that a number of Western viewers have had problems with all the women being middle-class—at least in their eyes. But dress codes are also class-informed and their (the viewers') being misled in their judgement by their own dress code is in itself a problem of class. There is no legacy of pride in dressing down among poor people or among people coming from Third World nations. On the contrary, the latter dress up when they are in a public situation—like being on film and being watched by thousands of spectators. So the women in my film also chose to dress up. I was time and again disconcerted by the combination of showy colors, but finally I stood by their choices because that's how they wished to be presented. As a result, the question of dressing became one of the threads of the film, as it wove in quite pertinently with the question of (de)territorializing the woman's body and Vietnam as a nation. So all in all, the person who was very narrow-minded in this instance was myself, not the women. These few examples are given here mainly to point to how fiction operates right in the heart of documentation. The truest representation of oneself always involves elements of fiction and of imagination, otherwise there is no representation, or else, only a dead, hence "false," representation.

AR: Going back to what you said about the devices that you use with the interviews—that you intend to set up an awareness of the manipulation that's operating. There is another process operating that goes beyond that idea of just an awareness of manipulation, which I see as a fairly sort of dry point. For me what happens with the device you set up in the interviews, with the delay between the written text and the spoken text, is an endless oscillation of uncertainty in the spectator. It's not as if at some point you realise that it's re-enactment but you are constantly being pulled back and forward in terms of how to interpret it. So it's not like you actually get to one point where it becomes seen as a fabrication but you are thrown around all the way through, back and forward between ideas of fabrication and maybe some sort of desire for naturalism. There is this process set up of endless tension—of a destabilization of meaning—which is much more dynamic and exciting than the idea of a simple recognition of manipulation.

T: Yes, I agree. You are probably referring to the earlier part of the film, and I was bent more on comparing it to the latter part of the film. Actually I think I never thought so much of the question of manipulation, so it's a rather awkward way of putting it. Many viewers, including Vietnamese, who have shared their reactions to the film would indeed not describe how it affects them in the terms I've been using. It would be difficult to point to this slippery realm, to pin down the effect it has on the viewers, when and how they start seeing a different pacing, a different structure of the film. All that I know from them is that this does hit them strongly, and whether it is a question of rendering visible the manipulations or not is not so much the point, as that something different is happening which would provoke awareness and reflection—and something very emotional can also be happening, as it has often been the case.

As for the tension created by a destabilization of meaning, I think there is also a very interesting problem raised in relation to the question of women and empowerment. A couple of women viewers did tell me they were extremely upset looking at the film, not so much in terms of ideological adherence as in terms of what happens between the spoken and the written words. They asked, by having the text appear while the women were speaking, am I not taking away from them the power of speech and undermining my own goal for the film? So, to be able to discuss the question, I had to ask the person what she thought I wanted to achieve, and she answered, quite annoyed, to show women's power, of course! to empower women through speech.

I can't say here that I only wanted to empower women, or as people like to put it, to "give voice" to the women involved. The notion of giving voice is so charged because you have to be in such a position that you can "give voice" to other people. And also the illusion that you "give voice," whereas the film is very much the voice of the filmmaker—the term "voice" meaning here the place from which meaning is produced, through both coherence and discontinuity. No matter how plural and diverse the voices featured, one always has to point back to the apparatus and the site from which these voices are brought out and constructed, and so the notion of giving voice remains extremely paternalistic.

Moreover, the question of empowering women through speech is highly problematic, because women's relationship with language and speech has always been an uncomfortable one. Language, of course, is never neutral. It is the site where power relationships are most complex and pernicious; yet it is also a place of liberation. Whether it frees or enslaves depends on how it is used, and it is pernicious only when its workings are invisible. So having the women articulate their oppression is not enough. One also has to do something to point to both the fact that language is a *tool* of power and the fact that possessing power is like owning a leaking boat. This was hopefully achieved in the film through the tension created between what the viewers hear, what they read, and what they see. The women's stories of oppression are important but the words and their meanings should not dominate in any single direction. When a speech takes itself too seriously (which is not quite the same as being heart-felt and passionate), it becomes abusive, because it tends to fix meaning, which would then be just a pawn in the game of power. At the same time as language is used to gain power, it should also be used to displace and undermine power. And the way I undermine it, I feel, does not take away the power of articulation of the women involved nor the importance of their stories; rather, it points to the nature of language itself.

The tension between what is heard, read, and seen actually came about in the process of making the film. The re-enacted interviews had been carried out in Vietnamese and translated into French for publication, and then translated again by myself into English. Instead of going back to Vietnamese for more authenticity, I rather deal with the notion of translation itself, and not claim any authentic retrieval. There is here no real desire to make people believe that what they have on screen happened (or did not happen) in Vietnam, so to have the interviews in Vietnamese would just be using the cliche. In other words, it is like going back to the illusion of unmediated reality, evading the staging by not acknowledging it. Whereas the use of English in the context of Vietnam and of Vietnamese in the context of the U.S. already creates a displacement, and a tension arises because not only do you have to listen to these Vietnamese faces speaking English, but you also have to understand a different sound of English.

LJ: Yes, there's a real unease in watching and hearing it.

A: For me it's not just an unease. You said something about that device allowing a space for the depth and quality of this speech to come out, which I think is what happened—that you retract from an automatic digesting of it, and you have to go with it through its whole unfolding. It draws you into a totally different sort of watching.

T: A tension is also created because the women were struggling with language. At one point in the rehearsal they really revolted against the whole idea of delivering their speeches in English and said, it's not an English that we speak in everyday situations so why are you making us go through this. They were sick and tired of

all the "ism"-words and they tended to skip all the conjunctions, prepositions, adverbs for which they had no use whatsoever. These arbitrary, grammatically correct "accessories" simply made no sense. But the words they rejected are words they use in their everyday Vietnamese, and as with the women whose voices they embody, it's a challenge to translate their silver-tongued delivery. I would rather remain true to their level of Vietnamese than to their level of English. What usually happens in the situation of refugees is that since they do not master the new language, the image they offer to the hegemonic culture has consistently been that of a people who are unable to conceptualize, to have any sophisticated thinking, or even to articulate their own condition. So once we openly discussed that problem, the women accepted it and went on rehearsing in English. This kind of crisis happening during the rehearsal was very important for the making of the film, hence the necessity to bring out, on many levels, the tension between the spoken and the written language. At one level, it is to have the text appear while they were speaking. At another, it is to make it possible for the viewer to compare the different forms of English by including fragments of conversation in which a woman who had been acting before was spontaneously telling her story in her "real" English. At another level yet, the viewer hears an entirely Americanized English from the conversation of a Vietnamese woman teenager. These differences in language are dealt with throughout the film.

Just a brief detour here back to the earlier question of power and speech. When you see the texts printed on screen, you see that sometimes the words correspond to what the women are saying, and sometimes they don't. In the shift from the written to the oral, the women have slightly altered them, and these little discrepancies were brought out on screen. So this is one of the moments when the women viewers quoted earlier suddenly realized it was a staged speech. And realizing this, they felt that the power of the women's deliveries were taken away from them—the illusion of the authentic kept on leaking here and there. For power to maintain its credibility—or for the "fake" to look "real" (that is, for the "real" to go on unchallenged), as cinema dictates—its workings must remain invisible. So if the speech is visibly a reconstruction, then it is thought that it loses all its power.

AR: Where in fact there are many voices in the film, so its not just the voices of the women being interviewed, but other voices that come in—the voice of poetry and so on.

T: Yes, perhaps not straight poetry, but let's say that poetical language is important to my critical work. People used to see theory and poetry as being miles apart, but I see the interaction of theoretical language and poetical language as capable of creating a new ground in which clear-cut oppositions are again thwarted. The mutual challenge between the two languages helps to alleviate the presumption and mystification existing on each side. The poetry you hear in the film is largely taken from oral traditions. The verses are proverbs and songs that help to derange the will to mean and to disrupt as well as expand language in its continuities. The narratives shift back and forth between being informational, reflective or analytical, and being emotional, trivial, absurd or anecdotal. Some examples: the stories about the refugees in Guam; the personal letter written to a sister telling her about the gendered fears and frustrations of a mother and her daughters when they fled the country. You have here a situation that is at the same time very personal and very typical of women's experience as refugees. Or else, the anecdote that tells us about the pleasure of going to an ice cream place in Vietnam as compared to the ones in the States. You alternate between the reflective and the non-discursive, between persuasive analysis through interview settings; straight confidences and storytelling in the form of letters; and elliptical commentary on the conditions of women in poetry, songs and proverbs. This multiple crossing of voices leads us back to the earlier discussion on the resistance to categories.

LJ: You say, "Reading a film is a creative act and I will continue to make films whose reading I may provoke and initiate, but do not control. A film is like a page of paper which I offer the viewer. I am responsible for what is within the boundary of the paper, but I do not control and do not wish to control its folding. The viewer can fold it horizontally, obliquely, vertically. They can weave the elements to their liking and background. The interfolding and interweaving situation is what I consider to be most exciting in making films." In relation to that, can you talk about how you create a structure that facilitates such freedom for the viewer more in terms of the montage and mise en scene? And is this related to the creation of what you call interstitial space?

T: It is a constant challenge to develop this notion of interstitial space which comes back in every piece of writing I have done. But to point to one of the more evident aspects of the interval or the interstice: I see the position of women, for example, as being radically difficult. As I have implied in the discussion on empowerment, as soon as you move from the position of a named subject into the position of a naming subject, you also have to remain alive to the renewed dangers of arrested meanings and fixed categories—in other words, of occupying the position of a sovereign subject. "Non-categorical" thinking sees to it that the power to name be constantly exposed in its limits. So in terms of subject positioning you can only thrive on fragile ground. You are always working in this precarious space where you constantly run the risk of falling on one side or the other. You are walking right on the edge and challenging both sides so that they cannot simply be collapsed into one. This is the space in between, the interval to which established rules of boundaries never quite apply.

If I expand on your question to discuss how one can create such a space in one's work, I would say that this does not just happen in the stages of montage or of mise en scene, but in every stage of filmmaking. Unless montage is here understood in its larger sense, since it involves not only the cutting, but also the preconception and shooting stages of the work. Very often, I have encountered viewers who ask, But how do you script the film? I usually do not have such a thing as a script that preexists the film. The only thing I started out with in *Surname Viet* was the few interviews I had selected and translated; but most of the choices in the film are dictated by what happened during the process of materializing it—the casting of the parts, the rehearsal, the shooting and so on. The script only came about with the film, not before it; and my role as scriptwriter is to provoke a situation in which things are allowed to happen and the choices I arrive at would have to be integral to the specific context of the film since they grow out of its making. The content here is the form, and vice versa. This has been very important to all the films I have made.

At the same time as you have this very thought-out structure you also have aspects of the film that escape the structure—even though the latter is not constructed linearly to give you the feeling that you know where you are going with the film. Many attempts have been made to theorize on this non-formulable realm of cinema, and you have approximate terms that circulate such as "excess," or concepts that Roland Barthes contributed such as, *punctum* vs. *studium*, pronunciation vs. articulation, "the third meaning," or "the blind field." All these to point to something that exceeds either control and intentionality in artistic creation, or rationality and analysis in criticism. So intention is certainly not all there is. One has to remain very much alert to these moments in film when even as one achieves control, one has to let go of the control. It's really a challenge, because what you get is not quite "natural" nor "accidental," but both—accidents that are created by the letting go of things while you are in full control of them.

LJ: That sounds a bit like what Bresson says about his filmmaking practice. He writes that shooting is to "put oneself into a state of intensive ignorance and curiosity, and yet see things in advance." . . How do you fund your films and what sort of distribution do they have?

T: It's a constant struggle. Although I do enjoy teaching, the fact that I have to go on teaching, when I would rather just spend my time writing and making films, is because I prefer to continue working as a so-called independent filmmaker and not to have to count on any commercial profit from my films for survival. In the States, the system of grants is such that there is no real support for "the artist." No matter how many films you've made, every time you apply for grants, you start from zero; you have to demonstrate that your project is worthwhile even before you start making it! So what exists is mainly support for "the project." This is somewhat ironic—although hardly surprising—in a context where the claim is overwhelmingly on "individual freedom of expression." There are certainly some advantages to this materialistic and noncommitted approach to art, but there is no structure here like in Canada, in Europe or in other parts of the world where once you have made a few films, fundings are facilitated because people trust the fact that you *will* be making films; what exactly, is up to you (and your conscience).

My films are all distributed by non-profit organizations. Since these distributors are motivated by what they believe in rather than merely by monetary profit, my films circulate mainly in film festivals, museums, media arts centers, educational and university networks, as well as different community organizations. Some people tend to react negatively to such a circuit of distribution, because universities, for example, connote right away privilege, hence a form of narrowness. But needless to say, any person who has been directly involved in media programming today knows that such a concept as "general public" is utterly naive and irresponsible. Some mainstream film directors do not hesitate to affirm, for example, that their audience is exclusively age group 13 to 17. And it is with money power that they promote their films and buy their audiences. I think it is very important to have my films circulate in educational networks, because the classroom is a workplace. And if it is a privileged workplace, it's because this is where changes in the production of knowledge can be effected, where film consumption can be challenged, and where different sensitivities and new forms of subjectivities and resistance are possible.

AR: I'd like to ask something about the politics of the film, in response to the uncertainties that a lot of people in the audience felt. You spoke yesterday about the fact that a lot of people want a film that either supports the North or the South, and you talked about how in the U.S.—and this also applies to Australia—there is an automatic support for the North, that goes back to the anti-war movement. I think there was a confusion, or unease, about what the position of the film is.

T: Well, I see it as a commitment to the feminist struggle more than anything else. When I was asked by anti-communist Vietnamese viewers what the political stance of the film was, I answered that it is the oppression of women which I see as being continuously obscured in many fights for human rights, whether from the Right or from the Left. To say this, of course, is to say nothing new, and yet history seems at time boringly repetitive. The conflict within the feminist struggle among those who believe fights can all be conflated, so that women's liberation comes de jure with socialism, and those who see it as a struggle of its own alongside other struggles, is an old conflict. Some called it "the longest revolution," and there are endless examples of feminists who have moved from the first position to the second one—Simone De Beauvoir was a well-known case. The question of women's oppression, that is of oppression *tout court,* is not something that can be quickly solved with an act of liberation. So it's not because a revolution has taken place that all forms of oppression are done with. On the contrary, everything has to start from zero again. And this is certainly not a problem specific to Vietnam.

What the Vietnam revolution has achieved can never be taken away from Vietnam's history. However, what I find most suspicious and deadening is the clinging on to an idealized image of Vietnam 15 years after the war has ended. To hold on to that image is to condemn Vietnam to invisibility. That's what I see happening in most of the spectacular movies recently made on the Vietnam war, as well as in such PBS products as the *Vietnam: A Television History* series. America can't just let it go, so even when the *mea-culpa*-breast-beating is at its height, the tendency is to say that yes, we have sided with the wrong side, but the American people is innocent of the wrong moves of its government. There is an urge to show the American people as being merely manipulated by the government rather than accepting the fact that it's a mutual responsibility, and that it's no easy task to separate the government from the people. The anti-war movement was not even and it was certainly not homogeneous. There were many anti-war stances that did not advocate socialism. If people are truly interested in Vietnam, they should be looking more curiously or carefully at what has been happening in the country since the end of the war—how its people fare in trying to cope with the challenge of recovery under the rule of a large post-revolutionary bureaucracy. Listen, for example, to what some of the more farsighted leaders in Vietnam have been publicly admitting in the last few years with regards to what they called their "ten years of mistakes." One has to maintain a critical space in order to contribute to the building anew of one's society. In deadening that space, in trying to reduce and cancel it, one comes to a very dogmatic, and actually very nostalgic, stance. This was what I was trying to avoid in the film.

As the saying goes,"Too far east is west." Above all, the film refuses to subscribe to the prevailing dualistic view on Vietnam. The Vietnam experience has been reduced to a question of communism and anti-communism, whereas its complexities—at least for the Vietnamese—go well beyond these two poles set up by the competition between the two world power blocks. The fight against imperialism was fought just as bitterly in South Vietnam as in the north, although the specifics differ markedly from one context to the other. Of great importance for me, then, is to break away from that First World–Second World dualism and to bring forth again the notion of non-alignment as being much more fundamental to the Third World. The risk that I take in relating the women's struggle to a radically non-aligned stance (which can be maintained even when some form of alignment is necessarily adopted), is not very far from the risk that Mai Thu Van, who initially carried out in Vietnam the interviews selected for the film, has incurred herself. It is still very difficult for her today to talk about what she went through. As a Marxist and a strong advocate of socialism, she was profoundly wounded by the ideological and emotional trial she underwent not only with the interviews she gathered, but also with the publication of the book in Paris. Most of the women interviewed spoke lucidly about their conditions and some eloquently smashed the idealized and highly misleading images of themselves as heroines of the war. And then, when Mai's *Vietnam: un peuple, des voix* came out in Paris (1983), the blow was probably just as hard since the book met with hostility from both the Left and the Right.

AR: The French Left or the Vietnamese?

T: Both, especially the French. From the little time I spent with her in public debates on the film when it was screened at the Women's International Film Festival of Creteil, I felt that she was very much disgusted with the righteous reactions that leftist foreigners—we are not even talking about the rightists here—tend to have when they speak about Vietnam. Disgusted is really the word I would use because, after what she had to go through to accept these interviews herself, it must have been somewhat both trivial and hideous for her to hear all these people who had never been intimately involved in the Vietnam realities question her Marxist stance. Who is more Marxist than whom? And who is more entitled than whom to decide how feminism should be represented? The situation is as absurd as that, and she was really put off by these paternal and maternal positions she constantly encountered. Some people seem to think they hold the right to decree how Vietnam should be talked about just because they belonged to the anti-war movement in the past.

For me, the effort deployed to preserve an ideal image of Vietnam remains extremely paternalistic. I find most problematic the fact that the West would always give itself a space to oppose its governments, while giving no space at all for Third World members to challenge their governments. Questions that keep on coming back about my film—such as, Did you show it back home? What did the Vietnamese think of your film?—really tell you, again, how narrow the space remains in which you are allowed to operate. Out of the 40 or more interviews that Mai gathered, the few only positive statements on women's conditions were voiced by high-placed official women representatives of the government. Even if you side with the revolution, why would you endorse a governmental stance? Since I am not interested in any official version of feminism, whether in Vietnam or in any other country, why would I include them just for the sake of objectivism?

LJ: You mentioned that despite your criticism of the Vietnamese government, the Vietnamese delegate to the United Nations had seen your film, and invited you to come to Vietnam to make a film. Are you going to take up that invitation?

T: I might, but right now I already have three projects waiting. You don't just go to a country to make a film because someone invites you, but you also have to let the idea of a project mature and to develop a relationship with it, otherwise you'll be doing just newsreel type of reportage. What is of interest in a film, as I've discussed earlier, does not merely lie in its subject. In other words, why Vietnam? I find it just as important to work on China or on India, for example, which is what I am doing now.

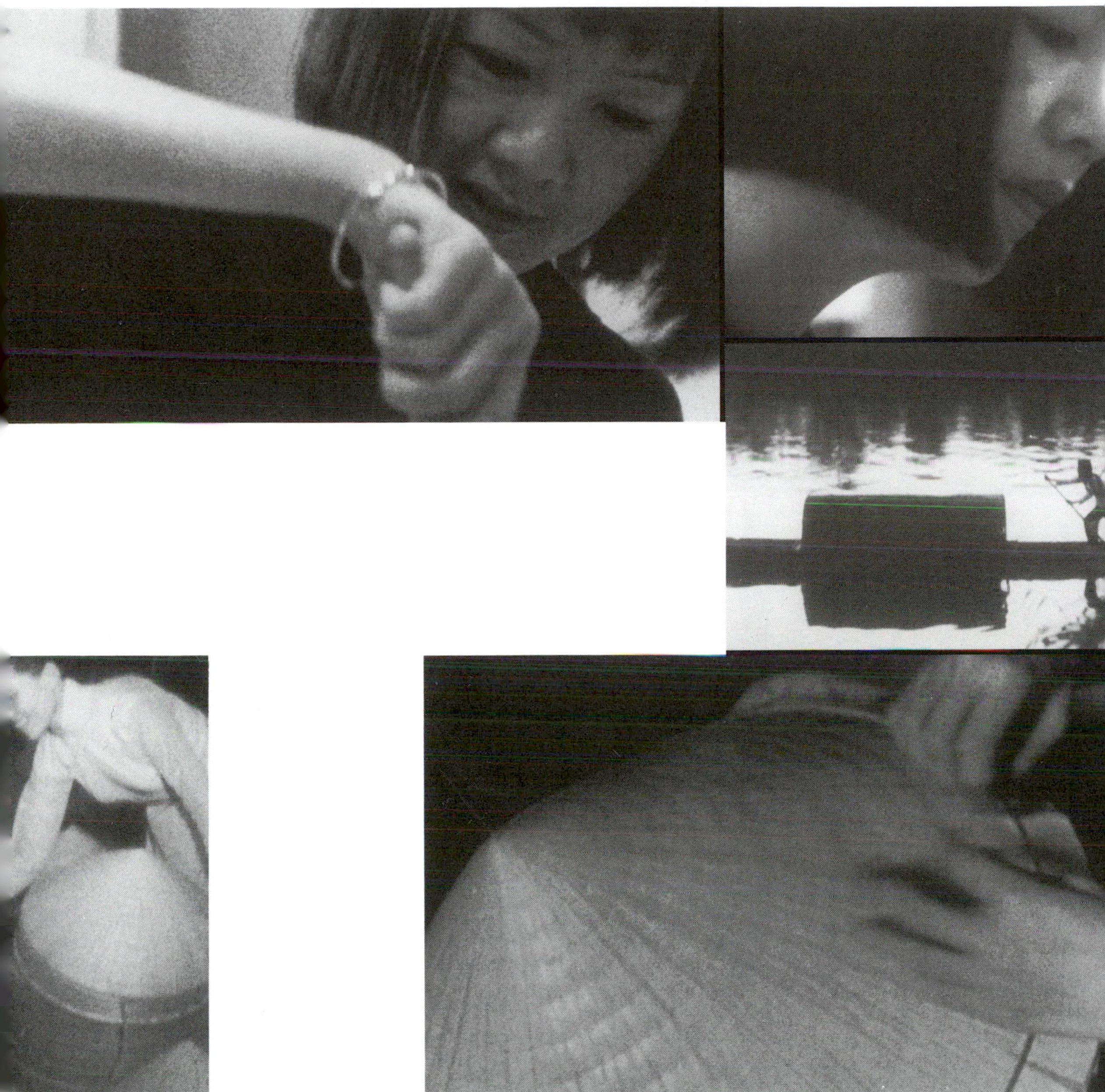

SV

NS

8

Questioning Truth and Fact

with Harriet Hirshorn

Hirshorn: How did you become involved in filmmaking? Can you give some general background about yourself, tell how and where you grew up, and describe your education?

Trinh: I was educated for the most part in Vietnam, then in the Philippines, in France, in the U.S., and since I learned more than what I taught during my three-year stay in Dakar, I can also add, in Africa. I left Vietnam for the U.S. in 1970 at the age of seventeen and was mainly trained in comparative literature and music: composition, ethnomusicology, and applied music—piano, organ, percussion and Vietnamese zither. I also painted for many years, and my interest in cultural anthropology dates back to the time in Vietnam when I discovered, with much bewilderment, the feeling of being "other," through reading about myself as a cultural entity offered up in writings by the European colonial community. My involvement in film came much later. It is difficult to say when exactly I first got interested in it. It would be easy to find some details in my childhood that would account for a precocious inclination for this field, but such myth-building practice easily generates complacency. Depending on who is asking and in what context, it is difficult to talk about

---

Interview conducted by Harriet A. Hirshorn. First published in *Heresies* (Feminist Journal on Art and Politics), no 22 (Fall–Winter 1987–88).

one's individuality without finding questionable the general tendency to determine a work mainly through the particularities of the filmmaker's personality.

H: *So, what compelled you, inspired you, to make the kinds of films you make? What was life like for you in Vietnam?*

T: I would join a number of Vietnamese women in saying that "if equality consists of being poor together, then the Vietnamese society in its non-corrupted sectors is truly egalitarian!" Those of us who were town-dwellers were and still are "uprooted on our own land," so thoroughly upset were we in our way of living. We all shared the insecurities of war. The burden has been such that it accounts for the profound and widespread silence that many Vietnamese still live with in regards to this war and its aftermath. What inspired me to make films like *Reassemblage* and *Naked Spaces?* Certainly Africa. But why Africa? In looking at these films, I would say that they lie somewhere between the very gratuitous and the highly motivated shores. On one hand, if they are so difficult for the audience as well as for myself to summarize ("What is the film really about?"), it's partly because they have no single story to tell, they do not build up around a center—be it a subject of documentation, a fiction with plot, or an individual hero's/heroine's achievement. They deal with a notion of film as critical process without a main or single motive. A perceptive review of *Reassemblage* by the writer Alberto Moravia in *L'Espresso* described the film as "an amorous invasion." However possessive it can be in its proffering, a love relationship does not allow one to speak *about* the subject filmed as if one can objectify it or separate oneself from it unproblematically; hence this statement at the outset of the film: "I do not intend to speak about / Just speak near by." On the other hand, these films are also strongly motivated by an experience that I lived through in formerly colonized Vietnam and that I clearly recognized, shared and re-lived in Africa; hence the necessity to make films that would always point to the process of constructing not truth, but meaning, and to myself as an active element in that process, both as a foreign observer of a specific culture and as a member of the general cultural zone and non-aligned bloc of countries known as the Third World.

H: *Who were your mentors? Who inspired or influenced you?*

T: No mentors. What inspires me most are usually people's sayings, music in villages, environmental sounds, and non-monumental "architecture." If I am to mention a few inspirational works, then I will say the poetry of Ho Xuan Huong (a Vietnamese woman poet), Thich Nhat Hanh, Basho, Aime Cesaire, Ezekiel

Mphahlele, and the prose of Assia Djebar, Clarice Lispector, Zora Neale Hurston. But these do not include many works of Euro-American artists and writers, which may or may not have an impact on me, despite my inclination for them. In film, I used to like Kurosawa, Ozu, Marker, Vigo, Mizoguchi, Godard, Satyajit Ray, Bresson. Today, I would rather see a film by Chantal Akerman, Valeria Sarmiento, Yvonne Rainer, or Sally Potter—recent encounters that have no influence on my film work. With a cross-cultural interdisciplinary background, it's difficult to single out a name or even a few names that have had a major impact on my work. The list is so long that I am afraid it would sound like name-dropping more than it would illuminate. In any case, naming is always a political choice: one gives the names one likes to be associated with or judged upon according to the times, often for the purpose of validation. On the other hand, there is no such thing as a one-way influence. What I do influences my understanding of others' doings, and vice versa; and I never understood certain aspects of the films I previously liked as well as now that I make films myself.

H: When did you realize you wanted to merge experimental with documentary filmmaking? Why?

T: I have never viewed them as being separated. "Experimental" for me is not a genre nor an approach to filmmaking. It is, in a way, the process of unmaking readymades, or more commonly put, of making visible what remains invisible (ideologically, cinematically) to many, including to oneself; what does not correspond to the established codes and is not always known in advance to the spectators as well as to the filmmaker. If "experimental" is a constant questioning of the relationship between the filmmaker and filmmaking, then it cannot be separated from the material, whether one chooses to call this material documentary or fiction. Some people may find such questioning "unnecessary." Well, I can't blame such a reaction; in this "one-dimensional" society, it is not always easy to draw the line between tracking down the oppressive mechanisms and aiding their spread. But for me, there is a certain naivete in believing that one could bring about changes in consciousness without challenging or uncovering the ideology of mainstream cinematic expectations. Realism, as practiced and promoted by many, consists of ignoring one's constant role as producer of realities (as if things can just speak by themselves without the intervention of the one who sees, hears and "makes sense" out of them) and, therefore, of taking one's view as immediately objective and absolute ("This is *the* reality"). With the continuingly growing feminist and Third World awareness, there is a strong necessity to make film politically, instead of settling down with making "political" or "non-political" films that remain oblivious to the workings of dominant ideology. Repression is as much in the *what* as in the *how,* and the two cannot be separated. Such a convenient opposition as—"political" versus "non-political"—dwells on a dualistic view of art and politics, art and science, art and life.

H: In Naked Spaces—Living is Round *you identified the voices in the soundtrack by giving them specific categories of things to say which were consistent even when overlapping. I liked the way you included yourself in the film you made—it was neither a heavy-handed signature nor an erasure of self in the pretense of objectivity. Why is it important for you to include yourself and to identify the sources of what is said?*

T: You give me a good opportunity to exemplify what I said earlier. In having three women's voices speak in relation to the music and the images, I was not so much concerned with specific categories of things to be said as with foregrounding problems of interpretation and translation. Whoever has attempted to "capture" an event and to make it accessible (if not entirely comprehensible) to others knows how delicate such an undertaking is, if one does not want to smother it under the omniscient voice of culture. In communicating what you have understood from a culture, where do you trace the line between what is specifically African (and within African, what is Joola as differentiated from Sereer, Mandingo, Peul, Bassari and so on), what is specifically Asian, and what is specifically Euro-American? Words, like images and sounds, connote different things when they are said differently. One cannot be so complacent as to claim that "This is what they said" or "This is how they see it" when one is content with translating the *content* of what one hears or sees, while remaining oblivious to oneself as translator, as inheritor of a different (verbal and aural) tradition, a different mentality. In my case, my pluralistic cultural background makes it even more problematic; as I wrote elsewhere, translation consists of grafting several languages, cultures and realities onto a single body. If it is important to involve my own subjectivity in my work or, as you said, "to identify the sources of what is said," it is because it is necessary to point to what has always been there but has almost never been outwardly acknowledged as such. There will be much less arrogance, much less it-goes-without-saying assumptions, much less taken-for-granted dominance of the First-World-Third-World/man-woman relationships, if the making subject is always vulnerably exposed in his or her making process. In *Naked Spaces* I work at differentiating the African/Euro-American/Asian personal voices without, however, opposing them, so that the viewer hears them not so much as contradictions or as separate entities, but as differences within the same subjectivity.

H: *I noticed in* Naked Spaces *that the soundtracks tended toward the universal: i.e., about human nature, approaches to living, and theories of creation, yet the images in the film focused on women, women's world and experience, with the exception of the dance scenes. Can you comment on this juxtaposition?*

T: Women and the Universal! Very interesting; one kind of giggles because women have always been confined to the realm of the Personal. In working with a notion of difference that is not synonymous with opposition or segregation, the apartheid notion of difference, I focus on the relationship between women and living spaces (or women and architecture) as the very site of difference on which both the Universal and the Particular (historical, cultural, political) are at play. As a statement in the film says, "the world is round around the round being"; women are the active producers and guardians of the roundness of life, literally as well as figuratively speaking. In many African societies, elder women inhabit round-shaped houses, which usually happen to be the more ancient ones of the village, compared to the squarish or rectangular buildings occupied by men or young couples. These houses have no angularities in their exterior as well as interior forms. All the elements that I see as being consistently attributed to women's domain and have foregrounded in the film—wall painting and sculpture; (curved) built-in features of enclosed spaces; pots and calabashes that contain their belongings, the water they fetch, or the food they cook; the general inside, inhabitable realms—are elements that diversely emphasize the womb-image of the house. As several statements in the film suggest, not only are spaces named after the human body, but their decorations insist on the house as fertility site, as life-giving force. Women being juxtaposed with approaches to living and theories of creation is hardly surprising in this context. For some viewers it might be difficult to associate what they relegate to the "domestic" realm with views of the world that they usually attribute to the "philosophical" realm. But the film brings forth the tight relationship between woman, house and cosmos. Even the dances which evolve around the circumcised young men are shot so as to show the circles they form and the participation of women in fertility rituals; the film ends on one of these dances, but the last sounds and images are those of the women dancers and their voices in chorus.

H: *Can you comment about yourself and your work in terms of feminism and how you view yourself in that context?*

T: I make a distinction between an alienating notion of otherness (the Other of man, the Other of the West) and an empowering notion of difference. As long as Difference is not *given* to us, the coast is clear. We should be the ones to define this difference, even if, as I said in *Naked Spaces*, "all definitions are devices." And this, for me, is one way of summarizing how feminism could be understood and practiced. One cannot rely on essences (the essence of being a woman and/or a non-white) and do away with the dialectic and problematics of things. In a way, a feminist always has at least two gestures at the same time: that of pointing insistently to difference, and that of unsettling every definition of woman arrived at. As a Zen saying goes, "Never take the finger pointing to the moon for the moon itself." While rendering Difference visible and audible in my films (as well as in my books and poems), I also have to move on, repeating what is shown or said earlier in different contexts, so as to remind the viewer that the not-quite-not-yet-it is always present. Thus my films have no single message, no wrapped-up package to offer to the viewer (hence also, as I mentioned earlier, the difficulty of saying what the films are really about). The messages foregrounded are necessarily plural as the film/filmmaker looks critically at itself/herself unfolding before the viewers. Being truthful to oneself and to one's making is, as said in another statement of the film, "being in the in-between of all definitions of truth."

H: *What does this exploration of truth and fact mean to you?*

T: It's not because one accumulates facts that one mechanically arrives at some truth; I don't see truth as something defined by a sum of facts. When one realizes the aberrations carried out in the name of truth, one is compelled to question the objectivity of any notion—of truth as well as the search for truth itself and its absolutism. If it sounds quite common to challenge facts vis-à-vis truth, it is quite uncommon to see this incorporated in documentary practice. I am thinking here of numerous films that claim (in their tone and in the way they offer information more than in any explicit statement) to give us a scientific view of the "natives." What is considered "scientific" or "objective" is often no more than the adaptation of a number of film codes and of an established approach in documenting, in other words, a question of ideology. Reality is necessarily always adaptive. With the spread of these films in popular consumer programs on television, it becomes more and more difficult for many of us not to confuse fact with truth; hence these statements in *Naked Spaces*. "The diagnostic power of a fact-oriented language"; "Truth *or* fact"; or "reality and truth: neither relative nor absolute." To the culturally/sexually dominant mind everything not qualified as "factual" is relegated to the realm of Instinct, Superstition or the Supernatural. The questioning of truth and fact is another way of dealing with the notion of difference as explained earlier in relation to feminism.

H: *I loved the editing in* Naked Spaces. *You used the overlaying of images very sparingly—why did you use it when you did? I noticed in certain segments a real building of images that would resolve sort of in the same way a circle closes. What were your concerns while editing* Naked Spaces, *both artistic and political/ethical?*

T: Many viewers have used the term "fluid" with regards to the editing of the film. I guess what I was preoccupied with is a fluidity of montage that does not rely on slick visuals or on smooth transitions, in other words, that does not bear the "professional" seal. The intent is not to settle down in a comfortably convenient relationship between sound, image and text (and further, between this statement and that statement, between this image and that image, and so on). If you remember, there is a comment on African music at the start of the film that says: "It [the music] does not simply "play" / In such a way as *not* to impinge on the viewing." The illustrative relationship usually found in film between sound, image and text; the cosmetic role often attributed to music; and the exclusively informative function assigned to environmental sounds as well as to people's talking lull the viewers into a falsely secure world that is fabricated so as to give them the comforting illusion that they know where they go; they know what to expect, and can even foresee what the outcome will be. In incorporating silence as one determining element in the film, I often remind the viewers of the flat (two-dimensional) reality of film, while not denying them the somewhat surreptitious pleasure of losing themselves in the flow of compelling images and sounds. The editing plays, therefore, with the viewers' expectations; the music is often cut off abruptly, thereby pulling them out of the atmosphere they have been bathed in, while the visuals incorporate casual jump-cuts, out-of-focus shots, and, as you have noticed, one or two seemingly "ill-placed" superimpositions. The latter are inserted more as a tease, although the images chosen are that of a woman's reflective face overlaid with that of a woman at work.

H: Are you working on another film? What is it about?

T: Yes, but as you can guess, I can't really talk about it. As I pointed out earlier, the film does not exist before its making.

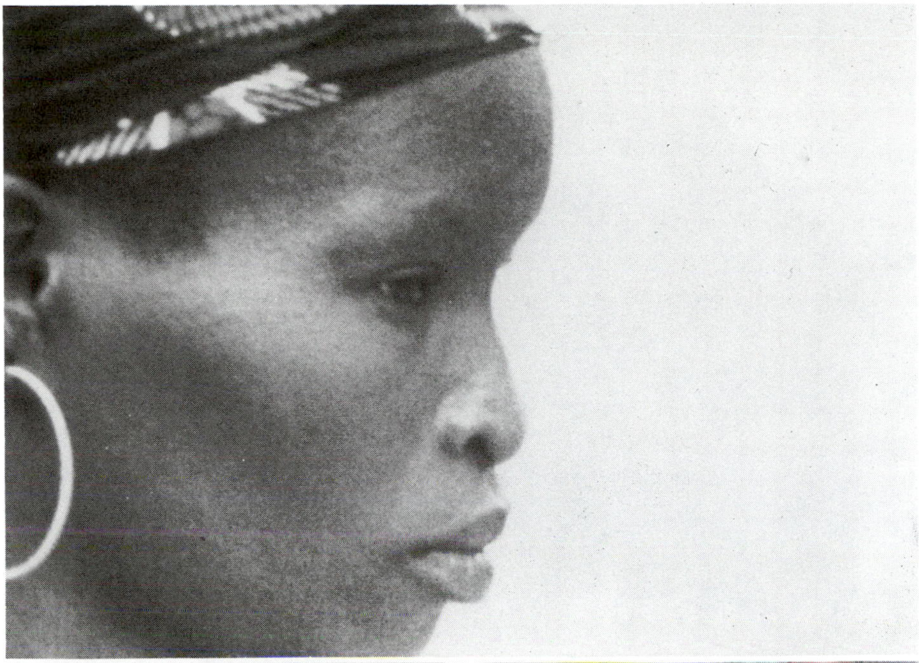

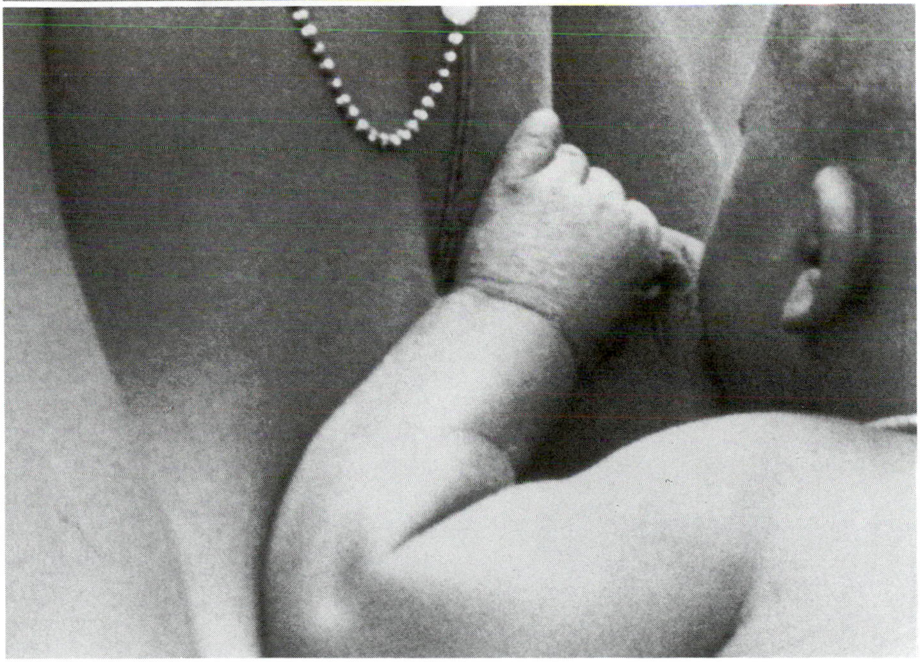

NS

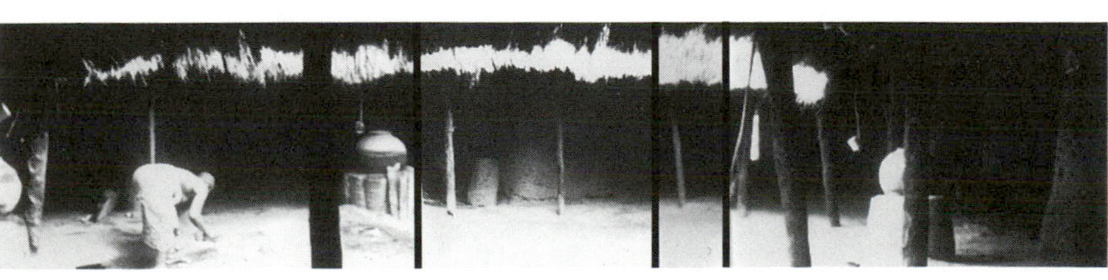

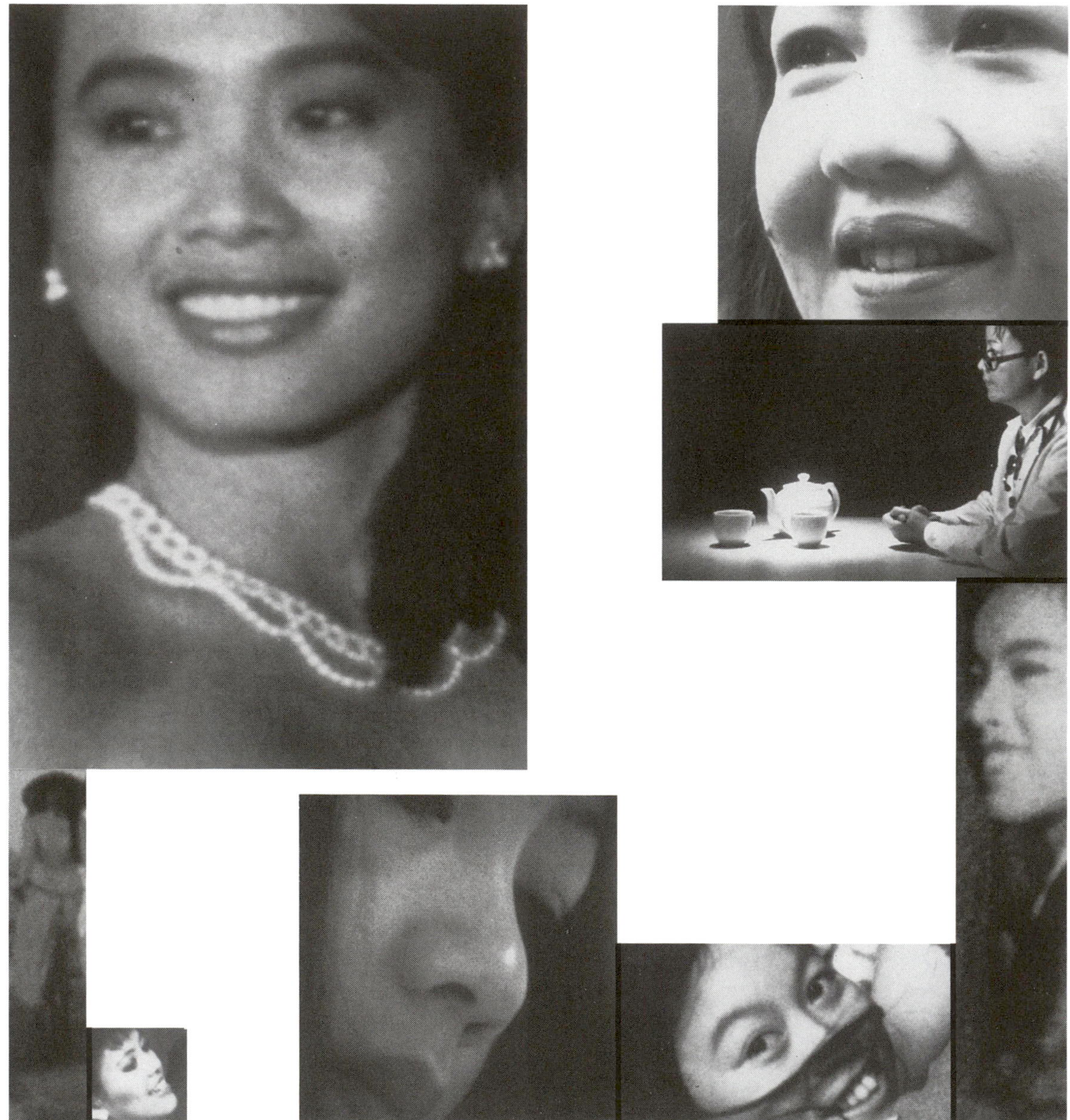

9

"Who Is Speaking?"

Of Nation, Community and First Person Interviews

with Isaac Julien and Laura Mulvey

Isaac Julien: Apart from the title being a pun, a play on, a parody of naming a country, a nation, there seemed to be a play with documentary form in the first instance—interviewees talking as first subjects—and then this deconstruction in the middle where we saw it break down, that it was really a constructed interview, rather than something that was first person, subjective. Then the third part was really a catharsis, subjective, a number of different voices coming together, a whole break down, and I just wanted you to elaborate on that kind of form, because it is different from Naked Spaces—Living is Round, *and harks a little more to* Reassemblage, *in terms of questioning documentary form, and deconstructing a number of devices.*

Trinh: You are the first viewer to talk about the naming of the country—or the attempt to name a country—and to relate that to a questioning of the first person interview in the film. It's a most perceptive reading; one that is pivotal, but that I have not yet had the opportunity to discuss, because it has not come up in the audiences' questions so far. The film, structured by multiple strategies of cultural

---

Interview conducted by Isaac Julien and Laura Mulvey after the screening of *Surname Viet Given Name Nam* at the London Film Festival, November 1989.

identification, is very much about how, even and especially for insiders, the naming of their own culture (the national narrative) remains plurally unstable. Vietnam cannot be homogenized nor subsumed into an all-embracing identity. Not only the explicit enumeration of all the names of the nation in the last third of the film recalls the different moments in its history, but the title itself, *Surname Viet Given Name Nam*, invites explanations and interpretations that differ according to gender, political affinity, and subject positioning.

This title, taken from a gendered context of recent socialist tradition in Viet Nam, suggests both a personalization of the country and a differential construction of the culture from within. It can also be read in the film's framing, as a feminist necessity to rethink the questions of community, nation, and identity, and to challenge nationalist assumptions of cultural mastery. On the one hand, *Viet* is the name of origin of the land and the ancestors of the Vietnamese people whom it is said migrated from meridonial China, while *Nam* designates their further southern relocation in relation to China—whose historical domination of Vietnam continues bitterly to mark popular memory. On the other hand, Vietnam as a name stands for the nation's (feminine-masculine, north-south) totality: to the question "Are you married yet?" of a man who makes advances to her, an unwedded woman would *properly* imply that she is at the same time engaged and not engaged by answering, "Yes, his surname is Viet and his given name is Nam." It requires wit to reply that one is married to the state; but such wittiness speaks volumes for both what it is supposed and not supposed to say on the question of gender and nationalism. And the risk incurred in this form of feminine-nationalist in/directness is, for me, the same risk taken in the simultaneous filmic construction and deconstruction of the first person interview in documentary practice.

In the making of this film, the politics of the interview emerges fraught with uneasy questions. As you point out very clearly, the first part of the film deals with interviews that set out to be first person witnesses to women's condition, but then as they unfold, it is also more apparent that not only their materialization borders the dialogue and the monologue, but it also fundamentally raises the question "Who is speaking?" Although the interviewee does address an ambiguous "you" (a "you" that is directed not only at the original interviewer and the filmmaker, but also at the English-speaking viewer, including here the Vietnamese viewer in exile), what is offered to the viewer in this part are long socio-autobiographical criticisms whose unconventional length and use of spoken language allow each woman her own space. It is, for example, at the difficult pace of her English utterances that the story of her life is unrolled, and the film structured. Lighting, setting, framing, camera movement, shot duration, and the use of visualized words are other strategies indicative of the carefully constructed nature of the interviews. The attentive viewer is bound at one point or another to puzzle over the voice of the film. I wanted to keep the reenactment ambiguous enough in the first part so as to solicit the viewer's sense of discovery, which may grow with means other than plot, story or message—means unique to cinema as a medium.

The interviews are made to look gradually less and less "natural" as the film advances. Only halfway through it does the staged quality of the visualized speech become more manifest: when a woman is seen pacing back and forth while she delivers her thoughts; when another woman is also seen speaking with her back to the camera in a denuded setting; or when the reflexive voice-over is heard with the synchronous voice, thinking aloud the politics of interviews. Thus, interviews which occupy a dominant role in documentary practices—in terms of authenticating information; validating the voices recruited for the sake of the argument the film advances (claiming however to "give voice" to the people); and legitimizing an exclusionary system of representation based on the dominant ideology of presence and authenticity—are actually sophisticated devices of fiction.

The play on the fictions of documentary is differently layered throughout the film. This is conveyed to the viewer, among others, by the diverse cinematic means mentioned earlier, which became all the more perceptible in what you could call the third part of the film: when the active-reductive, more documentary-like editing and cinematography of the "unstaged" life activities and snatches of conversation sorely stand out in relation to those of the "staged" material offered in the first part; hence this statement by a voice-over: "By choosing the most direct and spontaneous form of voicing and documenting, I find myself closer to fiction." It is certainly nothing new to say that every documentary practice fundamentally involves elements of fiction, just as every good fiction film has a profound documentary quality to it.

IJ: I know in my practice, and in Laura's practice as well, in using documentary there's always this tension if one wants to comment on the way documentary films are constructed, but then the way your subject is positioned within that text, is a problem. Then there is the extra, what I would call the burden of representation—making films about subjects that have not been given voice—that you face in relationship to trying to give that subject in some way its own voice without it being the "authentic" voice. In your film I felt these tensions. I avoided it because I didn't interview anybody, really. That was my way of dealing with it, but I know that to a certain extent that didn't work as well. I thought that your attempt was a brave one.

T: This raises another issue that came up, on a more simple level, when I approached the women for this film. In the casting process, it was important for me to hear about their own life stories before I decided on the voices that they would be incorporating. Within the range of their personal experiences, which were sometimes worse than those they were reenacting, they could drift in and out of their roles without too much pain. But in selecting them for who they are rather than simply for who they can play, I was not so much looking for authenticity as I was interested in seeing how they would draw the line between the differing fictions of living and acting. What the film tries to set into relief is precisely the fact that whether they act or whether they are telling us about their own stories, speech is always "staged" (or "tactical," as a statement in the film says).

Direct speech does not transcend representation. To a certain extent, interviewees choose how they want to be represented in what they say as well as in the way they speak, dress, and perform their daily activities. To push the limits of self-representation a bit further, the second, and even more so the third, parts of the film are organized around "documented" scenes that materialize the choices the women made when, as a structural device, I asked each of them how they would like to see themselves represented, after having been put through the ordeal of incorporating other women's pain, anger, and sadness. My own role thus shifted from that of a director in the first half to that of a coordinator in the last half. Hence you move here to what you called earlier a "catharsis"—or what I myself would see as the height of "documentary" fiction: the place where the diverse fictions of representation and self-representation come together. The result in this last half is a fabric of "excess"—of scenes that were sometimes fantasized and could be judged at first sight as being gratuitously unrelated: for example, a woman is merely cooking or quietly drinking tea; another is jogging solitarily in a park; yet another is sitting next to a fish pond; and a fourth one is performing her Tai Ch'i or doing a public presentation on the Vietnamese dress. These are things that, in a way, embarrass me [laughter]—at least initially, but afterwards I understood, because they are so much a part of myself as well. They embarrass me because I have problems with forms of presentation that tend to commodify ethnicity. This was for me the case with the live exemplification of Vietnamese women's historical and customary attires (the *ao dai* in its evolution). But seen in the context of this film, where women's bodies and the way they are clad constitute one of the critical threads woven through the entire texture of the work, it really adds a dimension to the critique and does not come out as just a commodification of ethnicity.

IJ: No. . . . In the beginning, where this question comes up about pleasure, where for me the beginning is very sensuous, there are the colors, the way this works to create a mood for it, I think, is important.

T: Yes. Commonly enough, I had to learn to give up much in this film and to burn all the intentions during the making process. In the reenacted interviews, we (the production designers and I) were partly going after the feminist "natural look"; thus, the women involved are clad in very simple clothing, which is what they would wear in socialist Viet Nam. But in the "real life" shooting situations where they had a choice, they would all prefer to wear make up and to dress up with showy colors. For the viewer, especially the Western viewer, this has been misleading in terms of class, because of the habit of attributing fancy garments to the bourgeoisie, and practical, if not drab, clothes to the working class. Not only such a habit is itself class-defined, hence indicative of the viewer's middle-classness; but it is also oblivious of circumstances and contexts. So while I was still trying to be "truthful" and to hang on to some vestiges of documentary practice in my choices as director, the women were, in fact, opening it up by insisting on what, in certain cases, is an imaginative flight from their working-class daily realities. As I state elsewhere, the legacy of dressing down in public occasions (here, on film), belongs in all probability to middle-class women who wish to ally with the cause of the working class.

IJ: That's very interesting, because for me that's about desire, and wanting to fictionalize yourself in a particular way, because to a certain extent they realize they want to present themselves in a way that may be different from the way they may be every day. Because it's a special experience. Andy Warhol spoke about this, "fifteen minutes of fame." . . . Those things are unavoidable really once you start interviewing people not familiar with different technologies.

Laura Mulvey: I've got a few general questions, then some specific things. The first thing is a way in which the film could be read, and judging from what I've heard you say in discussion afterward—I'm not sure if this is the way in which you intend it to be read, and that is, that there is a before and after structure in the film. Actually, not a before and after, more a kind of here and there structure: the experiences women are undergoing in Viet Nam, seen or understood through a comparison with women in the U.S. Is that a false reading?

T: I was not so much comparing—

LM: Would you say a kind of juxtaposition?

T: Yes, a juxtaposition, but with no linear intent in mind, so that's why I prefer it when you said here and there, rather than before and after, because there is no before and after.

LM: Yes, exactly. Because that's your point—a very beautiful point about people thinking that there's a moment when things start, but in fact they're just a continuum. I think you*

* Laura is referring here to a statement in the film which says: "There is always a tendency to identify historical breaks and to say 'this begins there,' 'this ends here,' while the scene keeps on recurring, as changeable as change itself." (T. M-h)

had the sound of a train on the soundtrack. . . . the sense of something running along on its own momentum, outside the way people may read history I wanted to ask you about the politics of that separation—juxtaposition—between the U.S. and Vietnam, especially as you were talking about the commodification of the traditional culture in the U.S., but then at the same time the picture of Viet Nam is very much one of oppression—the state of women in Viet Nam is one of oppression. So in some ways it's a rather bleak picture, of sexual oppression on one side, and the commodification of sexuality on the other side.

T: Actually, I would also see sexual oppression happening in the context of the United States. It's not only the commodification of ethnicity, but also the perpetration (with refinement) of many of the oppressive concepts in traditional Vietnamese culture. Despite its specific focus, this film is not in fact only about Viet Nam and the Vietnamese diaspora. Certainly, some elements in the film are more accessible to those who are familiar with the culture; nonetheless, many viewers, especially yesterday after the screening, have come to me individually and said that they didn't feel the film was just about Vietnamese women, but also about themselves and about the condition of the women they know. These viewers, mostly women of color from diverse nations, but also white American women, recognized the experiences of the women featured as their own. This is more important to me. When I put forth the fact that the question of women is still very much at issue in socialist Viet Nam, I do not see it as a problem of socialist Viet Nam alone, but as one that cuts across the borderlines of nations and cultures. It is with this in mind that I have selected the strategies and information advanced in the film.

The same problem exists in other socialist countries of the Third World and in any libertarian movement. This is nothing new because feminists of color have repeatedly been very vocal in pointing out how, within revolutionary movements, sexism remains a problem. One cannot simply equate left with feminist, just as the question of gender cannot be collapsed with the question of race; the differentiation of these issues has been very alive in feminist debates. The fact that one is a socialist does not mean that one is freed from patriarchal values; although, of course, there can be at an institutional level more caution and more of an effort to ameliorate the condition of women. This is not denied in the film; nonetheless that effort in Viet Nam has been reduced, for example, to texts that are written by men to be read by women in women's unions. With all these speeches on equality, what is more blatant is the fact that no women are in the political bureau. That socialist Viet Nam is still caught in the patriarchal system is nothing particular to Viet Nam. The criticism of the film is therefore not directed toward socialist Viet Nam per se; it is directed toward the condition of women—whether in socialist or capitalist context, whether back home in the nation-space or over here in the community-space. In forgetting this, I feel that the tendency is always to *obscure* the question of gender by reverting it to a question of communism versus capitalism and salvaging it in a binary system of thinking.

LM: What I thought was very interesting was the way that the question of women came out as taking a different form in each country—the way in which I thought it was important to show the Miss Vietnam pageant, in the U.S., so you could see the Vietnamese community and traditions becoming Americanized, as well as becoming kitsch. There was one monologue I felt was perhaps the most moving and the most difficult to interpret in the context of the overall subject of the film. That was the one with the woman doctor—very beautifully filmed. The one who talks about the problems at the hospital after the liberation, the disorganization of the hospital, the husband's arrest. I found it difficult to interpret because you bring on another soundtrack, during the interview which is about the condition of being a wife in Vietnamese culture, and I became confused at that point, the text became too textured.

T: I use that strategy more than once in the film, albeit differently each time. Aesthetically speaking, there is a moment within that passage which doesn't work for me either. That's when we hear, over the interviewee's voice, a poem read rather than sung; it's mainly a problem of distribution of dynamics that could be solved in mixing the sound. Since the aesthetic always acts on the politics, such a minor problem does influence the reception of the text. This being said, I'm glad you bring up this point, because one of the issues the film also addresses is that of translation. I am not really talking about the various meanings that one comes up with in translating, but of translation as a theoretical problem—the production of meaning, of identity, culture, and politics. The point you make reminds me of the time when I came to Paris for the International Women's film festival in Creteil. The translator for the festival ran up to me, and was at the same time excited, worried and upset. She told me that it was a most challenging task to translate my film, because in many instances there are simultaneously two texts, and which one to choose! She was all worked up by that, so I said, well, you couldn't do otherwise but make a choice, and in making the choice she was very aware that translation not only determined the way the viewer would read the film; it could also not strive for mere likeness to the original without betraying the latter. Although the situation is slightly different, this is partly what I wanted to achieve myself: to problematize both the role of translation in film and the role of film as translation.

To come back to the point you made about being confused, because the two texts come at the same time—

LM: It isn't just that they come at the same time, they seem to be also to some extent in contradiction with each other. She is talking in a sense not about her oppression as a woman, but the oppression of the southerners by the new administrative cadres.

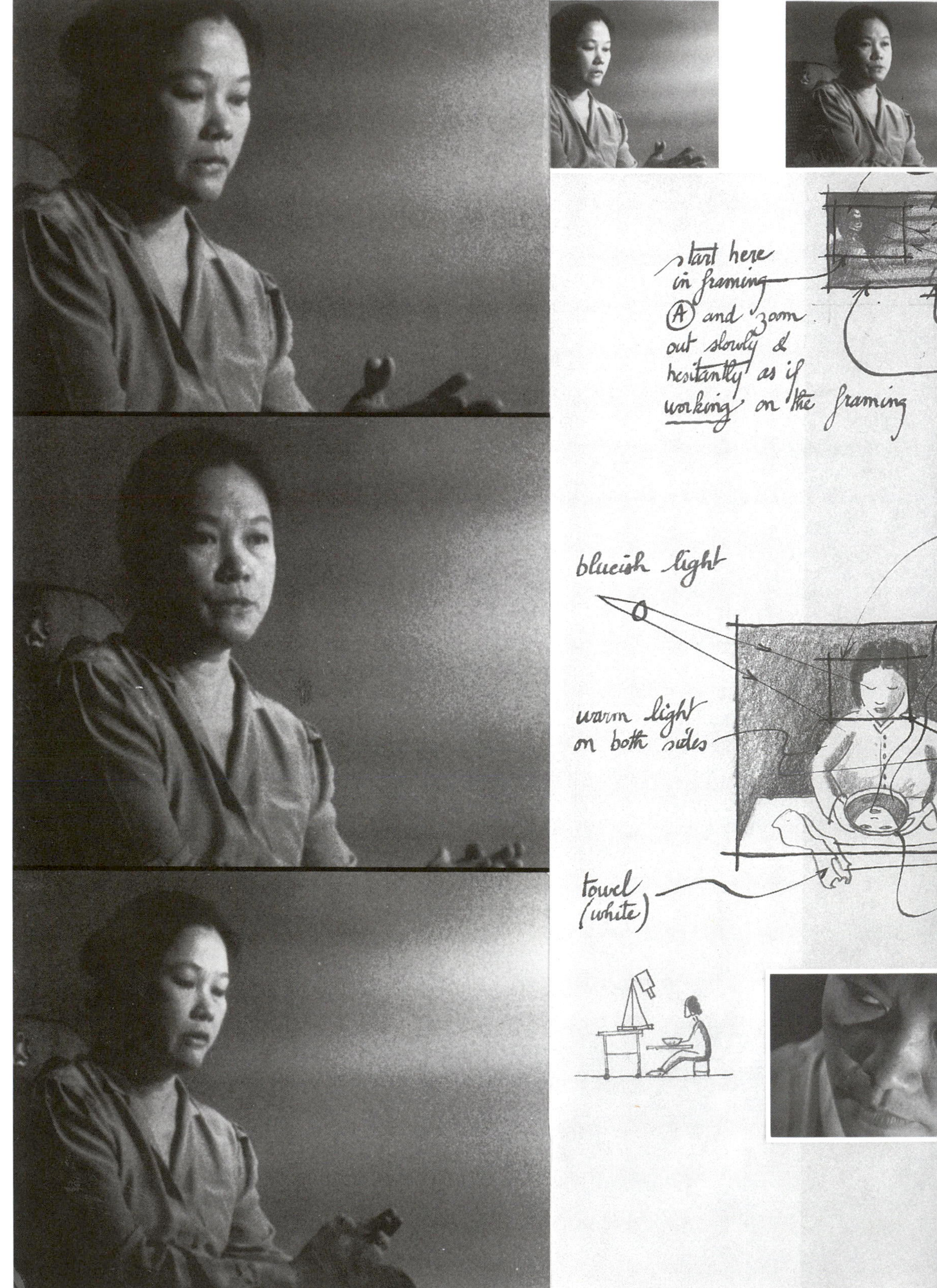

start here
in framing
(A) and zoom
out slowly &
hesitantly as if
working on the framing
bluecish light
warm light
on both sides
towel
(white)

t ... almost
tted
as intense as
le in scene 3
g B
o screen

frame (B)
vapor from herbs
frame (A)
'old fashion' dark blue
warm light
almost unnoticeable blue light on towel
herbs
tting of camera 

I lived at my parents' place with my
woman came to a stop. I became the
and spent my time at administrative
husband to come out from the camp.
went out. I was secluded. My whole f
liberty.
One of our surgeon-colleagues is stil
same time as my husband.... His wife
become a fruit- and vegetable-mong
earn a few dong. The children are le
themselves in such situations? the h
miles away, the family dismantled, th

You are interested in the condition o
women who are the misfits of history
economic distress. They sell everyth
support their children. They deny th
a socialist society.

(She stared at the interviewer and s
[You're asking me if there are social
You underestimate the drama of the
our women compatriots. This war we
as in a tornado. Crushed by the mach

The fragrant flower has already
lost its stamen

Why keep desiring it
when it no longer bears fragrance?

T: Oh yes, I see. That's a very nice reading; it also tells me that I have never seen the two as contradictory, only as supplementary. On the one hand she talks about the country, on the other she exposes the pathos of the family; and actually what appears as a representative case of a woman's and her family's distress also reads as the condition of woman in relation to the husband and the family. She was, in other words, suffering from a double cause. Although her story evolved around the deterioration of the hospital and the lack of competence of the new regime's staff, her real suffering began when her husband was taken away to a camp of reeducation. It was then that her entire perception of the working environment changed, so did her relationship with the hospital and her attitude toward her job and her children. The discovery of fear and the lonely endurance of humiliation on her side did not help the family. Finally as she told us, she quit her job and got out of that situation, simply because she decided she had nothing to lose, except some ration tickets. So I thought the two oppressions fed on one another.

LM: I see. I think I understand more now. So what she was exemplifying was the extent to which a Vietnamese woman who is middle class and a doctor internalizes her position of wife, and identifies with her very special position of wife.

T: Yes. But you see, the difficulty in that case was, I was not simply criticizing. Because I think it would be very abusive in such a case to be merely critical. The challenge was to present the plight critically without condemning. For someone who is in that kind of situation, it seems important to be caring at the same time as one is critical. That's something I find most difficult in working on this film. The same applies for many of the scenes of the Vietnamese community in the U.S., of which the Miss Vietnam pageant event that you mentioned is an example. How can a critique also be a compliment without being any less of a critique?

LM: That's what I think was a bit confusing for the viewer, because I think one felt that the emotion that this woman suffered when she lost her husband, is not something that one would criticize anyone for feeling. So to what extent you were associating it with an aspect of the position of wife as subordinate to the husband, which seemed to come in on the soundtrack at a certain point, did you think so?

T: No, even the proverb that is sung on the soundtrack at that point, simply evokes the loyalty and the sadness of the hard-working wife, who has to nourish her children while her husband is away. So once more it's not something that simply says she has submitted to her condition, but rather speaks of two sadnesses: one sadness that is proverbial and one that is historical, and the two go together. That's why even the word "criticize" here is not quite adequate, as you point out, because at the same time as one cannot condemn, one can still show to what extent we—women of Vietnam and elsewhere—are internalizing the four virtues, which are introduced and directly commented upon only later in the film, in the context of Vietnamese women in the U.S. The traditional four virtues prescribe how to behave to one's husband and by extension to the society. She must know how to manage the household skillfully; maintain a compliant appearance; speak properly and softly; and be faithful and respectful—all this to save the husband's face. In other words, a woman's identity is entirely defined by her demeanor toward her husband, and/or to recall the title of the film, by her adeptness at saving the nation's face.

Understanding this, how is one to look at this woman doctor? Her story is deeply moving, so are some of the proverbs and songs that tell us poignantly about the fate of women. But the doctor carries the four virtues in her very resistance and suffering. And to a certain extent, we all do. I cannot help but notice how these opressive criteria remain imprinted in my everyday behavior. Many of us, Vietnamese women living in the U.S. and in Europe, who have access to work and individual "liberty," may laugh when we hear of the three submissions and the four virtues, but that's only because the higher we climb, the more multiply sophisticated the forms of oppression prove to be. So in looking at this doctor, or at any other women in the film, I also see myself; one cannot criticize here without getting caught in the criticism itself. This also applies to the viewers in the audience.

IJ: . . . the way it brings us to the inside-out-outside-in dichotomy that you speak a lot about in your work. You speak about it in relation to nations—in every first world there's a third world, and vice versa. And then this is brought up again in the nexus of the problematic where you're talking about subjectivities and the way in which patriarchy has destroyed that. But I wonder if you could maybe speak a little about the way—I mean, I was very sympathetic to the film, because it's the whole thing about having ruled subjects and then the whole thing around the responsibility of the filmmaker, kind of boring questions in a sense, but they are questions that are important. This is not really different from my first question that I asked, but I mean how does one resolve that? This may be asking for closure on this kind of discourse, because maybe it not being resolved is a good thing, but it's like the relationship in this country to documentary practice, where the burden of representation, if you're a black filmmaker or a woman filmmaker, is very great still, and the grip of realism hasn't quite loosened from people's visions of seeing themselves, and I wondered what they thought when they actually saw it, because that's in the film as well.

T: You mean the response of the women acting in the film? They did watch themselves acting on video during the rehearsal of the reenacted parts. Although, one can certainly say that video doesn't quite have the same impact as that of film. They were aware of their acting, and actually, they were the ones to criticize themselves most harshly. But with regards to how they come out in the entirety of the film, none of us—including myself—really know. I started out with that limited body of interviews carried out in Vietnam by Mai Thu Van, but the way the film developed and got "scripted" came with the making of it, and I really didn't *know* it beforehand. So when the film was shown and the women saw themselves on the large screen, I guess it was a great surprise for them. On the one hand, it has always been an odd experience to look at oneself and one's self-consciousness as spectator; they had no flattering words for themselves and tended to laugh at what they perceived as their own awkwardnesses in acting. On the other, they didn't anticipate how complex all the issues were in relation to their own role, and how powerful film could be as a medium. They were somewhat intimidated by the packed audience at the premiere of the film, and one of them told me: "We just realize now with fright that thousands of people will be seeing this film."

Of course, there are some parts that also worried them, and it has to do with the way they wanted to be represented—which brings us back to your question. I love the way you keep on asking and saying at the same time that the questions (of responsibility and of non/representation) raised cannot simply be resolved. Precisely because the challenge is renewed every time one makes a film. The part the women seemed to prefer were the places where they chose how they wanted to present themselves. There is always a problem in relation to the part that they didn't choose; it was no fun to play the "ordinary" or to take on the role of a sixty-year-old woman. Some of them were even worried, as I said earlier, because if to the outsider these reenacted interviews can be highly critical of the government in Vietnam, to the Vietnamese viewers they are very nuanced. What is also apparent in these interviews is the fact that the women are not just aspiring for capitalism in criticizing socialism—there was none of that in their responses. On the contrary, they were saying very clearly that between two exploitations of man by man they don't know where to stand. Again, this is nothing unique to their situation in Vietnam; especially when one takes into consideration what is happening right now in Central and Eastern Europe, where the changes the peoples are fighting for have nothing to do with any simple transfer to the ideology of the "free West." With this nuance being very much present in the interviews, as well as the questioning of the feminine lady-maid-monkey condition, the women were quite concerned about how the community would judge them. These are examples of the kind of preoccupations they had at the first viewing, but with more viewings they apparently felt proud of the work they contributed and they wanted the film to circulate in the community like the commercial videos. . . . Two of the husbands said they were very moved by the film.

LM: How did you choose the texts that you used at the beginning? What criteria did you use?

T: As one of the voice-overs in the film states, some of the criteria are: the age, the work or the profession, the economical situation, the cultural region where the interviewee grew up, her critical ability and, sometimes, the question of personal affinity. When I first started out I was a little more "politically correct," in the sense that I was looking for a diversity of views and trying to include a wider range of professions, such as having a musician and a fish breeder, in addition to the employee in the restaurant service for foreign embassies, the two doctors and the health technical cadre whom you heard in the film. I chose the last three right from the start because of the scope that their stories and analyses covered. I think the fact that these women are helping other women-devoting their skill to relieving not only the physical but also the psychological pains of other women—makes them stand out as those whose interactions with women's bodies and mental health allow them to evaluate women's condition with both depth and scope.

Whether I agreed with their viewpoints or not, their stories struck me as being informed, rich, and penetrating—at once social and utterly personal. This, despite their critical denial of any intimate knowledge of their patients. Whereas some of the other interviews such as that with the fishbreeder would come out in the context of the film as being merely personal, hence reductive. Since the film was quite long, I had to cut down on the choices. The fact that the fishbreeder's account was too personal could not do justice to what she was trying to say, and it could be easily misread as some simplistic form of anti-communism. She was criticizing the system, but according to food metaphors, such as comparing the change of staple foods, from rice and fish sauce to bland potatoes, to the imposed consumption of the foreign doctrines of Marx and Lenin.

I would rather not have a representative of the manual labor class here, and maintain the integrity of the work by pursuing the links generated within the body of the diverse materials included. For example, the film also deals with the multiple appropriation and expropriation of women's bodies, and by extension, of Vietnam as a nation—her being possessed and dispossessed at different historical moments by different outside forces. In addition to the many stories of the beloved historical heroines of Vietnam, one love poem occupies a pivotal role in the film: it is the popularized story of Kieu, a woman who sacrifices herself for her father and becomes a prostitute, selling her body to save his honor. All these elements tightly interact with the choice of the doctors—one from the north, one from the south, and the third being the northern health technical cadre whose ideological control over the doctors is strongly evoked in the latter's analyses.

Finally, such a choice takes into consideration regional differences to which the Vietnamese remains extremely sensitive: culturally and politically speaking, the voices of the film must represent the three regions of Viet Nam—North, South and Center. This determines not only the choices of the texts as related to the interviewee's cultural background, but also the selection of the actors, whose accents differ markedly, especially when they speak Vietnamese, and last but not least, the singing of the folk poetry.

LM: So for example the woman that comes from the center spoke English with a voice that was accented differently from the others . . . I missed that.

T: It's normal. This is one aspect of language that remains inveterate and irreducibly idiomatic; I can't bring it out to the English-speaking viewer, and that's a limit of translation. For the Vietnamese, it is very evident since, by the feedback that I have had, I understand their attention is largely focused on this. As I just mentioned, such regionalist determination is also heard in the folk poetry, which was sung by one person, but in three accents, according to the context. However, if the demand for regionalism often springs from a hierarchically divisive attitude among certain members of the Vietnamese community, it can also be politicized and applied as a critical strategy. I found it very useful, for example, in trying to avoid reducing the Viet Nam reality to a binary opposition between communism and capitalism, to bring in the cultural role of the Center precisely in order to decentralize the North-South duality.

Nowadays, the center part of Viet Nam does not, as in the Western sense of the term, represent power and stability. On the contrary, physically speaking, it no longer constitutes the location where the seat of the government is situated; and politically as well as culturally speaking, it stands as the unstable ground between First World and Second World regulations. The central region has always been the one that remains closest to traditional culture, while the southern region adopted the modernization program of the West, and the northern region, under the influence of Russia and China, works at eliminating traditional practices considered to be "feudal and backward." So what's happening to this "tradition"—which people from all three regions keep on claiming in defining the Vietnamese identity? It is here that one realizes the potential of the Center as site of resistance—not in reinstating the authority of a national patrimony, or of an essentialist identity (a mere recovery of the authentic past is in any case an "inauthentic" and unrealistic goal), but in offering an "empty," non-aligned, always-and-not-yet-occupied space where the tension between past and present is politicized, hence neither negative nor simply positive.

LM: I've got a couple more things on the content, then we can talk about the form, because the form is so stunning. I had a problem as well with having set up the interviews—the monologues—at the beginning to show their fictionality, which I thought of not so much as a fiction but as a showing that the testimony that was being given was not coming from the people that were speaking. It was to make a separation between the actresses and the words, to show that it was not authentic subjectivity that was speaking. As a critique I felt that that became rather difficult at the end when the actresses spoke as themselves. It somehow came back to an idea of an authentic subjectivity, so that a relation appeared between the actress and the part, which kind of brought back the question of authentic speech.

T: That goes quite against what I said earlier in relation to Isaac's questions about the structural positions of the film. Of course, your reading can be just as valid, but I hope that there are enough cues in the film to engender another reading as well. I think speech is tactical, and with the unveiling not only of the fictionality of the reenacted interviews, but also the fictionality of the general nature of interviews in documentary practice, the subsequent words of the women in the "real interviews" can no longer be considered as being simply "truthful." Unmediated access to authentic reality via the interview has been questioned, so that the viewer's critical ability is solicited before the "real interviews" are introduced. These interviews in which a camera and a microphone are set up to catch the "spontaneous words" of a woman while she is having lunch, for example, are no less staged than the reenacted ones; but now the "staging" may be taken more for granted by the viewer, it's more hidden, concealed, because it is no longer perceptible via the mise en scene or the language, but more via the situating, framing, editing and contextualizing. Furthermore, when the women spoke, they mostly "chose" how to be heard, and perhaps—

LM: Can you give us an example?

T: The last interviews in Vietnamese with the two women who worked, one in a hydroelectric power company, and the other in a hi-tech electronics company. When they were asked the question why they accepted to be on film, one replied that she had consulted her husband, who encouraged her to contribute to "our native country"; and this was how she overcame her shyness to appear on film. She went on relating also how a friend of her husband teased her, saying: "Who knows, maybe you'll act so well that the Americans will notice you and you'll be a Hollywood star in the future." The other woman interviewed also considered her contribution not to be "an individual matter but one that concerns a whole community." She went on relating, similarly, her friends' reactions and how they "were taken aback when they heard I was acting the role of a sixty-year-old woman."

What stands out for me in these answers is the fact that the women were extremely aware of both the role they played earlier in the film and the role they were assuming as they spoke "for themselves." They were clearly addressing, not the individual filmmaker, but the community and its authority. And in a way, they were also voicing their desire as actors to a cinema public. There was no such thing as catching "life on the run," or capturing the words of "truth." Clearly, one truth that did not seem to come through their "real" lines was, for example, the tremendous difficulty one of the two women had to overcome, when the time came for her to answer "on her own" and to speak as first subject. She was absolutely stuck in front of the camera and couldn't utter a single word in response to the questions. In between long uncomfortable stretches of silence she said, "What should I say?" "How should I answer? . . . I can't talk." And typically enough, I said just answer it the way you usually talk to me; say anything that comes through your mind. But it took her a long long time finally to come out with speech. There is no question, really, of soliciting and reproducing the "ordinary" (or the authentic) in an "unordinary" (or inauthentic) situation. So whether it was by choice or by lack of choice (it was both), this "truth" didn't come out in the delivery; what materialized was not just "anything" that crossed the women's mind, but what they wanted the viewers to hear. It is in this sense that I find it difficult to see the last part of the film as a return to the voice of authenticity.

IJ: It is a whole process really, I mean your art must enter into that process with you in this kind of journey. . . . I know these questions are unresolved for myself. My practice is—since everything is fictional—to escape in fiction. And enter the realm of fantasy, then within those spaces, to try to talk about politics or representation. At the same time I'm drawn to documentary film as well because I'm interested in that kind of tension. They all have their different laws—

T: —and different sets of problems.

LM: Can't escape. No way out.

IJ: I wondered if you could talk about the use of text and image in juxtaposition, where you have the subject speaking, when in some cases they were using English, in the same way that my mother and father use English—it's half their own language and half English, so there's this kind of hybrid taking place, and then you use text as well when they talk, and when you think it might be difficult to decipher and disseminate what's being said, so I wondered if you could talk about the use of text and image in your film.

T: Sure. Since the film tackles the problems of interviews and of translation, it cannot avoid dealing with language and with the relationship between languages. Besides deliberately using English for the interviews carried out in Vietnam, and Vietnamese for those conducted in the States; and besides juxtaposing different instances of English as used by Vietnamese Americans, I have also worked on the relationship between what is read, what is heard, and what is seen on screen. The duration of the subtitles, for example, is very ideological. I think that if, in most translated films, the subtitles usually stay on as long as they technically can—often much longer than the time needed even for a slow reader—it's because translation is conceived here as part of the operation of suture that defines the classical cinematic apparatus and the technological effort it deploys to naturalize a dominant, hierarchically unified worldview.

The success of the mainstream film relies precisely on how well it can hide (its articulated artifices) in what it wishes to show. Therefore, the attempt is always to protect the unity of the subject; here to collapse, in subtitling, the activities of reading, hearing and seeing into one single activity, as if they were all the same. What you read is what you hear, and what you hear is more often than not, what you see. My desire, on the contrary, was to "unsew" them and to present them as three distinct activities endowed with a certain degree of autonomy. Since the task of translation is more than to impart information, the viewer is made aware, in this film for example, of the gap between what is said or sung and what is read, through the minimal appearance of the burnt-in subtitles.

The necessity to free these activities from the "stickiness" of sameness can also be found in the relation between the verbal and the visual, and between writing and speech. Although differently materialized in each case, the word-image relationship in my films has always been one that refuses the use of the voice as being homogeneous to the image, and vice versa. In such a relationship, the role of an element is never simply to *serve* another—that is, to explain, to illustrate or to objectify. For example, voice-overs need not be "fastened" to the visuals in an all-knowing mode; and the predicament of interviews lies here in its difficulty to solve the problem of talking heads, or to undo the fixity of synchronous sound and image—hence the name of "flat cinema" given to the talking film, and the need of a filmmaker like Marguerite Duras to break away from the habit of "screwing" (as she puts it) the voices to the mouths in realist cinema practices.

This discussion on the non-submissive relation between word and image leads us to the use of the text over the image in *Surname Viet.* The slight difference between the activities of reading and listening and its resulting tension is here created by the visibility of the small discrepancies between the text and the women's speeches (which are actually oral modifications of the text by the women themselves). The difference is also perceived in the fact that not only does the text not always enter at the same time as the speech, its shorter duration on the screen also makes it quasi-impossible for the viewer to hear and read at the same time without missing parts of both. The tension that the viewer experiences in trying to synchronize the two activities is, at another level, also the tension that the women experienced in reenacting a speech that has been transcribed and translated. The effort required from them is both that of transferring a written text into a spoken one, and that of delivering in a language that they have not mastered.

English as spoken by diasporic and Third World peoples has been widely treated by the media merely as a foreign language whose subtitling is a commonplace. I can't perpetrate such a hegemonic attitude, but I can't also ignore the amount of effort I require of English-speaking audiences. So as you rightly point out, I did use the text to help the viewer at moments when the women's foreign accents and articulations may start to make it difficult to follow the interview. But the texts are not presented as mere subtitles; they have a function of their own as discussed, and aesthetically speaking, they are treated as a visual superimposed on another visual. Framed and composed over and in relation to the image of the woman speaking, they often invade it in its entirety.

LM: About the rephotography, which you've used before . . .

T: No, I haven't used it in any other film.

LM: So it's the first time you've used rephotography; what does it mean to you in this context? Why did you use it, and what were its resonances?

T: There are a number of meanings possible. First, the question of time. Working in the realm of stories and popular memories, I was not interested in a linear construction of time, and I was not attempting to reconstruct any specific period of Vietnam history. Like the reenacted interviews, the archival images are indicative of the times, the places and the contexts to which they owe their existence. (One of the functions of the visual quotes preceding the interviews is also to date the women's accounts.) But the relations they generate among themselves as well as with the verbal texts of the film continually displace the notion of fixed time and place. Hence, the challenge is to use the very specificities of the black and white news footage and photographs to reach out both to a plural past and to an unspecified present and future.

An example: the 1950s footage of the north-south movement of the refugees is juxtaposed with a young woman's letter to her sister, reminiscing the time mother and daughters spent in Guam (in 1975) while waiting to be admitted into the States. Here the focus is neither on the plight of the refugees in the 50s nor on that in the 70s; rather, what seems more important to me is the specific nature of the problems women of many times and many places have to undergo—as women. This is brought out in the remembered story, through the mother's anguish and terror of rape in experiencing *again* "fleeing war on foot." So while the viewers follow images of refugees in the 50s with women clad quite unanimously in peasant attire and dark pants, they also hear about the mother's conviction in wearing dark clothes and persuading her daughters to do the same in the 1975 exodus "so as not to draw any attention to ourselves as women."

Another prominent example is the ending sequence of step-printed images of a group of refugees in the 1950s floating amidst the sea on a raft, seen with comments on the contemporary condition of the "boat people" and more recently yet, of the "beach people." The rephotography here stretches both the historical and the filmic time. It materializes the fragility of life, as it sets into relief the desperate and helpless character of such an escape. The insignificance of the tiny human forms on the drifting raft is seen against the vastness of the sea. But the fact that such a scene was recorded also reminds the viewer of the presence of a seer: the refugees had been spotted in the distance by a camera (and reproduced by another camera). Thus, hope is alive as long as there is a witness—or to evoke a statement in the film, as long as the witnesses themselves do not die without witnesses. In selecting the archival materials, recontextualizing and rephotographing them while acknowledging their transformations, I was, in other words, more interested in reflecting on the plight of women, of refugee and of exile through images, than in rehashing the mediated horrors of the war and the turmoil of the subsequent fall of Saigon—which accounted for the contemporary disquieting expansion of the Vietnamese diaspora.

To come back to a word you have astutely used, rephotography displaces, and displacement causes resonance. It is extremely difficult, on a certain level, to rationalize such "resonance" without arresting it. As Pushkin would say, "poetry has to be a little stupid." But if I am to further the discussion on another level without denying such a limit, I would add that the use of news footage and photography has its own problems in film practices—especially in documentary practices. The images have both a truth- and an error-value. In other words, they are above all media memories. This is where the desire to create a different look and reading becomes a necessity. In the film, the older news photography is not only selectively reproduced, it is also deliberately reframed, de- and recomposed, rhythmized, and repeated with differences. Needless to say, media images of Vietnam are not only ideologically loaded; they are also gender cliches. So the point is not simply to lift these news images out of their contexts so as to make them serve a new context—a feminist reading against the grain, for example—but also to make them *speak anew.*

Perhaps an example here is the very grainy black and white images of three women moving in slow truncated motion, right at the beginning of the film. They appear three times throughout the film, each time slightly different in their rhythms, framing and visual legibility. The third time the viewer sees them again, they are presented as they were originally shot, and with the original soundtrack, in which a male journalistic voice informs us that they were captured prisoners, whose bodies were "traditionally used by the enemy as ammunition bearers, village infiltrators and informers. . . ." A multiple approach to the same image is at times useful to cause resonance in the very modification of the material. Just as the story of Kieu has been, throughout centuries, appropriated according to the ideological need of each government, the media images of women during the war have been shot for causes in which women hardly come out as subjects—never fully witnessing, only glorified as heroines or victimized as bystanders of, spectators to, and exiles in their own history.

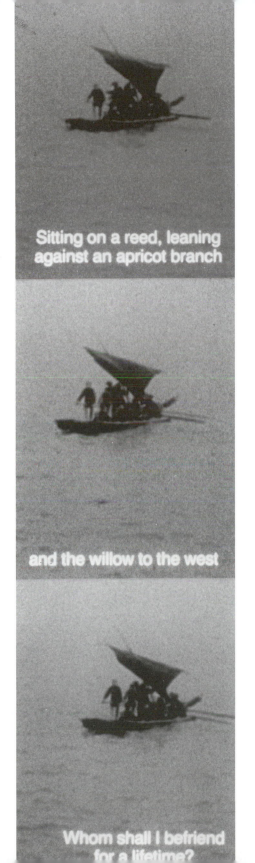

Sitting on a reed, leaning against an apricot branch

and the willow to the west

Whom shall I befriend for a lifetime?

SV

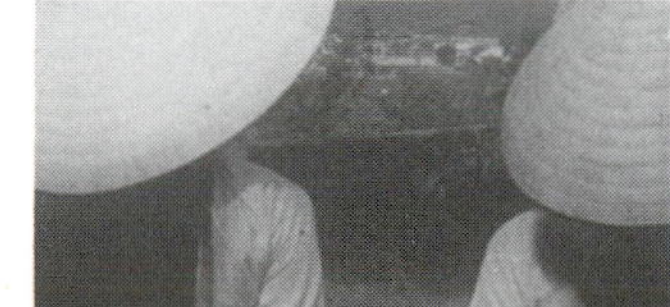

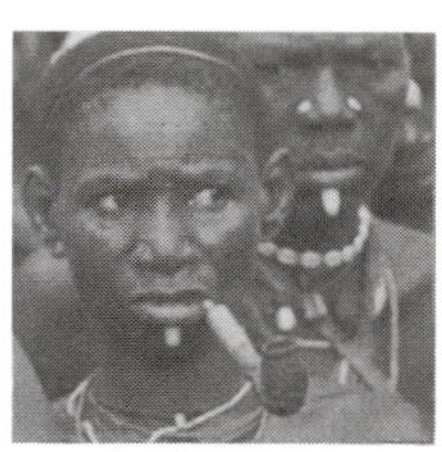

NS

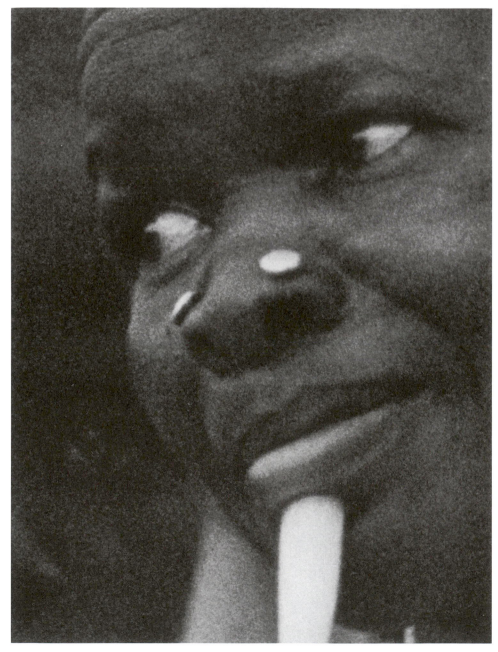

10

Professional Censorship

with Rob Stephenson

Stephenson: What are some of the differences between Reassemblage *and* Naked Spaces—Living is Round?

Trinh: The first, very evident difference is the length. *Reassemblage* is a dynamic short film, while *Naked Spaces* is an exactingly long film. It is long not only because its length exceeds the maximal time limit set forth by the film-television market—ninety minutes for documentary and two hours for feature. As some viewers relevantly remark, people do sit for hours in front of their television sets and they do sit through longer films that offer them a story to buy and to discard; if the film is long, it is also because the camerawork is carried out in such a way that each shot seems to kill time and to invite reflection. Or, as another viewer puts it, because people squirm when they are asked to reflect upon themselves. As in *Reassemblage*, the reflection always points back to the viewers as well as to the filmmaker, who is the first viewer of the film. The strategies adopted in *Reassemblage* in the shooting and editing stages—jump cuts, unfinished pans, fragmented compositions, mul-

---

Interview conducted by Rob Stephenson on October 31, 1985, after *Naked Spaces—Living Is Round* premiered in San Francisco at The Film Arts Foundation Film Festival and in Berkeley at the Pacific Film Archive. First published in *Millenium Film Journal*, no. 19 (Fall–Winter 1987–88).

tiple framings—are, however, very different: they prevent the viewers from appropriating the content of the images by their brevity and dispersion. The same intent prevails in *Naked Spaces* but is achieved through duration and empty (de-centered) circular motion. This shows that *Reassemblage* is only one way of dealing with difference; *Naked Spaces* is another way.

S: *For me,* Reassemblage *is much more disjunctive and more confronting.* Naked Spaces *seems to be smoother.*

T: Yes, the disjunctive aspect of the first film is evident; it is a step of deconstruction where you learn to say no (without reducing your "no" to a mere negation) and need to dot your *i*'s. It's my first film and the difference you refer to has to be brought out in a more obvious way. In the second film, I think the confrontation and the challenge come precisely from the fact that the work does not *appear* disjunctive even though it may be said to be profoundly and extensively so. It becomes clear in *Naked Spaces* that "disjunctive" is also "conjunctive." One does not exclude the other, and de-centering (a subjectivity) is not a simple matter of disjoining. There is a sense of continuity throughout the film, but not the type of linearly closed continuity that leads you from a starting point to an ending point. The continuous flow of life does not lead you anywhere, although you may want to mark your itineraries with departures and arrivals. What you qualify as "smoother" is probably what a number of viewers, especially women, have described as "a very gentle way of going towards things."

Coming back to the question of difference as related to a more obvious form of disjunction, I would say that the difference I work with cannot be opposed to similarity. It cannot be reduced to ethnic divisions and cultural separations. There are differences as well as similarities within the notion of difference. For example, the difference you see at the beginning of the film is closer to exoticism: the scene is that of a dance of social puberty where the circumcised young men are "exotically" clad in ensembles made of palm leaves. Toward the end of the film, the same dance comes back, amplified in importance by the larger context in which it subsequently appears. There is a sense of life that is overwhelming to me and "shocking" to some others because of the density of the crowd, the diversity of activities, and an inability on the viewers' side to reduce the scene to any single event. One "loses" control so to speak, and in my case, one loses the desire to control. The reception of the same scene has thus undergone a change.

S: *It has been changed by what occurs between the two showings of the event. Did you use the same idea with the text?*

T: This strategy is used throughout the film, not only in the visuals, but also in the music and even more often in the verbal commentary. Instead of enumerating all the interpretations arrived at when looking at an event or when listening to a statement, for example, I incorporate the shifting image-music-word relationship. A statement associated with a definite set of images may be heard more than once, each time in juxtaposition with a different visual context. Thus, the meaning resulting from the first association keeps on being displaced; it alters, extends, or supplements, and meanings interact with one another in the process.

S: So the film changes the more times you view it?

T: I think for many people, including myself, looking at this film is like listening to a piece of contemporary music (experimental music). The non-expressive, non-melodic, non-narrative aspect of the work requires another kind of attention: one that hears sound as sound, word as word, and sees image as image. Hence the necessity to clear one's heart and mind of the constant chatter of the soul. Just as in life, one can only really see and hear when one is in a state of availability; one can only absorb another culture when one is in a state of non-knowingness. If one looks at this film under pressure (time, need for immediate access, immediate decipherment, immediate consumption, and immediate gratification) or loaded with one's ideological baggage, then the experience can turn out to be quite irritating if not excruciating. You don't enter a piece of music when you are not in a state of reception, when the potential to hear every sound is clotted.

S: At a panel discussion on narrative and experimental filmmaking (San Francisco Cinematheque, October 27, 1985), you read all three voices from the film in one voice.

T: This was a tentative response to some people's reactions upon my using three women's voices for the verbal text. There is an understandable tendency to like one voice more than the others. A few viewers have asked: "Why three voices when yours (i.e., mine) works so well in *Reassemblage?*" I myself prefer the two others for the auditory qualities that mine does not have: musical (the combination is: low, high, and middle range), cultural and racial (Black, White, and Yellow), stylistical (assertive/non-discursive, non-assertive/ironical, non-assertive/vulnerable). These, roughly speaking, are the aural potentials of the voices. What these voices say is a different but related matter. Having one voice reading all three parts not only flattens the acoustical experience; it also blunts the critical edge of the film. In their statements, these voices constitute three ways of releasing information and of undermining the dominant documentary mode of informing.

Moreover, what seems to bother these few viewers is the lack of conflict they expect to arise (as a given) from these different voices. White versus Black, individual versus universal. For them, it is much more interesting to see differences through conflicts. In writing the parts for the voices (one remains close to the African people's sayings; the other, to the White man's logic; and the third, to the personal experience), I didn't want to oppose one voice to the other because the issues raised can never be clear-cut, and I do not perceive things in terms of oppositional conflicts.

S: *From the feedback you've had from the film, are people reading the three voices as one voice?*

T: Not really, but some of them think the difference is ambiguous.

S: *Do you feel that your preconceived ideas are received by the viewers?*

T: This is a question I often ask myself. It has always been useful to me to avoid speaking about my intentions until I get enough feedback from the audience. I think it is dangerous to assume that what one wants to say or not to say will be read by the audience as intended. Usually, when I get negative feedback that contradicts from one viewer to another, I know that my work is elsewhere and that its reading remains open. There are aspects of this film that I haven't talked about so far because I haven't had enough feedback from the viewers yet, and would have to wait until these come out through them. Very often, however, one also reads one's film by building on the many readings it yields to other viewers, which may not correspond exactly to one's initial ideas, but ends up enriching and filling out the cracks of one's intentions by their very controversial nature.

S: *In one film critic's review, it was suggested that your films are "anti-documentary." Do you think this term describes your work?*

T: Not at all. I think the risk we all incur in being critical is that a number of viewers will always call our work anti-this and anti-that. It's like the word "anti-anthropological," which has been attributed to me and to my previous film. That is none of my concern. If this is how viewers see my work, it's fine. But for me, to be anti-something is just a reaction and I am not concerned with reactions. Among the many other things I wish to bring out, I am more concerned with questioning the kind of specialized, professionalized "censorship" generated by conventions that exist to validate a certain ideology, than with breaking these conventions for

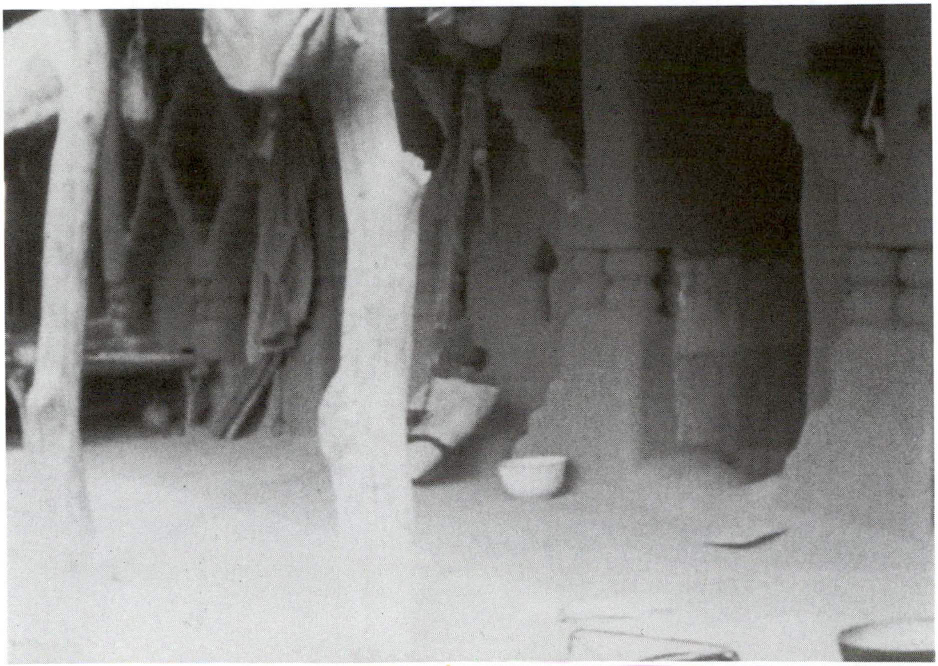

NS

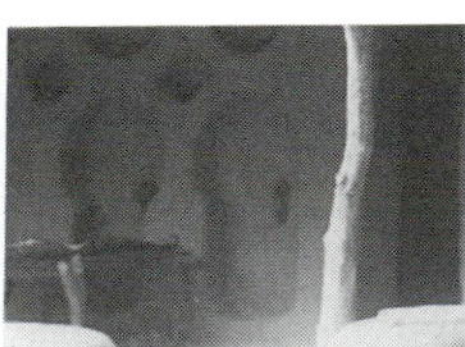

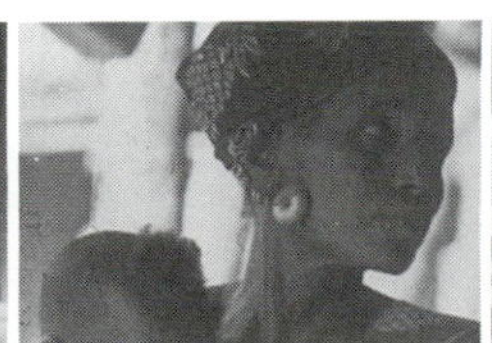

the sake of working against. Not letting oneself be intimidated by rules exterior to one's own work is quite different a matter from being merely "anti-." If my concern is mainly to line up a series of one-response-to-one-stimulus reactions, then the film is bound to come out very limited in its scope.

S: *Do you consider your work as* extending *documentary?*

T: Extending is a good word. I am always working at the limits of documentary and experimental. Working right at the limits of several categories and approaches means that one is neither entirely inside or outside. One has to push one's work as far as one can go: to the borderlines, where one never stops walking on the edges, incurring constantly the risk of falling off one side or the other of the limit while working at undoing, redoing, modifying this limit. *Reassemblage* and *Naked Spaces* have circulated in both documentary, and art and avant-garde film milieus, although the latter is a more recent opening as far as establishments are concerned. Festival categories have always posed problems for me; I have to decide quite arbitrarily what kind of jury I want for the films and in most cases the decision does not turn out to be a good one. Fact-oriented eyes do not like experiments and vice versa, as if science and experimentation can ever do away with each other.

S: *Do you think that it is important to show your films to the people in them?*

T: Not for reasons that make other people think it's important. There is a tendency among those of us who subscribe to the dominant ideology of authenticity to validate (consciously or unconsciously) our films by claiming: "We have shown this work to the people and this is how they react. They have told us to change this and that and we have followed their instructions," such as leaving out the music from a specific sequence "since the hunt had to be completely silent," and so on. Sometimes, the touch of authenticity is imprinted in the film and we see the natives watching the footage on the screen; instead of leading us elsewhere than where we were before, or adding dimensions to the culture that we would have missed otherwise, such insertion usually serves no other purpose than to show us that the natives enjoy or approve of the work. So what we get is not really the filmmaker's view, but a "shared" view, so to speak. The compromise reads as follows: this is the way I see them, but also the way they see each other.

S: *Have you thought of your film work at all in terms of preserving things that are vanishing from existence?*

T: No, I think in terms of raising consciousness. If the viewer believes that this film will help later on to keep things that are disappearing, that's fine.

S: How exactly do you mean "raising consciousness?"

T: Viewers have come out of *Reassemblage* saying they realize how racist they are. In viewing *Naked Spaces*, others have said they realize how much they have lost contact with their environment. Questions posed in the film lead to questions about the way we live in general. For me, the issue is not so much that of losing as that of forgetting or fearing: forgetting the contact; forgetting one's role as producer-produced; forgetting the dynamics of difference as non-separation, non-cooperation (with the system), non-alignment; forgetting, in other words, that one need not consent or contribute to hegemony.

S: Do you see your work as influencing ethnographic filmmaking?

T: That is not my goal. I would be happy if it does, but why would I make a film just to influence ethnographic filmmaking? The films speak to a much wider audience, and that is more important.

S: How do you work with Jean-Paul Bourdier?

T: We have done most of our field research together. Jean-Paul has a passion for vernacular architecture. For years he has been organizing research expeditions in West Africa; one of the works that resulted from these is a book that we collaborated on, *African Spaces: Designs for Living in Upper Volta*. We have other book projects at work on African architecture, and we have been involved with these studies for the last eight years. As the producer of *Naked Spaces*, Jean-Paul was responsible for the initial fundraising; for the planning of the several travels it took us to complete the shooting of the film (budgets, equipment, contact with and authorization from the administration); and for the selection of the sites where the shooting took place. Besides organizing and making the filming possible, he also participated in the editing process. Our works converge in many aspects, generally speaking; but we have different ways of going about them.

S: Naked Spaces *was originally conceived as a series of shorter segments called* Rites in Space. *At what point did the idea for a long film happen?*

T: At the beginning of the editing stage. I realized it was necessary to bring out an experience that requires a certain investment, a certain attention and patience from the viewer. As many of my African friends used to say, to understand African cultures, one needs to be very patient and very generous.

S: *I noticed an albino child in both films. Is this the same child?*

T: It's funny you ask that. I did go back a few places in Senegal to shoot some of the sequences in *Naked Spaces.* Some children in *Reassemblage* reappear in *Naked Spaces* changed, more grown up. But the albino child is not the same, and that shot was taken in Benin. I like to play with repetition in difference.

S: Naked Spaces *seems to explore the pleasant, personal, even beautiful aspects of African life instead of the turmoil, which is often the main reason we hear about Africa.*

T: Are images of turmoil and of famine the only "correct" images to depict Africa? If I were to make a film on the poverty of Africa, not only would I see poverty everywhere I go, but also, whatever I choose to show must correspond to my notion of poverty. The first point is: Why choose an apple instead of a pear? While the second amounts to: Is your apple the same as mine? Why should I see my apple the same way you see yours? All this has to do, on the other hand, with what you want to focus on and where you want to put your emphasis to bring out the subject matter of your choice, and with how you view yourself and the other in this First World–Third World relationship. Turmoil was not what I experienced in rural West Africa and I feel no necessity to contribute to images that the West has already had in abundance of Africa. Like much of the Third World, Africa may be restless; but for me it is also full of wisdom, a wisdom that always reminds us of this global village in which we all live. What I want to bring out in *Naked Spaces* is this living-is-round experience. One can talk about pleasure in this film as much as about unpleasure.

Again, this widespread tendency to condemn beauty in certain political and artistic milieus should be situated in an ideological context, which views beauty and politics, beauty and life as being mutually exclusive. Both those who believe in beauty for beauty's sake and those who avoid it like the plague partake in the same ideology. Much, not all, of the anti-aesthetic trend in the avant-garde scene today can be viewed as nothing more than another form of aesthetics. Instead of trying to understand how beauty functions in dominant ideology and drawing a possible difference with this same notion in your own or other non-dominant contexts for example, many merely censor it, indulging in the illusion that if you break with dominant narrative traditions (plot, dramaturgy, emphasis on technical sophistication and perfection as formal beauty), reality will yield itself up in its spontaneous, most authentic form. The kind of beauty I work with in my film is inspired by the beauty I see in people and in every element of their surroundings. As well-known folklorist Propp noted, "Folklore possesses not only aesthetic perfection but also a profound message." Here, aesthetic, function, and spirituality go hand in hand. Every house in the film is at the same time a tool, a work of art, and a sanctuary. As for the fear of turning this beauty into an object of consumption in Western context, all films are, in a way, commodities. I cannot escape this, for I cannot delude myself in thinking that I work outside consumption; but I can make it more difficult to consume the film. Hence, its length, the attention and patience it requires, as well as the commitment on the programmer's side to exhibit a product that is neither easy to digest not to discard.

NS

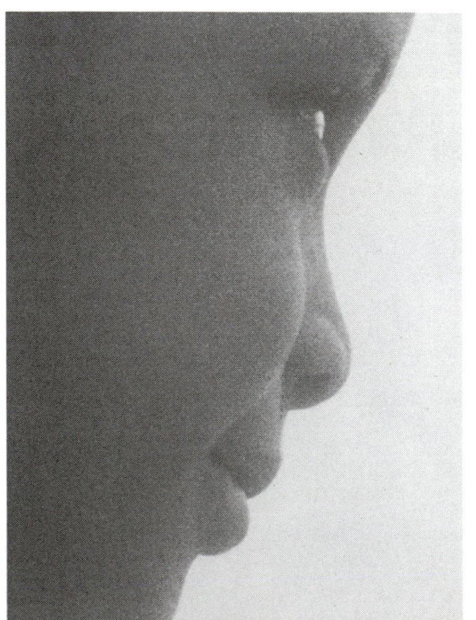

R

11

When I Project It Is Silent

with Constance Penley and Andrew Ross

Constance Penley: We would like to begin with some very specific questions about the way in which your film, Reassemblage, *comments upon the conventions of documentary film form and ethnographical method. We are especially interested in your use of editing, sound, music and voice-over. In the editing, for example, we noticed that some shots are too close and others too far away to be easily read, while at least one is blatantly out of focus; there are jump cuts within a single event or activity; the changes in angle are often less than the conventional 30 degrees; and the shot sizes vary more in accordance with rhythm than with the need to come in for a closer view or pull back for a more inclusive one. As the voice-over states, you're not following the ABCs of photography.*

Trinh: I would say that the strategies used are almost the same for the images, the music and the voice-over. The making of this film was, in a way, an experience of limits and limitations. It brought together a number of activities whose end-point was not known to me in advance. Neither my shooting and sound recording on the site, nor my writing of the script and editing off the site were carried out to conform

---

Interview conducted by Constance Penley and Andrew Ross in 1983. First published in *Camera Obscura*, nos. 13–14 (1985).

to a preconceived idea or a predetermined scheme. The work only took shape as the simultaneous montage of these diverse, nonfinite materials progressed. I knew very well what I did not want, but what I wanted came with the process. Any motive that I had before starting work on the film necessarily dissolved as I went along, so that creating consisted not so much in inventing something new as in rediscovering the links within and between images, sounds and words. The use, for example, of unfinished pans, of jump cuts and of distance itself as "readings"—that is, shots, as you have noticed, that travel without departure or arrival points, shots that are too short, too close or too far for the viewer to take full possession of the content of the image—may be viewed as an attempt to balance content and context, and are therefore aimed at unsettling our habit of seeing through the documentary "object-oriented" camera eye. Recurrent jump cuts within a single event may indicate a hesitation in selecting the "best" framing. They may also serve as rhythmical devices that disrupt spatial and temporal continuity, and suggest a grasping of things in their instantaneousness, in their fragility. Extreme close-ups remind us of the filmmaker's voyeurism; at the same time they lead us right into the image, into the texture of things instead of giving us just an image or focusing on the object filmed (the end point). Similar strategies are found in the way I cut the music or use everyday language as music.

CP: *And since you do not provide subtitles, we do not know what the voices are saying, but can only listen to them as sound or music.*

T: Yes. We can come back to this question of translation later on. One of the first contacts I have with any foreign culture is through the sound of its languages. When I travel across African countries, it is precisely by the inflection of the voices, by the music of people's utterances that I am often able to tell where I am and with whom, whether I've crossed a territorial boundary or not. This is what I would like to bring out in the film: language as musical communication and information. Even in situations where we understand a language perfectly, we often listen to a voice, not for what it explicitly says but for what it does not say. In the film, I was concerned with both the melodies and the grain of the spoken voice—the combination of tones and rhythms, the relation between body and sound uttered or heard. Thus, people's conversations, an old woman's voice as well as the English voice-over (my voice) are cut up and repeated in such a way as to put into relief the combinations and relations that appear most striking to me. Such a cutting of their conversations would be considered disrespectful by many documentarians who subscribe to a doxa which increasingly venerates the oral testimony of people in "factual" films. But for me, it is one way of bringing out the music in the language and challenging the tendency to consume language exclusively as meaning. The same applies to the editing of the music. It is commonly though that if you point a microphone during a dance, you can capture its general atmosphere. The technical device is taken for something that reproduces things as they are. But the music I record obviously sounds different from the music I hear on the site. Whether it sounds flattened out or more intense depends on the recorder's ear and how the technical device is used. This becomes even more obvious in the editing process. In film, on the other hand, music is one of the communicating links; it brings the audience and the screen closer. But its role, in most cases, is functional or cosmetic. It is used, for example, to reinforce an action or emotion, to intensify the inner thoughts of characters. Such an approach to music does not appeal to me. I use it once in a while to provide continuity, in apparent contrast to the shattered rhythm of the images, but music can also act to disrupt continuity.

Andrew Ross: And there are also some very ambivalent moments within this dialogue between sound and scene: when the drumbeats, for example, almost seem to pick up the rhythms of the women pounding the maize—both rhythms match up, but only for a second or so and then they go out of sync again. Clearly, these were the result of conscious editing decisions.

T: Yes, many passages are edited in that way. Another example is the section that opens with the statement "the land of the Sereer people." Here one sees the image of a woman and her child. She starts talking and then I—the voice over—begin to speak. For a moment one has the illusion of a synchronized sound, of my voice being her voice—a technique commonly found in documentary films: substituting one voice for another, speaking for or in the place of the "other." A few seconds later, however, one realizes that it is not her but me again that one hears. What you qualify as ambivalent, in other words, is an acknowledgment of the filmmaker's manipulations, a play on factualism and authenticity.

Since we are talking about music in film, I would also like to raise the question of silence. In many films the sound begins as soon as the titles appear on the screen and is typically used to get the audience into a certain mood. My film begins with silence over the titles and only later introduces music and mood. Silence is an important part of the work: it makes it breathe. I am aware that silence can also be disquieting and disorienting; whenever it occurs in the film, I can see by the reaction of the audience that some people are made uncomfortable. Good friends of mine have asked why I don't use natural sound as background instead of cutting off all the sounds and just leaving silence. But I do think that silence has more to offer than just being disquieting or disorienting. It suspends expectation (music usually tells you what to expect) and is necessary as a moment of restfulness or pause, just like the black spaces in the film. The rhythm of *Reassemblage* is very quick but it would lack dynamism and could become monotonous without the silences and the occasional darkness. Having the screen go black both indicates a transition from one geographical area to another and serves as a visual pause, in the same way as moments of silence in music are pauses that can make you become more aware of the sounds, or just leave you in peace, without any expectation.

CP: *Somewhat along these lines, we noticed that the film uses a great deal of repetition. You repeat sounds, silences, specific images, and black screen in a way that seems to serve as a kind of substitution for explanation. In other words, rather than have the narrator explain what is going on, she just repeats something and the spectator has to make the connection between those repeated events or elements.*

T: Of course. And repetition can serve many purposes. Those used in the spoken text, for example (fragments of sentences), are never identical. It suffices to pull one word out of the repeated sentence to shift its meaning. As viewers, we often fix a meaning or metaphor by identifying or associating the image with the commentary that accompanies it. Repetitions of the same sentence in slightly different forms and in ever-changing contexts help to unsettle such a fixity, and to perceive the plural, sliding relationship between ear and eye, image and word. In instances where repetition functions as a substitute for lengthy scientific-humanistic explanations, it leaves room for the spectator to decide what to make out of the statement or sequence of images in its diversely repeated forms.

CP: *A very effective example of your use of repetition to make a comment on anthropological methods can be seen in your juxtaposition of a shot of the distinctive pattern of the thatched roofs in a village with the similar designs of the weaving or braiding of the women's hair. The film does not, as an anthropologist like Levi-Strauss would do, offer an elaborate explanation of that striking correspondence.*

T: Yes. My approach is one which avoids any sureness of signification. In most anthropological presentations, the establishing of connections between signs and the deciphering of cultural codes is flattened out by the voice of knowledge, the voice of factual truth. This is reflected, in films, in the omniscience of the cinematography and the editing as well as the commentary and/or the "talking-head" strategy. The strategies of *Reassemblage* question the anthropological knowledge of the "other," the way anthropologists look at and present foreign cultures through media, here film.

AR: Nonetheless, the interpretation of this whole question of repetition with respect to the analysis of ethnic cultural events has been an important element of recent critiques of structural anthropology. Much of Clifford Geertz's work, for example, has been concerned with demonstrating that rituals are not expressions of universal functions, or rather that they do not conform to universal structural roles. Each ritual, inasmuch as it is repeated, attends to different, or specific, local circumstances each time. As a result, one can only construct "local" interpretations of any culture's social meanings, rather than an authoritative, structural breakdown of its workings.

T: I would agree with that. But, on the other hand, I think that Geertz's work, like most anthropological work, is replete with scientistic pretensions. If there is one thing that would always invalidate anthropology, it is precisely its claim to scientific knowledge. This claim can be conscious or unconscious. It pervades all the writings throughout the evolution of anthropology (notwithstanding its own criticisms of its methods of approach). What goes unchallenged here is not so much scientific knowledge itself (since many anthropologists do have a critical relation to it) as the diverse mechanisms used to validate and perpetuate the scientism of anthropological discourse. People like Geertz who criticize the claim to the universality of such discourse would be the first to declare that if anthropologists' interpretations differ from any one else's interpretation, it is because they are "part of a developing system of scientific analysis" and are professed by anthropologists. This implies the accumulation of specialized and institutionally legitimized knowledge. One of the intentions of my film is to suggest that you don't *know* a culture better by approaching it with an institutionalized or professionalized background.

CP: There is another strategy in Reassemblage that is also aimed at subverting the assurance of this authoritative pseudo-scientific documentary voice: your use of "fictional" techniques. You construct, for example, several false eyeline matches. At one point we see a shot of a little girl looking offscreen and then in the next shot we see a dead animal, thus giving the impression that she is looking at the animal, which she is not. And at another point, the narrator says, "I am looking through a circle in a circle of looks," and we see a series of eyeline matches of a woman looking offscreen to another woman, who in turn looks offscreen to yet another woman, etc. But it's obvious that this relay of looks, this fiction of these women looking from one to the other, has been created through the editing. A final example of the way you fictionalize "documentary" images can be seen in the theme of fire in the film. The narrator tells us that in the folk history of one tribe the women are believed to have been the originators of fire because they store it in their bodies. Thus when we see repeated shots of a forest fire we don't know if we are to read this image as a document of a real fire or as an image of that mythical fire housed in the bodies of women. It could refer to a real fire because, in another shot in the film, we do see a woman blowing on a cooking fire to get it going, but its status as either fictional or documentary is certainly ambiguous.

T: I have always, consciously or unconsciously, worked in a kind of in-between realm. The point you raise about the fire can also be found in the voice and in the text. For example, you have a very factual type of statement such as "Scarcely 20 years were enough to make two billion people define themselves as underdeveloped," and, immediately following that, you hear a statement that comes from a legend, such as the one about the fire coming from women. And where did they get this fire from? They got it at the end of a stick that they used to dig the ground, or in their fingers. You will find this in-betweenness throughout the film.

AR: Besides the more consciously polemical transgressions of filmic conventions we've already discussed, there are moments in the film when gratuitous or contingent details are allowed to take over the conventional role of ordering the film's meaning. I'm thinking, for example, of various punctum *effects caused by details which would otherwise be marginal but which the camera decides to linger over and foreground. I noticed the flies circling the woman's nipple, the bright yellow plastic cup in the villager's hand, the incongruous red bra on the woman pounding maize, the attention you devote to the two albino children. To what extent do you see the use of the gratuitous as a necessary aspect of your approach to the filmic material?*

T: First of all, I would say that my film is not just about transgression. Breaking rules is not my main concern since this still refers to rules. I do think that some of my shots and editing are very conventional. Often I would realize that I was shooting in conformity with anthropological preoccupations and expectations and have to stop in the midst of action! So that no emphasis is given to the finished product in the film. You don't follow an activity from a departure to an ending point. The objects and subjects filmed are purposeless; they are not governed by any single rationale. One example: the shot of the man carving wood is not included in the film to show what kind of sculpture he is making (hence the absence of information on the end product of his work); it merely offers a view of a man carving, while a correspondence may be drawn between his arm movements and the rhythmic music on the sound track. I would say that gratuitous images form an important part of the film, and, in order to convey a multiplicity of readings, much of the film should be that which I do not fully control. The most challenging and surprising moments that occurred to me during or after the working process were fleeting moments of plural encounter where something undefinable suddenly happens between the subject filmed and the cinematographer. The spectator unexpectedly sees what I see while I rediscover the materials through her or his eye. Whether it is a look, a smile, a gesture, a spot of color, these moments can hardly be put into words.

AR: This leads us to the question of subjectivity. As you've already suggested, one of the burning issues of documentary practice, or theory and *practice, is of course the question of objectivity, or the film's relation to the natural or the authentic—and this is usually seen in terms of an attempt to exclude subjectivity altogether. Obviously you are uncomfortable with those empirical assumptions about objectivity. Do you see your film, however, as a way of engaging your own subjectivity in some way or do you see it primarily in terms of a critique of subjectivism? (Assuming, here, that there is a distinction between subjectivity and subjectivism, which is to say that one can try to neutralize a domineering bias in the filmmaking or viewing, but one can never efface completely the subjective source of articulation).*

T: This is an issue I often have to deal with in public discussions on *Reassemblage.* Some people think that since the film explicitly criticizes objectivity, it is a counterstance to what one normally finds in documentaries. That is, instead of having an objective observer, one has here a subjective observer. Even people who understand that the critique of objectivity does not necessarily entail a subjective (subjectivist) position would come up with questions like (talking about the film I'm working on now), "Is your new film going to be pretty much the same as the previous one?" referring thereby to the strategies used. The question shows the conventional way that people look at films, but it is also highly justified. Conventional, because films making use of strategies validated as the norm can make use of them over and over again and nobody would say that these films are the *same.* Justified, because strategies, the subject filmed and the subject filming, are so interrelated in cases like mine that one cannot separate them. The distinction made between subjectivity and subjectivism might then be useful because it implies that there is necessarily a subjectivity in every objectivity. The question is that of degree and of differentiation within the same concept. When you realize the subjectivity is endless in its ramifications, you also realize that you can practice what has been called "the science of the subject" or, as I prefer it, "the trial of the subject"—a trial that is not limited to particular statements but which infiltrates every word, every image, every cut of one's work.

CP: Despite your film's debts to anthropology, it is Barthes rather than Levi-Strauss who seems to be the dominant influence on your thinking as well as your approach to filmmaking. How do you see the similarities or differences between your own position and Barthes' with

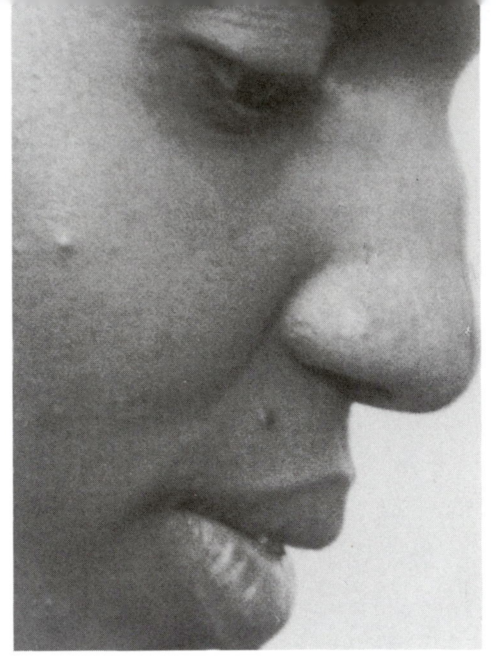

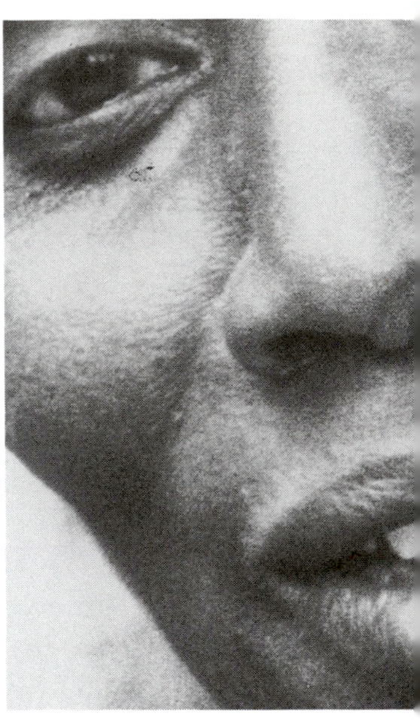

R

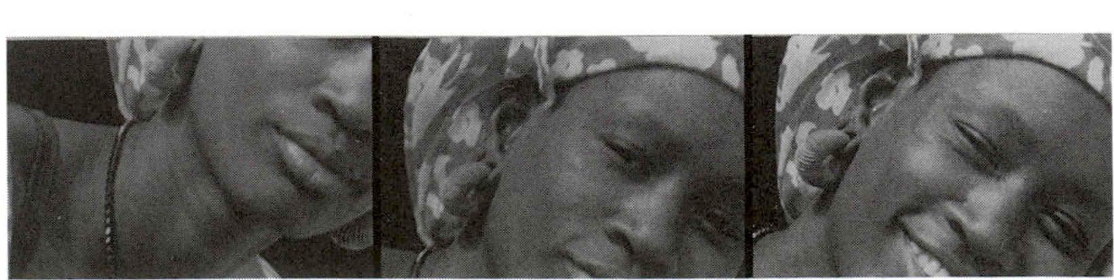

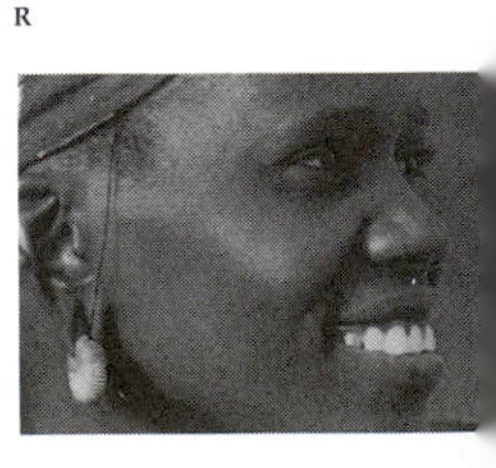

respect to his discursive adventures with the Orient (Particularly The Empire of Signs)*? Because, as you know, Barthes has been taken to task for what some have seen as his naive fascination with Japan and China.*

T: We can see it that way. But if I am interested in Barthes, in Western contemporary music, in feminism, in post-structuralism, it is mainly because, in my view, these ways of thinking do not *exclude* and therefore appeal more to non-Western thinking. So the influence goes both ways. To say that my work is Barthesian is already to take on a hegemonic stance. I think post-structuralism is what it is today thanks to non-Western thinking. If contemporary music has succeeded in breaking loose from its classical frame, it is thanks to the infiltration of non-Western music into the Western world.

CP: In the same way throughout your written work we are asked to recognize a strong similarity between Derrida and Zen Buddhism. You seem in fact to understand Derrida primarily through Zen Buddhism in its similar critique of the metaphysics of presence and identity. Are you saying that your interest in Barthes too comes from the way you were able to assimilate it to a previous interest, or a previous way of thinking, a non-Western way of thinking?

T: Yes. There is, for example, a text by Barthes entitled *Alors la Chine?* which struck me by its mediocrity (compared to Barthes' other works) and which I like very much because of this mediocrity. In this relatively unknown, privately published text, Barthes talks about his difficulty in saying anything about China under (his colleagues') pressure and hence the problem of finding the "right" discourse in which to write about Her. The affinity I have with him here is the attempt to suspend utterance—neither affirm nor negate—in other words, the refusal as I said in my film, to speak about the other.

AR: Perhaps if we address that question of the other in a more general sense, or more specifically in terms of the infiltration of non-Western ideas into the West, we would touch upon something that seems characteristic of much of your written work—a tendency to accept or promote monolithic descriptions of East and West as a set of dualistic oppositions: Western logic versus the otherness of Eastern non-identity. But those cultural oppositions are challenged by the conventional practices of your film (notwithstanding the additional irony of your position as an Asian woman subverting a Western conventional vision of the Third World). Would you like to comment on these oppositions and the difference between the way in which they are assumed in your writing and then eroded in your film work.

T: This is a meaningful critique in the sense that I often have the tendency, in a first stage of my work, to approach the West with monolithic conceptions. And then, in the process of the work, to let them crumble away as East and West keep on meeting and moving away from each other. I don't think, however, that these are more eroded in my film work than in my writing, nor do I agree with the word "oppositions" and the setting of one work against the other. In the book I wrote on contemporary arts, *Un Art sans oeuvre,* the examples I used to discuss and illustrate the trend toward nondualistic thinking—characteristic of Eastern philosophies—in painting, literature and music were all precisely Western examples. And in my latest work on Third World feminism, I had lots of problems with personal pronouns because "I" stood for both white and nonwhite values and so I had to use the entire range of personal pronouns—we, they, she, capital I, small i, you—in order to bring out this nonmonolithic position.

AR: As a kind of supplement to this response, we're very interested in knowing a little more about your attitude towards the contribution of Buddhist thinking to these ideological East-West distinctions. How, for example, does your own cultural absorption of Buddhism differ from the Western interest in Zen, say, during the 60s, with Cage and Ginsberg being the obvious examples?

T: In this country, there are people whose mode of absorption is very close to mine, but there are also those whose mode of absorption is closer to other Asians' absorption of Buddhism. Perhaps two very well-known examples in the West would be Alan Watts, who has written a great deal on Zen, and John Cage, whose work has been deeply influenced by Buddhism and, more particularly, Zen. The way Cage works with Buddhism is very dynamic in the sense that there is no such thing as Buddhism. It has to change everywhere that it appears. It's not a doctrine or a philosophy; it's a way of living. So Zen in America is as undefinable as Zen in Asia. Someone like Alan Watts would say that Cage's approach is entirely Western and very remote from that of a traditional Zen person in Asia. This implies, in my opinion, a way of looking at Zen which is very fixed, a way which corresponds nonetheless to some Asians' way of looking at Buddhism.

AR: Clearly, a notion of authenticity lies at the center of this debate. With regard to your own work, both literary and filmic, we tend to see a shift in your attitude towards the political effects of a celebration of authenticity.

CP: I think we tend to see the distinction open up across a period of time. In other words, we see more of a critique developing as your work comes up to date.

T: You mean that what I've been doing recently is more critical of the idea of "authenticity" than the earlier work?

*AR: Yes. There does seem to be a contradiction, if you will, between the position which you adopt in your book on modernism in the arts—*Un Art sans oeuvre*—and this more recent perspective in* Reassemblage. *In the book you end up privileging those modernists who value attempts to extinguish all forms of identity or subjectivity—Cage, Artaud, Mallarme, Duchamp, the Dadaists. And by contrast, more conscious artists like Warhol, Stockhausen, Boulez, and Buren, are criticized for their over-calculated understanding of the concrete political circumstances and effects of their work. To our minds, however,* Reassemblage *would seem to belong with the latter group, with the need to take up a position, rather than with the former group, with the desire to eschew all positions. We were wondering if you agreed with that distinction, and if so, does that represent a shift in your own thinking?*

T: I'm very surprised at this interpretation, but I'm also very curious to know why you put the film in the second group.

CP: Perhaps it boils down to a rather hackneyed question of whether it is possible to write a haiku and *make a critique of white male biases in anthropology. In your written work—I'm thinking in particular of your article "The Plural Void: Barthes and Asia"* (Substance, *Winter 1982)—you contrast the reductiveness of scientific method to the more epistemologically open structure of the haiku. You describe haiku (partially quoting Barthes) as a "grasping of things in their fragile essence of appearance," and celebrate it as a "vision lacking commentary." Is there a contradiction between your earlier strategy of neutrality, manifest in your appreciation of the haiku, and the very real polemical needs of what you now want to do?*

T: I don't see the two as contradictory; they are supplementary approaches to problems that are very related—the question of non-origin, non-authorship, non-identity in the earlier work and the question of non-authenticity, non-objectivity and non-meaning in the more recent works. To summarize Cage's position as a stance of neutrality or to see in it a strategy of neutrality is already to misread him. Cage's indeterminacy is *not* the same as Warhol's stance of neutrality and non-individuality, which I criticized in my book. It is also this reading that makes you think of Cage's (and those whom you classified in the first group) position as an attempt, as you said earlier, "to extinguish all forms of identity or subjectivity." I see no such illusion in his work nor in Buddhism. With respect to my own position, however, I understand your question. I think it has to do with my rationalizing the film after it was done. Because of certain audience's reactions and because of the nature of the questions asked, I feel compelled (and have trained myself accordingly) to speak lucidly

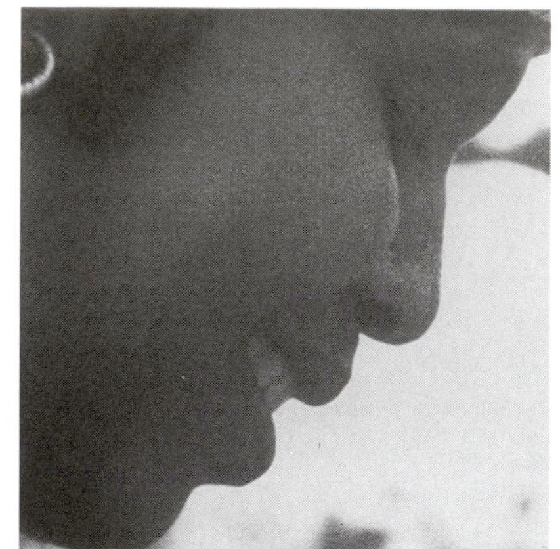

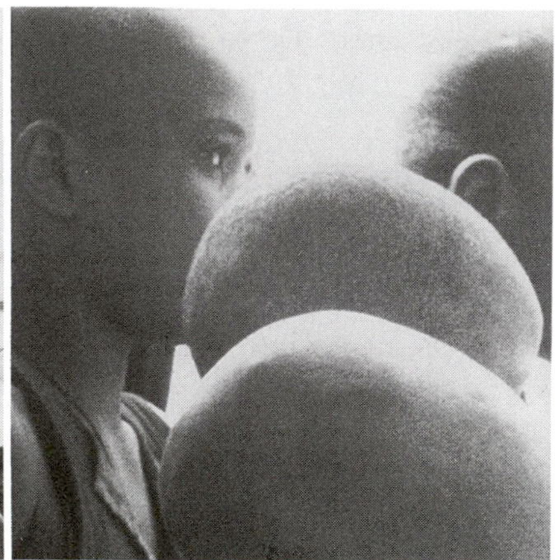

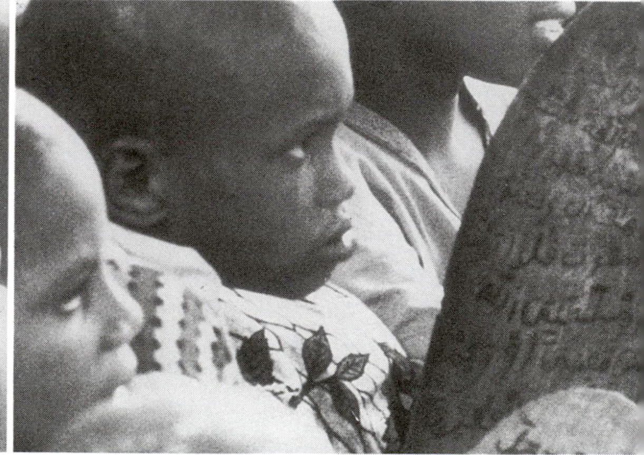

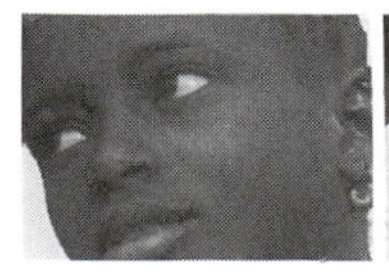

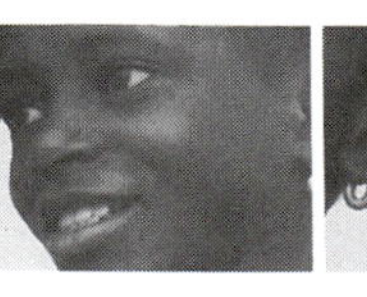

about my work. This is a defense mechanism that may have little to do with the work itself. The truth of reason is not necessarily a lived truth. So that if it is a question of intentions, then every event in the film can be given an intention. But any prior motivation for my film—what you call the need to be consciously political and polemical—simply did not enter into the working process. Hence the link to my earlier work and my affinity to Cage. (But we seem to diverge in our understanding of "political," for I think it is precisely thanks to his very concrete political consciousness that Cage's work has such a wide-reaching effect as to revolutionize not only the entire field of music but also the other arts.) On the other hand, there is definitely, as you point out, a change in my position. The approach I adopted earlier differs from the one I have now in that, in the former case there is no "I"—I alternatively and anonymously speak through the voices of those whose works I discuss—in the latter case there is a fragmenting and weaving of a multiplicity of I's, none of which truly dominates—a subject on trial.

AR: If we were now to think of these positions in terms of feminist strategy, which would you be more willing to condone: guerrilla-like anonymity, or the responsibility of identifying yourself (albeit in a "multiplicity of voices")?

T: It depends on the context. Generally speaking, I think the second approach might be more useful in a Western or pro-Western context. With respect to the first approach, the risk of going unheard is too great in a context where anonymity bears a strong negative connotation and silence can almost never be understood as a will not to say but only as a lack, a weakness or an effacement. The two can however overlap, for any position that allows me to break away from or undermine a dominant system of thought would appeal to my feminist stance.

AR: Can we extend this to talk a little about Third World feminism, discussed in your recently completed book, The Story of Nativism**? It seems that Western revolutionary politics must always, by necessity, look to the most distant cultural example in order to support its own imaginary position, and at this moment it seems as if Third World feminism has been chosen to fulfill that supporting role. Is this choice, on the part of the Left, as problematic for you as the anthropologist's demand for an imaginary cultural Other?*

T: Yes, it is, although it is difficult for me to reduce to a few sentences what I have been trying to say in so many pages in my last book. One of the traps that anthro-

---

* By the time this interview was published, the book was retitled, *Woman, Native, Other*—T M-h.

pology has fallen into is to claim objectivity via the "other." Or, in other words, to think that object can be separated from subject. The idea that there is a hidden truth in the other's culture that needs the joint effort of the outsider and the insider to be fully unveiled is highly misleading. On one hand, it allows the anthropologist to justify his role—the outsider sees more objectively while the insider understands more subjectively (this is how he perceives and arranges the marriage between objectivity and subjectivity)—on the other hand, it favors the development of what Zora Neale Hurston called "the pet system": the outsider "tames" a native whose participation would give weight to his words, if not turn them into facts. A similar situation can be found in feminism today. Just like the anthropologist who invites the native to sit down at the table with him because he needs this native's presence to validate his arguments, feminists have come to a stage of consciousness where they can no longer talk about women in general without taking into consideration the participation of minority or Third World women. So the introduction of a Third World woman's voice in major feminist events can, in some contexts, function to validate what Western women have to say on certain issues and to give it a touch of universality.

*CP: We are interested in your opinions of some other documentary filmmakers, in particular those who are working at the very edge of documentary, somewhere between documentary and fiction. I'm thinking, for example, of filmmakers like Kidlat Tahimik from the Philippines (*The Perfumed Nightmare*), as well as earlier filmmakers like Rouch and Franju. Does any of this work have a particular significance for you, even in your choice to work within the area of "documentary film"?*

T: Perhaps I can say a few things about Tahimik and Rouch, although I'm always reluctant to comment on other people's work, at least in situation like this where I have the feeling of being put in a position of authority. With respect to Jean Rouch, I think he is one of the rare few to have done such a substantial amount of work in ethnographic film. But if, at one time, he did help "documentary" to advance, his influence today is detrimental to the younger ethnographic filmmakers. His cinematographic language has become the accepted norm in this field, in French-speaking countries anyway, and his name, the seal of authority. Despite his many innovations, the voice in his films is always the voice of an unacknowledged dominant. A voice that makes everything else in the film appear as if it were there only as camouflage for this unavowed dominance. Of equal importance is the promotion of the concept of the cinéaste as catalyst-observer which gave rise to the cinéma verité style. The artificial intervention of this observer is thought to trigger off reactions or events considered to be *more true* than those found in normal situations. As

I pointed out earlier with regard to anthropology, this whole idea of catching and revealing the *hidden* truth of people through created situations is somehow very illusionistic, for it does not really deal with the complexity of the cinéaste's subjectivity.

I love the work of Kidlat Tahimik. It is unpretentious and it deals with issues like the infiltration of foreign values in the Philippines or the assimilation of these values in a very non-selfconscious way. He has this rare ability to laugh aloud at himself and to keep a certain innocence in his look. Instead of making the audience uncomfortable, as I do in my film, he offers a view that is simply other and free of colonial values.

CP: In your work on Cage you stress the importance of the concept of nonsense, that is, something that doesn't make sense in our *terms, but is nonetheless very funny. Isn't there something of this in Tahimik's work?*

T: Definitely. And that is very close also to the language of Zen and Tao, for example, which sounds absurd to many people at first hearing. But the language itself is perfectly clear in the sense that there are no words in a sentence that you *cannot* understand. Things are just put together differently. Tahimik's work is the same; one cannot say that it is sophisticated or that it puts you in a state of nonsense because everything said does actually make sense; it's just the total effect that may not.

CP: The stereotypical idea of "Third World film" (serious, politically inflected drama or documentary) does not include films that are self-reflexive, modernist, and funny. But Tahimik, for example, adopts many avant-garde strategies such as elliptical narrative and repetition, which upset conventional expectations.

T: There is a general assumption that playing with film criticism and filmmaking itself in the work or questioning the form in which you present a film is something Western. Such an assumption is usually unfounded and, again, hegemonic. In many cases, it comes from viewers who had preconceived ideas of what Third World cinema is or should be. Ironically enough, what they consider more authentic to the Third World are precisely films that have well assimilated old narrative techniques of Western Cinema and deal with a specific socio-political problem of a country. This is not to say that we from the Third World should not make conventionally narrative and political films, but that assumptions of this kind are often voluntarily or involuntarily used to set us up against each other.

AR: One last question about feminism that we'd like to ask is related to problems that are raised by the promotion of cultural specificity within America itself. We were thinking of the way in which minority-marked cultural forms chosen by Asian, Hispanic, or black artists and writers generally appeal to a straightforward celebration of ethnic identity. Now one of the more incisive arguments in The Story of Nativism *is that this is reminiscent in many ways of the dominant strain of essentialism within American feminism.*

T: The question of ethnic identity and the question of female identity are one to me. They have been treated as two, as if they could be separated at all, and as if identity could be separated from oneself and treated as an absolute that one can lose or reclaim. The claim for an ethnic and/or female identity is necessary at a certain stage of the feminist fight, it helps us to beat the master at his own game. But it is not an end in itself. If it were, then it would be oppressive, for it would have become just another product of the dominant discourse. For a long time our ethnicity and our femininity have made us the objects of contempt; now the situation is turned around: we are supposed to search for them and recover them as *lost* properties. We have thus come to adopt the cause of the anthropologist whose role it is to help us redefine our authenticity. It is easy for me, for us, to get caught in this game and not to realize that we are just bouncing back and forth within the same frame of reasoning. As I say in one of the statements in my next film (with respect to truth, to ethnicity and femininity): "I can't take hold of it nor lose it / When I am silent it projects / When I project, it is silent."

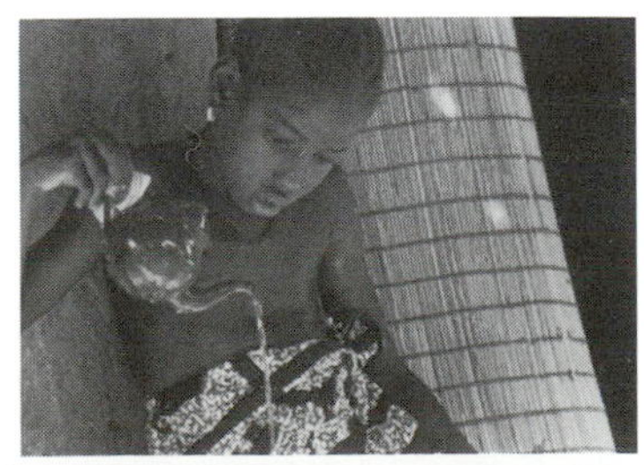

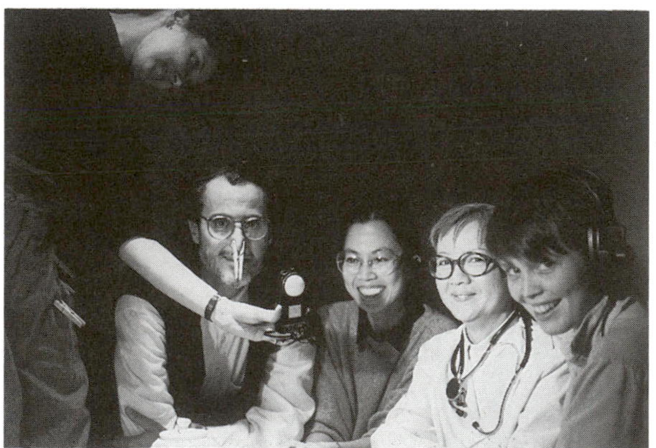

Nearest above: crew during the shooting of *Surname Viet* in Austin, Texas. From left to right: Kathleen Beeler, Jean-Paul Bourdier, Trinh T. Minh-ha, Tran Thi Bich Yen, Linda Peckham.

12

"Which Way To Political Cinema?"

A Conversation Piece

with Laleen Jayamanne and Leslie Thornton

This conversation piece is composed of two dialogues presented here separately, in juxtaposition. It was originally conceived as a single talk gathering Leslie Thornton, Laleen Jayamanne and myself. But due to the fact that she had recently become a mother, Laleen, who lives in Australia, was unable to come to New York when her film *A Song of Ceylon* was shown at the Collective for Living Cinema in May 1988. We have therefore decided to carry on a conversational exchange by correspondence, hence the (written-in-the-interlocutor's-absence) nature of some of the questions which I have kept.—*TM-h.* First published as "If Upon Leaving What We Have To Say We Speak" in *Discourses: Conversations on Postmodern Art & Culture,* eds. Russell Ferguson et al., New York: New Museum of Contemporary Art and the MIT Press, 1990.

Trinh: One way of discussing your film work is to talk about avant-garde filmmaking in the late eighties. How do you see the changes taking place?

Leslie Thornton: I think there is an avant-garde practice within cinema, but that it is dispersed, or rather, not constituted as a coherent movement. It depends on how we define "avant-garde"; for myself it means work that actively challenges accepted forms and the divisions between forms. I see this work as having a difficult relation with the established exhibition circuit, though the New York/San Francisco-based circuit has a particular history and focus. I think work that stretches the form is often hybrid in genre, crossing the traditional categories of narrative, documentary, and experimental film. My own interest is in the outer edge of narrative, where we are at the beginning of something else.

T: Before we discuss your interest in questions of narrative, let's come back for a minute to your affirmation that avant-garde film practices continue to thrive mostly outside the more visible experimental film circuits. You are aware of Fred Camper's essay in the twentieth anniversary issue of the Millennium Film Journal, *on "The End of Avant-Garde Film," in which he specified what a "great film" is for him and also addressed the question of how the viewer individuation in avant-garde film can constitute a social challenge to the mass culture conformity of the postwar decades. The insights he offers on the historical avant-garde, and the social dimension he incorporates in the notion of "personal" work are very useful in explaining the cultural impact it had during the years 1946–66, which he terms "the individual period" of American avant-garde filmmaking.*

Of importance to me is his rejection of a reductive and isolationist overemphasis of the "personal" found in recent experimental films. Camper also analyzes the teaching of avant-garde film technique within institutional structures as "a recipe for the end of avant-garde film." This is certainly a challenge, on the one hand, to filmmakers eager to rank themselves among the avant-gardes by simply working with the established vocabulary of the movement; and on the other hand, to those of us who teach in order to continue to make films, even if we count ourselves among the teachers who play a tight game with academism and provide students "with a whole system both to learn and rebel against."

Yet, as Camper recognized himself at the end of his essay, his concept of great film can be and has been considered the very source of his problem with newer work. Numerous other notions he advanced, such as "originality"; "authentic expression"; the artist's visionary role in society; the need to "find a new artistic mode to work in," or to "reinvent cinema"; and the idea of opposing "a state of decadence" to "a genuinely avant-garde movement," are central objects of the postmodern attack. These notions may be said to partake in this vertically imposed form of individualization whose ideology of separation ultimately helps to maintain the status quo. The problem of our time, as Michel Foucault would say, is not to liberate the

Trinh: Your film A Song of Ceylon *and your writings situate your work at the intersection of postmodernism, poststructuralism and feminism. Do you agree with this? If not, why? If yes, how would you describe this intersection?*

Laleen Jayamanne: Situating *A Song of Ceylon* (1985 Australia) at this intersection now would validate it in a way that is not very useful. Such a maneuver leaves no room at all to examine what doesn't work in the film, which is the only thing about it that still interests me. Constantly referring to the theoretical discursive apparatuses that make certain films possible or readable, has also become a way of blocking *critical* engagement with "x" number of "independent radical films." When I introduced the film at a Sydney screening in 1985, I half-jokingly called it a postcolonial dance film. On other occasions I have called it an ethnographic film of the body.

Since the *Standard Oxford English Dictionary* defines "conversation piece" as "a kind of genre painting representing a group of figures," I am reminded of another intersection—that museum relic of a film, Godard and Gorin's *Wind from the East,* which has the charm of an intensity or passion spent and utterly dated. The scene I am thinking of is the one in which the late Brazilian film director Glauber Rocha stands at an intersection with his hands extended in a Christ-like gesture. A pregnant woman with a camera approaches him, asking"which way to political cinema?" Rocha gestures in one direction speaking of a marvelous Third World cinema, but the pregnant woman strolls off in another direction—(I may be embellishing this, as it has been at least five years since I last saw the film and used that scene and dialogue in a live performance).

My writing now is distracted by an identification with that pregnant woman with a camera articulating differences between Western and Third World cinema. I like the way the woman negotiates that intersection via a simultaneous gesture of engagement and deflection. The urbane relaxed felicity implied in the term "conversation" is made difficult by that state of distraction called "motherhood."

We know that the "maternal" and the "feminine" are not isomorphic with mothers and women, just as we have been told not to confuse the "phallus" with the penis. After Barthes refused to show us his mother's image, some men engaged in theoretical work in the anglophone world have initiated an autobiographical discourse about the maternal/the mother, the function of which in their respective discourses may be worth thinking about; but in my state of distraction I can't sustain that interest and want, instead, to talk about the ritual in *A Song of Ceylon* which is governed by two mythical avatars of the maternal found in the South Asian religious imaginary. One is Pattini, the good mother, and the other Kali, the evil mother; both are figured very differently from the beautiful spaced-out virgins of Western Christian imagery. The film yokes these two contradictory figures, whereas in the ritual

individual from the state and its institutions, but from both the state and the type of individualization inscribed in its power structures. What is your view on these issues?

LT: As a filmmaker it is odd to read so many commentaries bemoaning the demise of experimental cinema. A lot of this is misleading, because what is really happening is that people are speaking in a generational way, and are feeling a passage. They see the passing, and also the diminishing, through derivative work, of what they trust and found expansive.

I think there is also an element of sexism at work here. Experimental film of the fifties and sixties was a male-dominated practice and involved considerable grandstanding. Jonathan Rosenbaum made himself unpopular when he said as much in his book *Film: The Frontline.* Now when much of the most interesting recent work is made by women, it is amazing to me that so little attention has been paid to this development, even among feminist writers.* The development marks not only a shift in sexes, but also in the kinds of work being done. In my own case, I have been accused of working in a manner that is "feminized." Perhaps this is because the work doesn't announce its agenda, it is not confrontational in the usual sense, and it does not take an overt position in relation to power as it is currently constituted.

I do agree with some of the reservations about an academic/experimental film link. It's difficult when teaching not to be put in a position of authority, even if everything you do is intended to counter such a position. This and other factors endemic to academia can lead to a kind of reinforcement of status quo. Despite everything, though, I think academic institutions provide at least one kind of meeting ground, which becomes more interesting when it cuts across generations and disciplines.

T: Perhaps you can say something about the avant-garde energy that continues to stimulate you, and try to describe the situation in which, as you put it, we are "at the beginning of something else" and straight anti-positions no longer appeal to a feminist sensitivity.

LT: That is a huge question. One thing I see happening in work which is vital is that the focus is shifting from film as an art *form,* to film as a vehicle to approach problems or issues—to tell or untell stories. The lessons of a more formal investigation have been absorbed and have become part of a working language; the parameters are greatly expanded, maybe they are dirtier around the edges, in a positive

---

* One notable exception is the work of Bérénice Reynaud. See her *Film: The Frontline,* an annual publication from Arden Press—LT.

of spirit possession and cure the reigning figure is Kali. The disturbed biological familial relationships are restored at the end of the ritual under the auspices of the priest dressed in drag as Kali. The maternal as the space of primary narcissism is an atemporal, eternal concept of that dual dynamic, and if women want to bring the maternal into the flux of time, then different operations are required, though what these might be is a matter for film to explore.

I suppose I'm rambling on about the feminist thematics of the film. *Song of Ceylon* attempted to work through an impasse in an aspect of feminist film theory overdetermined by what I call protestant feminism. But the film's impulse was not purely reactive. The possessed woman interested us because her body was not one—in fact, here was an example of the infamous poststructuralist "decentered, heterogeneous, subject-in-process" displaying the very processes of subject formation and displacement in extremis. We loved this possessed body which could say to the priest and audience and the gods, "Do you know who this woman is? This woman is Somawathi. Do you know me well? Do you think I am a woman? Ha! Do you? Do you?" We loved her verbal and bodily dexterity, even as she enunciated the cultural text of a body in extremis. The problem then was how to stage this dynamic without presenting THE MAD WOMAN. So we thought we'd spread the contagion of possession democratically across gender boundaries, across many bodies so that the difficult pleasures of masochism, narcissism and hysteria could be viewed and voiced with the cinematic means. And here the most interesting question to keep in mind is the one Homi Bhabha asked me at an Edinburgh film festival forum: "What was it that resisted the theoretical discourses you were working with (at the time of making the film) even as you used them?" This question is vital if one wants cinema to do something other than simply mirror theoretical discourses.

As for my writing, I wish to comment on the use of my late mother's name, Anna Rodrigo, as the interviewer in the fictional interviews I did for *Discourse* and *Fade to Black*. The maternal as the space of primary narcissism for the son is part of the history of the Western genre of painting called "Mother and child." For me, the interest in working with the maternal is not an autobiographical one. To converse with the maternal in an unsticky tone, where there is space for tonal shifts and distancing, I find very appealing. Is this a way of writing a poststructuralist feminist biography?

T: In an interview with Geeta Kapur and Yvonne Rainer for Art & Text, *you asked whether the notion of postmodernism has any relevance to contemporary Indian art. I would like to rethink the connotations of this question. For me, to affirm (like some of us Third World members) that postmodernism is mainly a phenomenon of American culture, or to assume (like some First World members) that the avant-garde is spurred and controlled by the West,*

way. An avant-garde cinema cannot understand itself in the simple oppositional terms which were originally used to mark off the field. Rather, there is a positioning of an avant-garde within a range of possibilities in cinema and media. I don't see this as a capitulation, but as a potentially subversive deepening—a maturing. When boundaries begin to break down between the political and the personal, the popular and the obscure, truth and fiction, some interesting elements begin to slip through cracks. We have to look again at what we mean by these categories.

T: Yes, one way in which what is named "postmodernism" distinguishes itself from (a certain concept of) modernism is with respect to the question of novelty. As some have said, we live in an era of the decline of the new. While the modernist project is promoted through a claim to create from zero and to make tabula rasa of traditional values, no such conception of language could be confidently relied upon in today's context of critical thinking without appearing naive. Postmodernism, in a way, has always existed; it does not merely come after modernism, but exists before, with and after it. This is what Jean-Francois Lyotard is probably pointing to when he affirms that a work can only be modern when it is first postmodern. These two qualifying terms do not stand in opposition to each other and postmodernism is here defined as modernism at its nascent stage—one that is always recurring. As in all "ism" histories, however, the urge to circumscribe and unify the situation is often unavoidable, hence the tendency to turn the postmodern condition into "another version of that historical amnesia characteristic of American culture—the tyranny of the New," as Stuart Hall puts it. One can never situate oneself outside mainstream values. In challenging them, one has to go constantly back and forth between the center and the margins.

LT: It is important when considering the possibility of an avant-garde to draw a distinction between newness, or novelty, and change. We do suffer from a certain "tyranny of the new" in our culture, but what has somehow become lost in all of this is the possibility of change, which I see as a more fundamental process, not always visible or comfortable in its moment. My reservations about postmodernist theory relate to a lack of distinction on this count, and to its resignation with respect to present and ongoing political, social, aesthetic forces. In the arts, for instance, I believe it is essential to imagine a marginality, to perceive an edge from which to work. One can be entirely cynical and say that this edge is illusory, that it is already absorbed, but then it becomes impossible to work. So I think one has to combine any cynicism with a (cynically) constructed dream—a space for yourself.

Another reservation I have concerns our culture's voracious appetite for naming. In some cases the deployment of Theory, as a prescriptive or legitimizing device, becomes just another mode of commodification. This has been especially true in the arts. I first encountered the term "postmodernism" when I was finishing the film

is in a way to concede "history" to the West all over again. In other words, it is to assent to the West's cultural hegemony. This does not mean, however, that postmodernism as promoted by Western theorists and artists is not context-specific. What is designated as postmodernist on the New York scene, for example, does not really indicate what is happening in other parts of the country or the world. One cannot overlook the heterogeneous nature of the histories of all socio-aesthetic movements. The "failure" of modernism, as Lyotard viewed it, is due to the resistance of the multiplicity of the worlds of names (a resistance which your answer to my first question exemplifies so well) and to the irreducible diversity of cultures. Postmodernism depends upon a re-reading of culture, and this re-reading is a "transversal" struggle not limited to any single country or context. As Third World subjects, we run the constant risk either of falling into the Master's hands by making his preoccupations central to ours, or of giving up our parts in the struggles by denying our very contributions to the process of questioning modernist ideals—of bringing forth new forms of subjectivities (hence of socialities)—by rethinking the self in relation to the political.

J: The historical avant-garde is after all a Western phenomenon. The valorization of the new and the denigration of the old (i.e., tradition) is a Western avant-garde attitude made necessary by the historical exigencies that the various movements faced in their particular cultures. I don't think the notion of an advanced garde is very useful in the context of late capitalism and the mass culture it produces. As for postmodernism being mainly a phenomenon of American culture—that is true in a restricted sense as it defines art work that circulates in galleries and journals where pastiche is a defining feature of signification. As Geeta Kapur said in the *Art and Text* interview you mentioned, Indian art is not postmodernist in this sense, it is rather eclectic, because of the differences between cultures of surfeit and those of scarcity.

But if postmodernism is defined in Fredric Jameson's sense, as the cultural logic of late capitalism, then in so far as the world is American, as a Sri Lankan (and here the distinction is from Indian culture, which has strong regional traditions), I am interested in the effects the project of modernization has on visual culture in the postcolonial era—the era *after* the introduction of indigenous film production in 1947 and the electronic media (both TV and video in the early 80s). I think the latter marks the postmodern moment in our culture, along with major economic policy changes. Due to a complex number of factors involved, the statement about the "irreducible diversity of cultures" needs to be tested in particular contexts rather than simply asserted like a mantra. I know ethnographic views on the matter are sharply divided and maybe one has to repeat the slogan like a mantra even as "diversity" is homogenized in an international media culture. This is where filmmakers can intervene, the conditions for the rapid transformation of the culture are there,

Adynata, a kind of pastiche of images of Orientalism, meant as a condemnation of a certain Western or colonial gaze. Yet the film, the making of it, the discovery of it, happened in muteness. I don't mean to naively suggest that the film came out of nowhere. In fact Edward Said's *Orientalism* helped trigger the project. The strategies employed, however, and the film's refusal to situate itself within a recuperable political discourse, while remaining somehow political, this was born of muteness.

Then one day you sit down over coffee and read about postmodernism and it is like a recipe book for what you just had such difficulty locating. The problem is not that the theory reduces a precious experience, but that it is partial, comfortable, and taming. I feel that in *Adynata,* I was attempting to tap a certain "unspeakable," and that it was important for the audience to have this experience as unspeakable. However, a difficulty arises when, under the name of postmodernism, a descriptive reading of the work's attributes precludes an in-depth reading and compromises its political thrust. What I'm addressing here is really an ambivalent relationship to theory; the irony in this is that I see my work as somehow "theoretical," or at least as converging with related trends.

This brings me back again to the idea of an avant-garde, which I do not see as a well-considered reworking of established codes, but as an improvisational act, drifting back and forth between reason and the unfamiliar.

T: *Instead of engaging in a discussion on the specific relationship between theory and practice (which is another endless topic; so is the question of the role of criticism in the making and exhibiting of a work as well as in the building of an audience), I would rather try to talk around this place from which you make films. It's not that we need to identify it to fortify the presence of the artist as the one who fully controls the creative process. I am more curious to understand what I see in your work as a certain uneasiness with regard to the avant-garde scene, or perhaps I should call it the* arrière-garde *scene. Your films are identified as avant-garde, exhibited mainly within avant-garde milieus, but they remain marginal within their own category. I guess this is also a way of saying that by their marginality, they contribute to keeping the notion of "experimental" alive, hence to resisting modernist closures often implied in the very label of "avant-garde."*

LT: I see my own work as a kind of "minor literature"—in the sense that Deleuze and Guattari talk about this, "like a dog digging a hole, a rat digging its burrow," working through that language which is given to us, in this case, that of dominant cinema and the historical avant-garde. They speak about being nomads, immigrants, Gypsies, in relation to one's own language.

I do think that when you work this way you are carving out for yourself—no place, at least in any immediate, practical sense. Working this way produces a dis-

and can be deployed in the service of either an extreme traditionalist reaction or a joyous indiscriminate acceptance of all that is foreign. Real women are now emulating an image of femininity made popular by the Sinhalese cinema that has been invoked in a call for cultural purity. The phenomenon suggests that work can be done in other directions too.

T: *With the growing awareness of different ways of thinking about knowledge and reality (Third World, feminist and so-called philosophical "antihumanist"), it has become more and more difficult today to turn a blind eye to power relations and to take the referential status of one's images and meaning for granted. One way of understanding the current deconstructive thrust in the arts and the humanities is to inquire about the ways the "real" is dealt with within the representational limit of a specific work or medium. How do you deal with this question in your films? In other words, how is the filmic text construed?*

J: In an era of simulation where the image precedes and determines the real, can one really make images or does one need to maintain that as a fiction in order to work?

T: *Among the many textual strategies in vogue such as simulation and pastiche, which you mentioned, those of appropriation and parody, or of bricolage, dissemination, suspension, quotation, grafting, spacing and mapping, which, if any, come closest to speaking the displacements effected in your film on the cinematic body as spectacle? Also, since the script of* A Song of Ceylon *is adapted from an anthropological text, its title reappropriated from Basil Wright's* The Song of Ceylon, *and its visuals formed by five main sequences composed around a "possessed" body as related to film stills from Godard's* Passion, A Married Woman, Pierrot le Fou, *and Hitchcock's* Vertigo, *do you think that, in order to understand your film, the viewer has to be knowledgeable with regards to these references? Can one refer to tradition as a store of styles and symbols to expropriate without questioning this tradition's status as tradition, or challenging the accepted notion of tradition itself?*

J: Even if one has to maintain the fiction of making images, sooner or later one becomes aware of how one's images echo previous ones. But what is essential is to try and rework and rethink the material one is using. Quotation is perhaps the main device used in structuring the images in my film, but I hope that the quotations do not rely upon the erudition that a knowledge of the original material would entail. Visual culture today is so much a collage that my preference in using quotation is not simply to take a bit from somewhere and stick it in my piece, but to try to rework what is derived from tradition in some way. For example, in the section derived from *A Married Woman* (which is in black and white) we alternate (more or less)

ease, and what is surprising, a resistance from even those factions that claim to support the advancement of film as an artform.

It is a rather discouraging time to be involved in a marginalized activity within an already marginal network. Financial pressures and general burnout make this a conservative period, a time of getting by. But that doesn't mean that challenging work does not continue; it is there; and when there is an adequate summoning of energy, changes in the support system will follow. Unfortunately, today the inverse is often the case—works are being produced to meet the funding and exhibition priorities which are already in place, institutionalized, commodifiable. I think it is up to the artists and writers and scholars who are feeling the limits of their systems to provoke change. Otherwise we doom ourselves.

T: It's necessary to point out that we do not operate outside the exhibition network, but that we play an active part in its making, even when we think our actions can only remain passively circular within a delimiting system. I would, however, like to persist in another facet of my question concerning the work itself, or rather the filmic text that is being produced. If your work meets with difficulty circulating within the established network, and even within the already recognized alternative exhibition venues, it is perhaps because it addresses its own ambiguous relationship with the established, predominantly male tradition of avant-garde filmmaking. It has not crossed the borderlines separating works that concern themselves with paradigms of modernist artistic practice and those that grow with contemporary theoretical practices. Adynata, There is an Unseen Cloud Moving, *and the series on* Peggy and Fred *deal with the discourse of feminist film theory, but only to impulsively "cross" it or to instantly disperse and undermine its authority. (This is not far from Teresa de Lauretis' notion of feminist* deaesthetics.*) Perhaps the dis-ease you mentioned has to do with the concept of the "personal" we discussed earlier. I would relate it here to the deconstruction of the opposition between the private and the public implicit in feminist activities and the emphasis these activities have consistently laid on the political personal. What is implied here is a critical stance that resists the collapsing and the convenient separatism of the two notions, and offers insights into the direct relationship between institutions and individuals, sociality and subjectivity, language and consciousness. Where does language start, where does it end? In a way, no political reflection can dispense with reflection on language. The working with language and with the process of producing meaning is precisely a concern with which purist avant-gardists have problems. Visualism and its tendency to reject the verbal image (or sound) as elements of pollution in the safeguarding of the purity of the vision, partake in this ideology of the visible, which links the purist avant-gardist's discourse to the one that dominates the film industry.*

LT: I agree with much of what you are saying, including your last point, but where we may differ is in the value of delineating contrasts between an avant-garde prac-

between fragmenting the male body and the female body and hopefully at some point it is not clear if it is male or female but just a nice piece of ass. In Godard's film of course, it is the woman whose body is viewed tenderly by the man. In the scenes derived from *Vertigo* and *Jeanne Eagles* the role of Kim Novak is played by Juan Davila, a voluptuous man. So the burden of embodying the classical (Hollywood) lineaments of the feminine is borne by a man. By making the human bodies of the performers more like still sculptural forms, the idea was to foreground affective (possessed) gestures which seize the body, but without getting involved in character because the voice-over enactment of the ritual of cure carries the narrative.

T: One type of reality that continues to be widely discussed and challenged in Third World contexts is the one characterized by a transition between tradition and modernism. What is at stake, on the one hand, is the recycling of these concepts within the framework of dualistic thinking and vertical ranking (East/West; North/South; Developed/Underdeveloped; Regress/Progress; Instinct/Reason; Nature/Culture; Heart/Mind; Woman (guardian of Tradition)/Man (advocate of Modernity)—hence the impasse that results from such a perceptual stagnation; on the other hand, the denial of, or blindness to, the collapse of the modern project and our confidence in its enlightening and emancipatory potential. In other words, Tradition as the Past is a modernist idea. It is in such context that the urge to break with tradition and to install a better and entirely new way of living and of thinking is made an indispensable goal. It is also in this context that the reactive impulse to retrieve tradition in its authenticity becomes a need. Postmodernism therefore does not come after, *but* with *modernism; it does not work so much against modernism (hence the modernist character of any anti-position) as it sets into relief its fissures and its blind fields. Since you are working now on a feature film in Sri Lanka, I assume that you must be confronting these problems.*

J: Yes, women have functioned as the killjoy guardians of tradition, resistant to change. What is very interesting now is the way in which "Woman/women and modernity" has become a topic of investigation both in theoretical work and filmic work. The coupling of the terms is a relatively recent development which seems to me to hold a great deal of hope for opening up certain impasses within feminist work. In fact, in the new film I am researching now, *Image in the Heart*, I hope I will not make the opposition Heart/Mind. The heart of the film is the paradox of the very first star of the Sinhalese-language cinema, who is an ethnic Tamil but has never been perceived as such by the predominantly Sinhalese audience. As the star was both a singer and an actress I have the chance to explore in a fairly complicated way the processes of modernization (i.e., the introduction of indigenous film to Ceylon, as it was then called) via the image and voice of a woman who galvanized audiences for several decades. It will not be a biography but a ruse to explore strategies for addressing new kinds of questions vis-à-vis women and modernization,

R

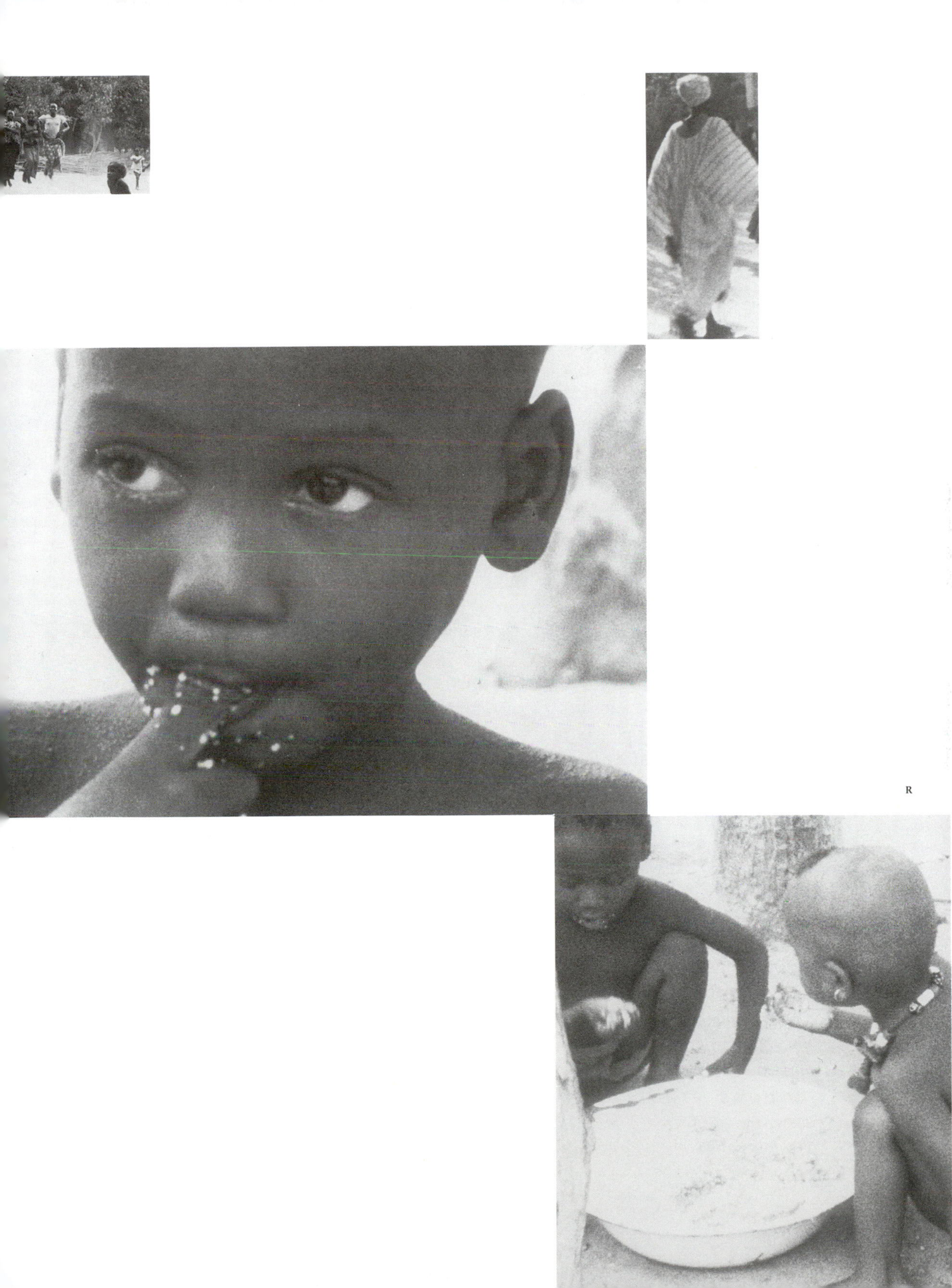

R

tice then and now. As in the notion of post-feminism, I would prefer to say we are in a different place, a developing place, the kinds of priorities that are emerging within a marginalized practice in cinema—a focus on language and subjectivity, for instance, or a rediscovering of narrative—this is where we can invest our energies.

What is more interesting to me is the way in which a commerce can develop across works—the way a visualist practice can be taken up, the way a feminist practice can be taken up—not as a prescriptive strategy, but as one of many traces, in a mesh of traces. The danger is in any totalizing agenda, any "master discourse." Even feminism is susceptible to this kind of reification.

The point you make about the relationship between the public and the private is an important one. Maybe the "Self" is not that interesting, I don't think it is, but what flows through it can be.

T: *In the film series* Peggy and Fred, *for example, by pointing to something very close, very familiar to American culture, you allow those who, like yourself, are part of it, to look at it very differently. You make this culture "other" (an other among others). It is here that I feel what is very personal becomes a site for cultural resistance. Can you talk about some of the displacements effected in* Peggy and Fred?

LT: Yes, *Peggy and Fred in Hell* is a science-fiction-like chronicle of two small children making their way through a post-apocalyptic landscape. It uses mundane everyday images and concepts to construct a kind of devious phantasmagoria. It creates an unstable picture, in terms of character, plot, set, language, and time. Signs are stacked up arbitrarily, madly, one on top of another. Because they are decontextualized, moved just slightly, there is an estrangement which occurs, a disturbance; the mundane becomes exotic. The project looks for the structures we rely upon to make sure "reality" flows by us invisibly, that we flow within its stream. It achieves this in part by working with children, because children are not quite us and not quite other. They are becoming us, or they are becoming other. They are at a dangerous point.

T: *In listening to your description of the process in* Peggy and Fred, *I hear a difference. The stacking up of signs of a culture in order to understand it is an activity common to cultural analysts; but more often than not, they are stacked up in order to make something coherent out of them. Although every making is a way of playing with order, the urge to generalize, interpret, and "clearly" communicate is usually not dealt with as an element in the making process, so that the analyst usually comes out on top of his stack, in a position of power above the work. With such attitude, what you have on the one hand is the claim of transparency of representation and immediacy of experience, and on the other, the sovereignty of the personal/meaning subject or the decoder. A film like Christ Marker's* Sans Soleil, *for*

including the "feminization of labour" in the hi-tech division of the international labor economy. So we will have a contemporary film director—a woman in her sixties—and an actress in her late thirties researching and rehearsing the film about the dead star. It will employ a film within a film structure which will permit the space/time needed to pose certain questions about the contradictory and conflicting temporalities that women are brought into through the processes of modernization. Woman as figure of modernity in torsion is something that the cinema can explore very well.

T: *Another, not unrelated, question concerns the very negative reactions of a large number of feminists to the term "postfeminism." Why see postfeminism mainly as a term that declares feminism outmoded or as a form of going beyond feminism? Why not understand it in the sense of postmodernism, both as a disengagement of the feminist liberating project, and as a resistance to Woman and to monolithic Feminism? In other words, as a different form of subjectivity that does not come "after" feminism so much as "with" feminism, remaining alert to the movement's political closures, and keeping it from reproducing the centered, unitary, masculine subject of representation? Is the difficult work of differentiation effected between modernism and postmodernism already always effective in feminism, rendering the prefix "post" unnecessary and even destructive because of the risk it incurs in deepening the fissures that already exist in the women's movements, or are the rejections of the notion of postfeminism equivalent to modernist claims on behalf of the authority and autonomy of the signifier and its reification in a legitimation of power?*

J: Just putting "post" in front of feminism will not make the problems that Feminism foregrounded go away, but feminism itself has produced its own problems, so your definition of postfeminism as a way of remaining alive to the political and aesthetic closures of feminism is a good move. I think it is necessary to question and shake up feminist smugness and legitimation when certain discursive operations are exhausted. As Baudrillard said in Sydney, the unconscious may disappear but psychoanalysis will certainly go on regardless, and I sometimes feel when reading work that comes from the U.S. in Feminist Film Theory, that due to the powerful academic industry there, some of the work tends to repeat a certain limited number of propositions, even when terms are changed. This is connected with what I said earlier about not having much space to consider film X a bad film despite the fact that it "deconstructs patriarchal modes of perception and that the sound and image are montaged etc. . . ." By now these strategies can amount to a too-familiar rhetoric of validation.

T: *Postmodernism, isolated as a* fin-de-siecle *phenomenon, can also be seen in conjunction with what is often called today the death of man/the author/the subject and the end of the real/*

example, may stay away from objectivist modes of textual production by offering the viewer a subjective layered interpretation of the cultures presented, but in spite of its impressive ability to weave images from disparate places, liberal comments and insightful analyses, it is still caught up in the process of filiation and it leaves the speaking/making subject in position as master and decoder. The difference in your work is that you do not really separate yourself from this process, not even to offer a subjective position; so that the stacking of signs is experienced mainly as an activity of production, the reading of which requires that the viewer in a sense recreate the filmic text.

LT: Yes, the effort is to displace any authoritative discourse. The viewer is then put on the spot to invent, along with the film, a way of reading.

Will you indulge me for a moment? I will try to point to an aspect of my own "dream space for working." Two virtues in my book are what I'll call "stupidity" and slowness. I see stupidity as a strategy of resistance to authoritative discourses and to fashion. It offers another path to thought. I have a reference which helps me tease this through. In certain of the Gnostic tests, "thinking" is broken into various stages—Forethought, a present-thinking, and Afterthought. In other words, thinking doesn't happen in one place, in Language, for instance. Furthermore, forethought doesn't always proceed to thought, and more complex, afterthought may come first. I see the thinking in *Peggy and Fred* as happening in a "fore" and "after" space, and not so much in the middle. For example, to some extent it is true, and to some extent I affect a certain blindness to conventional narrative codes in cinema. This resistance is visible in *Peggy and Fred*. It is as if Story is being discovered. In some ways, hopefully, this describes the viewer's experience as well. It is as if this were early cinema—a proto-cinema—in which Story has taken a different turn.

And slowness—you give yourself, and your work and your audience time. This project has gone on for six years now, and it is taking that long to fully understand its potential. Nothing in our culture is organized around slowness—another site for resistance?

T: What accompanies the discovery of "Story" is a process of reversal in which the self is displaced. The self becomes foreign. It becomes self-other; it does not negate itself not assimilate the other.

LT: Right. It is in the interplay of difference and recognition that otherness is revealed. By working closely with our traditions, our stories, *Peggy and Fred* destabilizes the familiar. It points to an otherness within. To recognize an otherness within is to see ourselves.

the political/philosophy. Thus the overall sense of impotence, if not of doom, attributed to this postindividualist experience. As Baudrillard puts it, in this "social void" and "system of deterrence," no distinction can be made between active and passive, between resistance and hyperconformity. As for me, rather than talking about death, I would prefer to talk about threshold, frontier, limit, exhaustion and suspension; about void as the very space for an infinite number of possibilities; about the work effected on one side and the other of the limit, refusing to settle on any reductive position outside or inside, and instead making possible the undoing, redoing and modifying of this very limit. The work is brought to the borderlines, to a certain exhaustion of meaning, thereby suspending its closure, and this seems quite different from either escaping or annihilating meaning. Where do you draw the fine line between "anything goes" and "anything may go" (when nothing basic is taken for granted)?

J: It is an exhilarating moment to be in when "nothing basic can be taken for granted," and this also goes for feminism.

T: You have just provided me with a link between what I've said earlier on the prevailing type of individualization in the system and the myth of filiation in producing works. Actually, when you insist that works have to interact among themselves, this reminds me of the by now familiar differentiation proposed by Roland Barthes, between the notion of work *and that of* text. *One can say very broadly that the notion of work implies a finished product, "a fragment of substance" that closes on a signified, whereas that of text brings to the fore the question of relations, the interaction among texts.*

The text has a generative quality that allows it to always defer the signified. This notion, while it does not exhaust what is seen, is quite useful when one wants to talk about, for example, your video There Was an Unseen Cloud Moving. *Perhaps, however, you could continue on* Peggy and Fred *and discuss its structure?*

LT: The project is being produced and released as an ongoing series of 16mm films and videotapes. Though they are intended to be screened in chronological order, they can be shown individually. In an ideal screening situation, both mediums would be used—film screen in front, and TVs off to the side and in the audience. Each medium would retain its own kind of presence—cinema its epic and ethereal quality, and the television its intrusive intimacy. The seriality allows for an open-endedness in the narrative and means that new issues, strategies, and styles, can continually emerge. At this point I see the series continuing indefinitely.

Now, this brings up something we talked about earlier, which is funding and distribution. The sprawl of *Peggy and Fred* makes it questionable as a commodity.

Funding agencies require a specific agenda, if not a script, then at least a confined product. In setting up shows, programmers ask when the project is going to be finished. I respond that it is happening, that I would like to show it as it develops. But I have encountered skepticism about showing something that is incomplete, a "work-in-progress." Yet its tentativeness is one of its most essential qualities. So it is important, though sometimes frustrating, to stick close by the necessities of the work, rather than succumb to the demands of the marketplace.

T: *Two points arise from your statements. First, I would take up again what you said earlier regarding our active participation in the process of creating possibilities for exhibition, and suggest that perhaps in the case of a work like this, you may have to change the way you present it to programmers and audiences.*

It seems to me that the term "work-in-progress" which has been used in relation to Peggy and Fred *has to be redefined or used differently. As long as you retain the term "work-in-progress" in an unqualified way people will adopt habitual attitudes toward what they consider to be an unfinished work—a work awaiting a "better," more finished version. For me, every book or film I've made is a work-in-progress. So, what you have is what you get. The step you take is the finished step. But every finished step is still a step, a work-in-progress.*

LT: I agree.

T: *The second point concerns a certain notion of the actor that is implied in the way you work with the children and conceive the series, which continues to be formed as the protagonists grow (in life as well as in their acting) and as the audience feeds the process with their expectations. This notion reminds me of Godard's concept of the actor-medium, in which the actor is capable of seeing and showing at the same time, rather than just acting.*

LT: Yes, I've come to understand the presence of actors in this way. It was Bill Krohn, who writes for *Cahiers du Cinéma* who first pointed this out to me. He felt that I was making quite literal the documentary recording of the actors acting, in both *Peggy and Fred* and in *There Was an Unseen Cloud Moving*—the simultaneity of what is "acted" in the presence of the "actor." I think it creates a real tension in viewing. The actors leap out of the same fictional space they are constructing.

T: *Yes, talking about the simultaneity of the act in the presence of the figure, the text is precisely a notion that foregrounds the density of experience. In other words, instead of having a meaningful narrative line representing an experience, one would present an experience in its thickness or density.*

LT: Exactly. Even cinéma-vérité does not have this "thickness," because it too is usually organized around a storyline, so that "real life" gets naturalized into a stable narrative figure. The tension occurs in the combination of fiction and document. Both are rendered volatile.

I can give a specific example. In *Unseen Cloud*, I worked with four different women playing the lead role of Isabelle Eberhardt, the Victorian traveler and adventureress. None of these women were actors. At times they were basically being themselves, at times, they were asked to do or say specific things. In one section, one of the Isabelles describes "paradise." What she recites is actually an interpretation of the Islamic conception of paradise, as interpreted by a nineteenth-century Englishman. It appears as a footnote in what was incidentally the first English translation of the Koran. So this is already a derivative reading, a Western reading of an Islamic image. I wanted her reading to have about it a kind of absence, to mark this distance. I recorded the text and then, through a hidden earphone, she heard it for the first time as she spoke it. She describes an exotic lushness ("and there is a tree so large that it would take over a hundred years to ride from one end of it to the other," etc.) in a manner that is both haunting and absent.

T: The idea is very close to Godard's way of working with actors, but your text has a very different effect.

LT: I later heard that Godard uses the same earphone technique. One of the qualities of the work which is disturbing to people is that they are uncertain of how to position the individuals involved—where they are and what their role is.

T: It seems to me that there is currently a renewed interest in the science fiction genre among filmmakers who have long worked with the limits of the documentary and fictional modes. They usually find fiction unsatisfactory, and documentary too limiting. Peggy and Fred *has been referred to as a science fiction; would you talk about this aspect of the film series?*

LT: When you make the effort to construct a different kind of story, another framework for time, space, social intercourse, language, etc., you might also imagine that this is possible, some time, some place, in the future. The future becomes a richly imaginative site for speculation, for an otherness, which puts you in the realm of "science fiction." However, I am cautious about using the term as an apology for certain interventions—"Oh well, that strangeness in time—that's just science fiction time." I prefer a position which is less clear—maybe science fiction, maybe not.

What is more interesting to me is the process through which we may come to recognize alternatives, to the kinds of stories we tell ourselves about ourselves. One way I think this can happen is through encounters with difference, across cultures, or across times. Last night I had a strong experience of this in the film we saw together, *Sambizanga*, by Sarah Maldoror. Apart from the film's ostensible subject matter, what I could not stop watching was the time, time as ongoing, and the time involved in looking at an event or situation. It was different from what I experience in Western cinema. Even though all of the familiar codes were there—the shots and angles, the continuity—there was something which completely exceeded the accepted form. It must reside in a cultural difference.

T: The factors of time and difference you point to are also strong experiences and very inspiring elements for me in Sambizanga. *Although I would agree with you that the difference is a cultural one, I do think it is also more than culturally specific. Indeed, Sarah Maldoror said herself that through the rhythm of the film, she was trying to recreate "the slow pace which characterizes African life." And when one looks at films like Safi Faye's* Kaddu beykat, *Haile Gerima's* Harvest: 3,000 Years *(which remains a fabulous film for me, in its different mode of storytelling as well as sense of time), or even my film* Naked Spaces—Living is Round, *one can easily say at first sight that it's "African time." But if one goes a bit further one may realize that it is not just a question of African time versus Western time, but also a question of the relations between the viewer and the context of viewing. In other words, this is not a mere case of cultural difference which people can easily dismiss ("Oh well, it's cultural . . ." or "You see, I'm not from your culture . . ."). This element of time which stands out so strongly for both of us in a Western viewing context, would probably not strike me the same way if I were sitting in an African audience. I think that it retains our attention because it is situated in the context of a dominant mode of action-cinema. To work with the notion of time in such a context is to resist that very notion of time that is synonymous with action. As this latter conception is common, it is hardly surprising that most people simply understand time only in the sense that derives from the editing of the film and constitutes its overall length. The time in* Sambizanga, *like the time in the films of Chantal Akerman and Marguerite Duras, is not merely the synthetic time of the film, it is constantly at work within the image without being subordinated to actions and camera movements.*

Julia Kristeva, for example, wrote about extrasubjective and cosmic time—a form of jouissance she attributes to female subjectivity. This "time" inserts itself in history even as it refuses the limitations of history's time—linear time. Working with *time means therefore working differently with the image. Gilles Deleuze classifies the body of cinematic works according to two categories, those primarily characterized by movement, and those in which time is the dominant factor, hence his two volumes on* The Movement-Image *and* The Time-Image. *There is a reversal process involved in which time is not made the measure of movement, but through movement, a perspective of time is made visible. The film takes on this pensive quality which Barthes considered subversive, not because it frightens, repels, or strikes, but because it thinks. The filmic image becomes a thinking image. This different relationship to time is the result of a mutation in the way one works with the image—a way not submitted to the "perception-action-affection" system.*

LT: Yes, to respond to your first point about *Sambizanga,* it is always a question of context. Yet it was in that combination of difference and recognition that time became salient. How different is this from Orientalism? On the other hand, how different is this from learning from a friend? It depends on how and why it is done, how it is used. I think that is where we must make the distinctions.

Regarding the idea of a "time-image," if I can digress for a moment, I think one of the more interesting aspects of much of the earlier avant-garde cinema was its address of time (curiously, this was seldom a focus of its criticism). Ernie Gehr's work, Peter Gidal's, Hollis Frampton's, Andy Warhol's, each produced what we might call an excruciating "time-image." This accounts in part for its affect of pensiveness.

T: Talking about Deleuze's theories in relation to your films, I have another question. Deleuze sees two things happening simultaneously in the time-image. On the one hand, the image tends to become cliche; this civilization of image, as he wrote, is in fact a civilization of cliches whose powers work at hiding from us (certain things of) the image. On the other hand, the image endlessly attempts to perforate the cliche and free itself from it. This need to extract a real image from the cliches comes from the difficult knowledge that an optical or a sound image are not in themselves cliches, unless images are re-used as formulas. But to overcome cliches, it is not enough to parody them, to try to empty them, or to disturb the sensory-motor links. One has to bring to the image forces that belong neither to a simply intellectual conscience nor a social one, but to "a profoundly vital intuition," as he puts it. This way of looking at what could strongly disturb the system of action-perception-affection-image seems to me precisely what you have been working on in your films. Would you like to expand on this?

LT: Let me do this with an example. When collecting material for a new episode of *Peggy and Fred in Hell,* I had copied all of the music, large stretches of silence, and occasional dialogue for Polanski's *The Tenant,* thinking I might surreptitiously weave some small trace of it into my film. Upon listening to the recording later, I realized this is it, this is the sound track for the next film, as is—grand larceny. My work had incorporated found material before, but never such a complete and unadulterated quotation.

The music is eerie and suspenseful, as are the silences. The dialogue is fleeting and provocative. Through working an image back into this sound—mostly nature images, a flock of ducks, rushing water, trees shuddering in the wind, and eventually the children, climbing out of a hole in the earth—a strange kind of horror developed, one both invisible and pervasive. There is a schism between what we see and hear, an impossibility, and in this dislocation the horror becomes unmotivated, random, and hence more threatening. It is not *The Tenant*. It is not the children's story, but they are its victims.

Perhaps this is a kind of thinking through film not unrelated to what Deleuze talks about, again, through an intrusion into the familiar.

T: Is it necessary for viewers to be knowledgeable about the sources of appropriation to understand the appropriation?

LT: Yes and no. With knowledge it works one way; without, it works differently. If you happen to have watched *The Tenant* that morning, it would have another kind of resonance. In all cases, one experiences a borrowed narrative space, superimposed.

T: I see. I asked that question because I've always found very questionable the tendency in certain postmodern works to merely plunder a number of historical styles without suggesting a different reading of history. The historical status of the material from which theses styles are extracted is taken for granted. So is the notion of history itself.

LT: Yes, what are the ethics of appropriation? As a device or strategy it quickly exhausts itself. At its best it is a matter of problematizing judgments, at its worst, it simply defers judgments

T: Where appropriation is deployed unproblematically, the old opposition between form and content prevails, with form maintaining its decorative function. The work becomes a mere vehicle for the transmission of knowledge. It becomes a closure: you wrap up a story—some information, an analysis for the viewer—instead of keeping filmmaking alive as a mode of knowing. Working always involves a desire to modify one's consciousness or the limits of one's thinking, and to shift, not from one place to a better one, but intransitively. One is quickly bored with one's work where this generative quality is absent.

LT: Right. I have been reading *Nomadology* (Deleuze and Guattari) and I feel very drawn to their notion of becoming, and the commerce they describe between a "royal science" and a "nomadic science." There is a wonderful metaphor they use, and that is in the building of the first Gothic cathedrals. The possibility of such height and grandeur in architectural space is something that happened originally and literally from the ground up. The stones were carved one by one to fit onto the preceding level, with an active role in the part of the maker (stone-cutter/engineer), who would see how far this possibility could extend. And what is wonderful is that sometimes the buildings actually fell down. There was that kind of risk involved. Soon, other parties in the Church and State became aware of and concerned about a certain anarchic side to this practice. It became necessary, instead of just building, to first submit plans, which would be approved and then stored some place. This brought about a whole different kind of practice and maker.

In general, the codified practice of royal science would lay a groundwork for the next intervention or layering brought about through a nomadic practice. This distinction may also be useful in considering the arts, and actually touches on many of the issues we have been talking about today.

R 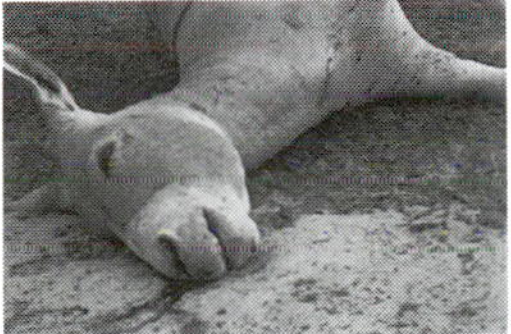

Selected Bibliography

Film Reviews and Analyses

Surname Viet Given Name Nam

Auer, James. "Vietnamese Women Topic of Film Study." *Milwaukee Journal*, 22 October 1989.

Berenstein, Rhona. "Remembering History: Films by Women at the 1989 Toronto Film Festival." *Camera Obscura* 22 (1989), pp. 161–162.

Crane, David. "Trinh's *Surname*—Between 'Nam and A Hard Place." *Shepherd Express* (Milwaukee) 26 (October 1989), p. 17.

Gabrenya, Frank. "'Surname Viet' is Intellectual Delight." *Columbus Dispatch* 25 (May 1990), p. 10.

Heung, Marina. "Haunting Film Probes Life and Art in Exile." *New Directions for Women*, 19, no. 1 (January 1990).

Hoberman, Jim. "Mekong Delta Blues." *Village Voice* 11 (April 1989), p. 61.

Jaehne, Karen. "The 18th New Directors/New Films." *Film Comment,* May-June 1989, p. 68.

Kaliss, Jeff. "Vietnamese Filmmaker's Unusual Work." *San Francisco Chronicle,* 12 February 1989, Datebook section, pp. 28–30.

Kapke, Barry. "Surname Viet Given Name Nam." *High Performance* (summer 1989), p. 74.

Klawans, Stuart. "Films: Surname Viet Given Name Nam, Heathers, Slaves of New York." *The Nation,* 17 April 1989.

Leventhal, Frances. "Trinh Minh-ha Breaks Convention in Film." *Asian Week* 17 (February 1989), p. 24.

Manuel, Susan. "Vietnamese Women Pulled from Obscurity." *Star-Bulletin* (Hawaii) 1 (December 1989), p. B-1.

Peckham, Linda. "Surname Viet Given Name Nam: Spreading Rumors & Ex/Changing Histories." *Frame/Work* 2 no. 3 (1989), pp. 31–35.

Rich. "Surname Viet Given Name Nam." *Variety,* 27 September 1989.

Rosenbaum, Jonathan. "Undermining Authority." *Chicago Reader,* 23 June 1989, p. 14.

Sterrit, David. "War's Impact Seen by Vietnamese Eyes." *The Christian Science Monitor,* 3 April 1989, p. 11.

White, Armand. "Surname Viet Given Name Nam." *Film Comment,* May-June 1989.

Wolff, Kurt. "Local Filmmaker Questions Authority." *The San Francisco Bay Guardian,* 15 February 1989, p. 22.

Naked Spaces—Living is Round

Brown, Georgia. *Village Voice,* 18 June 1991.

Camper, Fred. "Unsteady Gaze." *Chicago Reader,* 21 November 1986, p. 1.

Hoberman, Jim. "Pagan Rhapsodies." *Village Voice* 31, no. 20, 20 May 1986.

Jensen, Steve. "Critic's Choice." *Bay Guardian,* 11 December 1985.

Reynaud, Bérénice. "Toronto Film Festival." *Afterimage* 13, no. 4 (November 1985), p. 20.

Rosenbaum, Jonathan. "Critic's Choice: Naked Spaces—Living is Round." *Chicago Reader,* 11 September 1987, p. 22.

Sterritt, David. "Hanoi-born Filmmaker Turns Her Lens on Africa." *Christian Science Monitor,* 19 November 1986, p. 31.

Viviano, Frank. "From Charlie Chan to Hyphenated Cinema." *Far Eastern Economic Review,* 30 July 1987, p. 35.

Viviano, Frank, and Sharon Silva. "The Next Wave." *San Francisco Focus,* December 1986.

Reassemblage

Aufderheide, Pat. "Dislocations." *Village Voice* 28, no. 40, 4 October 1983.

———. "Provocative Statements from the East." *Chicago Reader,* 23 September 1983, p. 14.

Kruger, Barbara. "International Women's Film Festival." *Artforum* 32, no. 3 (November 1983), p. 79.

Mayne, Judith. *The Woman at the Keyhole. Feminism and Women's Cinema,* pp. 213–217. Bloomington: Indiana University Press, 1990.

Moravia, Alberto. "C'e del marcio in Turchia." *L'Espresso* (Italy), 16 September 1984, p. 117.

Nix, Shann. "Ethnic Women in Film." *The Daily Californian,* 30 October 1987, pp. 16–17.

Peckham, Linda. "Peripheral Vision: Looking at the West through *Reassemblage.*" *Cinematograph* 2 (1986), pp. 1–5.

Rosenbaum, Jonathan. "Avant-Garde in the 80's." *Sight and Sound* (Spring 1984), p. 131.

Scheibler, Sue. "When I am Silent, It Projects." *The USC Spectator* 7, no. 2 (Spring 1987), pp. 12–14.

Wallis, Brian. "Questioning Documentary." *Aperture,* no. 112 (Fall 1988), pp. 60–61.

Vietnamese Reviews

Ha Chau. "Trinh Thi Minh-ha la ai?" *Nguoi Viet,* 25 September 1988, B1–9.

———. "Cau chuyen mot phu nu Viet lam dien anh." *Nguoi Viet,* 21 May 1989, B1–10.

"Hanh dien phu nu Viet," *Thang Mo* (San Jose), no. 283. 19 September, 1987.

"Ho Viet Ten Nam," *Chinh Nghia,* 24 February 1989.

Nguyen Sa. "Nu Dao Dien. Doat Giai Dien Anh Quoc Te." *Doi* (Los Angeles magazine), no. 51, August 1987, pp. 12–14.

———. "Mon Qua Nam Moi." *Doi,* February 1984, pp. 3–6.

Catalogs

Ditta, Susan. "In-between Spaces/Interstices: The Films of Trinh T. Minh-ha." *Film and Video by Artists Series,* National Gallery of Canada, 10–27 May 1990.

Furlong, Lucinda. "Images of Cultures: The Films of Trinh T. Minh-ha." *The New American Filmmakers Series 32,* The Whitney Museum of American Art, November 1986.

Hanhardt, John. *1987 Biennial Exhibition Catalogue,* p. 149. New York: Whitney Museum and W. W. Norton, 1987.

Ladely, Dan. "The Films of Trinh T. Minh-ha." *Film/Video Showcase,* Sheldon Film Theater, University of Nebraska-Lincoln, November 2–4, 1989.

Additional Interviews

Freeman, Mark. *Lightstruck* 7, no. 1 (January-March 1990), p. 9.

Hulser, Kathleen. "Ways of Seeing Senegal." *The Independent,* December 1983, p. 16.

Kearny, Stephen. "For Filmmaker and Teacher Trinh T. Minh-ha, Curiosity and Sensitivity Come First." *Film/Tape World* 2, no. 8 (September 1989), p. 13.

Passaretti, Gayle. "Challenging Objectivity: One Filmmaker's View." *Phoenix* 17 October 1985, p. 6.

Sherman, James, and Laurie Sosna. "Trinh T. Minh-ha: A Multi-Dimensional Maker of Film." *Mindport* (San Francisco), Fall 1986, p. 4.

Thielen, Laura. "Women in Film." *Cinezine* (San Francisco), October 1984, pp. 4–5.

Interviews on Video

Access Video of Western Pennsylvania (Cable Television), "Women in the Director's Chair" Program, June 26 and 27, 1987. 50-minute interview.

Video Data Bank (Artist Series), Chicago, October 30, 1989. 31-minute interview.

Other Works by the Filmmaker

Books

Trinh, Minh-ha T. *When the Moon Waxes Red. Representation, Gender & Cultural Politics.* New York: Routledge, 1991.

———. *Woman, Native, Other. Writing Postcoloniality and Feminism.* Bloomington: Indiana University Press, 1989.

———. *En minuscules.* Paris: Le Méridien Editeur, 1987.

———. *Un Art sans oeuvre.* Troy, Michigan: International Book Publishers, 1981. (out of print)

——— and Jean-Paul Bourdier. *African Spaces. Designs for Living in Upper Volta.* New York, London: Holmes & Meier, 1985.

———, Russell Ferguson, Martha Gever, and Cornel West, eds. *Out There: Marginalization in Contemporary Culture.* New York: New Museum of Contemporary Art and MIT Press, 1990.

———, ed. (Un)Naming Cultures. *Discourse,* no. 11.2 (special issue, Spring-Summer 1989).

———, ed. She, The Inappropriate/d Other. *Discourse,* no. 8 (special issue, Winter 1986–87).

Articles and Poems

———. "Not You/Like You." In *Making Face, Making Soul/Haciendo Caras: Creative and Critical Perspectives by Feminists of Color,* ed. Gloria Anzaldua. San Francisco: Spinsters/Aunt Lute, 1990.

———. "Panel 3: Responsibility and Strategies in Representing the Other." *Motion Picture* 3, no. 3/4 (Summer/Autumn 1990), pp. 48–50.

———. "Refugee," "Flying Blind," "For Love of Another" (poems). *City Lights Review,* no. 4, 1990.

———. Poems and photographs in *Aperture,* no. 112/Storyteller, 1988.

———. Six poems in *Poésie 1* ("La Nouvelle poésie francaise), no. 136 (Paris, October-December 1987), pp. 71–76.

———. "On the Politics of Contemporary Representations." In *Dia-Art Discussions,* ed. Hal Foster. Port Townsend, Washington: Bay Press, 1987.

———. "On Naked Spaces—Living is Round." *Motion Picture,* no. 1 (Spring 1986), p. 13.

——— and Jean-Paul Bourdier. "Traditional Rural Dwellings of West Africa." In *The Encyclopedia of Architecture,* vol. 5, pp. 306–334. New York: John Wiley, 1990.

Works Cited

Ba, A. Hampate. "Animisme en savanne africaine." In *Les Religions africaines traditionnelles.* Rencontres Internationales de Bouaké, Paris: Seuil, 1965.

Bachelard, Gaston. *The Poetics of Space,* trans. M. Jolas. Boston: Beacon Press, 1969.

Barthes, Roland. *Roland Barthes,* trans. R. Howard. New York: Hill & Wang, 1977.

Baudrillard, Jean. *The Evil Demon of Images.* Sydney: Power Institute of Fine Arts, 1987.

Blier, Suzanne Preston. *The Anatomy of Architecture. Ontology and Metaphor of Batammaliba Architectural Expression.* New York: Cambridge University Press, 1987.

Chernoff, John Miller. *African Rhythm and African Sensibility.* Chicago: University of Chicago Press, 1979.

Cixous, Hélène. *Vivre l'orange.* Paris: Editions des femmes, 1979.

Diop, Birago. *Les Contes d'Amadou Koumba.* Paris: Présence africaine, 1961.

Eisenman, Arlene. *Women and Revolution in Vietnam.* London: Zed, 1984.

Eluard, Paul. *Capitale de la Douleur,* 1926. Reprint. Paris: Gallimard, 1966.

Gabus, Jean. *Sahara bijoux et techniques.* Neuchatel: Les Editions de la Baconnière, 1982.

Glorious Daughters of Vietnam. Hanoi: Vietnam Women's Union, n.d.

Griaule, Marcel. *Conversations with Ogotemmeli.* London: Oxford University Press, 1965.

Hama, Boubou. *Le Double d'hier rencontre demain.* Paris: Union Générale d'Editions, 1973.

Heidegger, Martin. *Poetry, Language, Thought,* trans. A. Hofstadter. San Francisco: Harper & Row, 1971.

Illich, Ivan. *Celebration of Awareness: A Call for Institutional Revolution.* New York: Anchor Books, 1971.

Johnson, Barbara. "Taking Fidelity Philosophically." In *Difference in Translation,* ed. J. F. Graham. Ithaca: Cornell University Press, 1985.

Larsen, Wendy Wilder & Tran Thi Nga. *Shallow Graves. Two Women and Vietnam.* New York: Random House, 1986.

Mai Thi Tu & Le Thi Nham Tuyet. *La Femme au Vietnam.* Hanoi: Editions en langues étrangères, 1976.

Mai Thu Van. *Vietnam: un peuple, des voix.* Paris: Pierre Horay, 1983.

Marr, David G. *Vietnamese Anticolonialism.* 1885–1925. Berkeley: University of California Press, 1971.

———. *Vietnamese Tradition on Trial.* 1920–1945. Berkeley: University of California Press, 1981.

Nguyen Du. *The Tale of Kieu,* trans. Huynh Sanh Thong. New Haven: Yale University Press, 1983.

Nguyen Ngoc Bich, ed. and trans. *A Thousand Years of Poetry.* Ithaca: Cornell University Press.

Rattray, Captain R. S. *The Tribes of the Ashanti Hinterland,* 2 vols., 1932. Reprint. London: Oxford University Press, 1969.

Sister Cao Phuong with Thich Nhat Hanh. *Songs of Vietnam.* Produced by Other Americas Radio, Santa Barbara, California (cassette tape).

Vien Van Hoc. *Ky niem 200 nam nam sinh Nguyen Du* (1765–1965). Hanoi: Nha xuat ban Khoa Hoc, 1967.

Yutang, Lin. *The Importance of Living.* Bombay: Jaico Publishing House, 1977.